STUDIES IN ISLAM CIVILIZATION

STUDIES IN ISLAMIC CIVILIZATION

THE MUSLIM CONTRIBUTION TO THE RENAISSANCE

Ahmed Essa
with Othman Ali

THE INTERNATIONAL INSTITUTE OF ISLAMIC THOUGHT

© The International Institute of Islamic Thought, 1431AH / 2010CE

The International Institute of Islamic Thought
P.O. Box 669, Herndon, VA 20172, USA
www.iiit.org

London Office
P.O. Box 126, Richmond, Surrey TW9 2UD, UK
www.iiituk.com

ISBN 978-1-56564-350-5 paperback
ISBN 978-1-56564-351-2 hardback

The views and opinions expressed in this book are those of the contributors and not neces-sarily those of the publishers. The publishers are not responsible for the accuracy of URLs for external or third-party internet websites referred to in this publication, and do not guaran-tee that any content on such websites is, or will remain, accurate or appropriate.

Typesetting by Abdallateef Whiteman
Cover design by Shiraz Khan

Printed by Cromwell Press Group, UK

Dedicated to my family: my mother and father, sisters and brothers; my wife, daughter and son; and my cousins, nieces, and nephews.

CONTENTS

ACKNOWLEDGEMENTS

I REGRET THAT it is impossible for me to express fully the gratitude I owe my wife Eva. She has shared my enthusiasm for this book, and has been helpful and encouraging in more ways than I can remember. She assisted me for over ten years in its development and while I was writing, from the project's inception to the editing and manuscript stages. During this period, she also cared for me during two open-heart and other surgeries and medical procedures.

I am also indebted to Muslim communities in South Africa – particularly those in Durban, Pietermaritzburg, Johannesburg, and Pretoria – for financial assistance to study in the United States in 1952 and 1960. This book is a fulfillment of a promise I made to use my knowledge to do something worthwhile for Islam.

I am grateful to Larry Michalak for valuable counsel and help with research at the University of California at Berkeley. In response to my call for consultation, Bill Graham went out of his way to visit me at home soon after I returned from the hospital after my first open-heart surgery. For that I am deeply grateful. Of considerable value in the writing of this book were discussions I had with Muhammad Asad, Ismail al-Faruqi, and Salma Khadra Jayyusi.

I am grateful to Husain Haddawy for extending my horizons, especially in my understanding of Islamic art. I am thankful to Farida Kuraishy for doing some of the research for this book and to Bob Harvey for his encouragement. That I was able to do considerable research is due to helpful librarians at the University of California at Berkeley and the University of Nevada, Reno. I am grateful to the UNR Foundation for funding a year's leave of absence to do full-time research and travel for this book. I also appreciate the encouraging responses from a number of people – in the United States and in other countries – when I discussed this book with them.

AHMED ESSA

FOREWORD

*Of knowledge, we have none, save what
You have taught us.* (The Qur'an 2:32)

THE INTERNATIONAL INSTITUTE OF ISLAMIC THOUGHT (IIIT)
has great pleasure in presenting this outstanding work on the
achievement of Islamic civilization and the intellectual legacy of a
faith that transformed the world.

Muslims today find themselves in the rather strange position of
being viewed through the eyes of a lens that for the most part depicts
the Muslim presence as a backward product of a one time lascivious,
violent prone and generally undesirable culture. So estranged is the
popular historical account from documented reality that the word
civilization is rarely employed as an appropriate epithet to describe
the achievements of a culture that at its height was considered the
model of human progress and development.

However, according to Aldous Huxley "Facts do not cease to
exist because they are ignored." *Studies in Islamic Civilization* is a compelling attempt to redress this wrong and restore the historical truths
of a "golden age" that ushered in the Islamic renaissance, and as a
by-product that of the West. Islam's brilliant contribution to science,
art, and culture are systematically explored in a highly informative
work, offering a detailed yet succinct view of the great panorama of
learning that formed the bedrock of a religio-humanistic vision that
gave precedence to intellectual development and scholastic endeavor.
Whilst charting the Muslim preoccupation with studying, mapping,

and investigating the world, the writers also offer fascinating insight into the many intricate workings of religion, culture and knowledge, whose point of reference and source of inspiration would invariably be the Qur'an and Sunnah.

The book, realistically and not idealistically written, is divided into fifteen chapters. These examine Islam's Role in History, Learning and Islamic Civilization, the Establishment of the First Community, the Islamic World Order, Islamic Civilization in Europe and West Asia, Trade, Agriculture and Technology, The Flowering of Islamic Learning, The Sciences, and Medicine. The work goes on to explore the absorbing but often neglected area of Arabic and Persian Literature, culminating in chapters on The Arts, and Islamic Art, focusing on The Ottoman Contribution. The final chapter on the Islamic Impact on the Renaissance is an important analysis of not only the enormous learning that the West acquired from the Muslim world but the enlightened vision it bequeathed humanity, forming the catalyst for the development of modern Western civilization.

We all stand on the shoulders of giants and the West is no exception. The need for cross-cultural understanding is perhaps greater today than at anytime in history and works such as this are not only a mine of information but vital for a better understanding and recognition of our common human heritage.

Not all history is traitorous however. In point of fact, the authors are not alone in their call for an appraisal of history which has betrayed the Muslim presence. Mired in Eurocentric rhetoric and underscored by spurious assumptions, this pseudo scholarship misrepresents all progress in favor of the West whilst distorting understanding of the Islamic historical phase and the great debt owed it. By contrast works such as, *The Theft of History* by Jack Goody, *Lost History: The Enduring Legacy of Muslim Scientists, Thinkers and Artists* by Michael Morgan, *The Colonizer's Model of the World* and *Eight Eurocentric Historians* by J. M. Blaut and *The Miseducation of the West, How Schools and the Media Distort our Understanding of the Islamic World* edited by J. L. Kincheloe and S. R. Steinberg, are examples of serious scholarly attempts to separate fact from bias.

Since its establishment in 1981, the IIIT has continued to serve as a major center to facilitate sincere and serious scholarly efforts, based on Islamic vision, values and principles. Its programs of research, and seminars and conferences, during the last twenty-eight years, have resulted in the publication of more than four hundred titles in English, Arabic, and other major languages.

We pray for the soul of Dr. Ahmed Essa who has passed away and express our thanks to Dr. Othman Ali for his invaluable work in producing the final manuscript. We also express our thanks to the editorial and production team including Sylvia Hunt and Shiraz Khan at the IIIT London Office and all those who were directly or indirectly involved in the completion of this work.

IIIT LONDON OFFICE, MUHARRAM 1431 AH, JANUARY 2010

PREFACE

MANY WORLD HISTORIES either minimize or completely overlook the presence and contributions of the entire Islamic civilization. This book tries to bridge that gap and surveys the accomplishments of the Muslim world from its first society. Subsequent chapters focus on the expansion of Muslim communities into other regions, and on areas omitted from most discussions of Islamic civilization: trade, agriculture, and travel.

At the heart of this civilization's accomplishments is its pursuit of learning, which is a significant aspect of Islam and the focus of the early chapters. Other chapters discuss how learning led to advances in philosophy, the sciences, and medicine. These chapters present in detail Islam's synthesizing, creative, and intermediary role between the ancient Romano-Greek civilization and the Renaissance in Europe.

Three more chapters cover the Muslim world's immense flowering of creativity in literature and the arts, as well as the civilization's contribution to and impact on the literary movement in the medieval world. Islamic learning, especially in the sciences, was far more extensive than has been recognized. For example, very few scholars know that for over seven hundred years, the international language of science was Arabic. How all of this has affected Western civilization is reviewed toward the end of the book.

Today, there is widespread prejudice against Muslims in the Western world, so there is a greater need now to understand them, their history, and their achievements. Misunderstandings are most evident in common stereotypes regarding the subjugation of Muslim women and Islam's legacy in its treatment of non-Muslim minorities. Instead, ample data support the creative roles of both women and non-Muslim minorities, especially Jews and Christians, in the development of Islamic civilization.

Islam created a civilization that changed the world for the better. Islam's civilization spanned a greater geographic area than any other, across the eastern hemisphere from Spain and North Africa to the Middle East and Asia. Islamic civilization also formed a continuum between the Classical world and the Renaissance. Peter Jennings emphasized the significance of that bridge when he introduced a National Public Radio series on Islam entitled "World of Islam," first aired in 1985, then rebroadcast in 1991: "It is doubtful whether the European Renaissance could have taken place without vital contributions from Islamic civilization."

The Muslims were, said author Gabriele Crespi, "the harbingers of science, culture and art; of values the West could avidly draw on in the interests of revival."[1] Marshall Hodgson, the most eminent Western authority on Islamic history, wrote that Islamic culture has "been very important in influencing the present condition of mankind...because it represents the highest creative aspirations and achievements of millions of people."[2]

Islamic Civilization speaks from a Muslim perspective while drawing upon the works of Western scholars. This study emphasizes the need for the dialog and engagement of civilizations, instead of confrontation and friction, which do no good to any party.

AHMED ESSA

EDITOR'S INTRODUCTION

TO TELL THE story of Islamic civilization in a single manuscript is by no means an easy task. Islamic civilization's achievements and positive contributions to the world and the European Renaissance have not received due recognition. There are many reasons for this oversight, including a lack of relevant research, the uninspiring present condition of the Muslim world, and the Eurocentric approach in Western academic discourse.

The studies that have tackled Islamic civilization to date fall into two main categories. First, a trend in modern-day academia denies Islam's outstanding and far-reaching role in its service to medieval civilization and the subsequent development in the West. These writers try to succeed where the medieval Church failed: by denying a respectable recognition of Islam and the positive traits of its civilization. Instead, their presentation of Islam and Islamic civilization has been confrontational and exclusivist. The recent coinage by this trend in academia is "clash of civilizations."

However, as this book demonstrates, there is a second trend in Western academia that recognizes Muslim contributions to the unfolding of both Islamic and Western civilizations. These scholars have performed resourceful and painstaking fieldwork, as well as discovering and editing hundreds of manuscripts from libraries across the world. As a result, they have uncovered an immense number of treasures of medieval Islam. George Sarton, for example, is a leading authority on the history of science. He maintains that until the fourteenth century, Muslim civilization was "still at the vanguard of humanity. There was nowhere else in the world, in those days, a philosopher who could at all compare with al-Ghazali, neither as an astronomer like al-Zarqali, neither a mathematician like Omar Khayam."[1]

These same Western scholars were clear that the Renaissance and modern Western civilization owe much more to Islamic civilization than has been acknowledged. They have also noted that Islamic civilization was neither dogmatic nor exclusive in its dealings with non-Muslims.

Nevertheless, owing to the continuing confrontation between Islamic extremists and the Western world as a result of the tragic events of September 11, 2001 in the United States, the discourse of a segment of politically-oriented Western scholars emphasizes extremist views. This trend, with considerable influence in political and academic circles, grossly understates the openness and creativity of Islamic civilization throughout history. This approach has created an atmosphere in the West in which, as journalist and historian Karen Armstrong has pointed out, "Tolerance is not a virtue that many Western people today would feel inclined to attribute to Islam."[2] The current politically-oriented reading of Islam and its civilization contends there is no moderate Islam, and that Islamic history and tradition have nothing to offer other than bigotry, violence, and holy war. This book adopts a historical perspective and points out the errors and flaws in this reading of Islamic civilization.

The book also demonstrates how Islam as a religion and the law of the land has always sought peaceful co-existence with others. Historically, the Islamic concept of unity was unique and not totalitarian. Islamic society in the medieval period sought unity in diversity, and diversity meant accepting the contributions of non-Muslims, borrowing freely from the preceding civilizations, and using this knowledge as a basis on which to build a progressive society. The result was a civilization that was free from religious bigotry, universal in its outlook, and humanist without ignoring the Creator.

It was indeed an honor to contribute to the preparation of this manuscript for publication. The author spent a decade of painstaking research on various aspects of Islamic civilization, despite his ill health. The International Institute of Islamic Thought approached me to edit the work in the light of evaluations from two other scholars. The study is well-documented and constitutes a standard text on Islamic civilization, in many ways supplementing the work of the late Professor Ismail al-Faruqi in the field.

OTHMAN ALI

NOTES BY THE AUTHOR ON WORD USAGE AND SPELLING

FOR CONTINUITY, I have adopted the following usages and spellings throughout the book. *Muslim*, for example, is a more accurate rendition of "Muslim." I use *Muslims* in the text rather than the customary "Arabs" often used when referring to the early Islamic period. I do this for several reasons. It is only when Arabs became Muslims that they achieved what they did. But they were not alone. From the very beginning, the closest companions of the Prophet Muhammad included an African, a Persian and a Caucasian. Iranians, too, contributed a great deal to both the initial and subsequent stages of Islamic civilization, as did, later, Indian and African Muslims and the Muslims of other parts of the world.

I also prefer *Muhammad* to other spellings, because of its pronunciation. On the other hand, I most often refer to Muhammad as the Prophet, rather than by his first name. In doing this, I am following the Qur'anic usage, where Muhammad is named only three times and is instead identified as a Prophet throughout the Sacred Book.

In another respect, to keep the pronunciation accurate, I have used *Qur'an* for Islam's Sacred Book, instead of the more popular Western "Koran." The divisions of the Sacred Book are referred to with the Islamic designation of *surah*, rather than "chapter" because the latter label is inaccurate. A reader sees the word "chapter" and expects all of it to discuss that particular subject, as in practically any book. The Qur'anic heading is not the subject of a surah but a means of identification of that particular segment of the Sacred Book.

My use of *Iranian* rather than "Persian" needs to be clarified. I prefer *Persia* and *Persian* for the pre-Islamic period and *Iran* and *Iranian* from when the region became predominantly Muslim. However, I have used *Persian* in a few instances, and especially in reference to the art and literature of Iran, because such usage is deeply ingrained in the discussions of the country's literature.

With regard to the spelling of names, I have made every attempt to be consistent, except when I quote directly. In such instances I have retained the spelling the author uses.

Regarding dates, as is becoming more customary in histories of Islam and the Muslims, I give the Islamic date first, followed by the date of the Common Era (CE). Also, since the Muslim calendar is lunar and hence shorter than the "common" calendar, the number of years of the two dates – the Muslim and the "common"– is not identical. Birth and death dates of important people are given in the text.

My use of *man* is generic and does not mean only the male. In a number of places in this book, I have found it necessary to repeat some things I have already said in a previous chapter. This is for a number of reasons: for the sake of clarity; because the context demands it; or, more important, because many Muslims were polymaths, in that they excelled in a number of disciplines and therefore needed to be discussed under different chapter headings. Nevertheless, I have avoided such repetitions where possible. The result is that a discussion might seem incomplete. It is not. I return to it where it is relevant in another context.

I

ISLAM'S ROLE IN HISTORY

ISLAM FORMED A unique bridge between the civilizations of the East and West. Muslim scholars rescued knowledge that would have been lost, if not forever, then at least for centuries. The Muslim body of scholarship synthesized and built on existing knowledge and hence brought forth something new each time. In these bursts of creativity, Muslims made their own contributions to the world over many centuries.

These accomplishments stemmed from the unique features of a religion that was in many ways new to humankind. Contrary to the largely negative view of the human race in many parts of the world at the time, Islam conferred dignity on human beings. Muslims saw the quest for knowledge as a religious duty and, as a result, changed the ways of looking at the world. Also unique was how Islam made clear that people should enjoy the bounties of the earth, provided they did not ignore morals and ethics. Furthermore, Islam eliminated the social distinctions between the classes and races of humankind.

Geographically, Islam created a civilization where a person could travel safely from Europe through North Africa, the Arab countries, Iran, India, and all the way to China and Indonesia. All that was needed was a copy of the Qur'an in one hand and a prayer mat in the other.

Islamic civilization created further changes, for it transcended not only geographical boundaries but also temporal, and thus achieved unity among divergent peoples. The position of women improved in its communities, at a time when women in many parts of the world were treated as chattels and soulless creatures.

For almost a thousand years, Islam could be said to have been one of the leading civilizations of the world. For over seven hundred years its language – Arabic – was the international language of science. J.M. Roberts, an eminent Oxford University historian, evaluates civilizations according to the contributions they made to the world and cites the Islamic civilization to be one of the major contributors.[1] The progress of every aspect of Muslim society affords the world the best example of how civilizations emerged from near-primal, semi-literate conditions, how they developed, and how they ultimately emerged to become true civilizations. Islamic civilization, owing to its reach across the world, its productivity, and its long existence, thus earned its high position in human history.

Yet even those who are widely read in history might never know any of this. In many history books, Muslims, who occupy vast stretches of the earth, are treated summarily as enemies of the West. From these texts, readers would hardly know that during the Middle Ages, this viable civilization made valuable contributions to other civilizations, particularly that of the West.

Where these studies mention the achievements of Islamic civilization, these accomplishments are either minimized or attributed to borrowing. For example, the Muslims' philosophy came from Greece, these historians insist; their form of government from Persia; and their scientific knowledge from Greece, India, and China; Sufism was an incarnation of Hinduism; and Islamic architecture and art were borrowed from Byzantium and Persia. Some historians are fond of emphasizing these borrowings, as though their own societies never did the same.

These historians prefer to devote their attention to the West as the only civilization of the Middle Ages. Their focus is primarily on Europe, which they label *the* civilization of this period. Although they write in the present time, their minds are rooted in the Dark Ages. Their descriptions and judgments come from tomes written from the seventh century AC onward, attacking Islam, the Qur'an, and Prophet Muhammad. The pejorative language of those days might be couched in today's academic terms, yet it is blatant in its rejection of Islam and especially its civilization. The technique in perpetuating this attitude is common: the historians dwell lengthily on Greece and Rome and the early development of Christianity, summarize the Islamic period, and make an enormous leap to the Renaissance.

This book intends to fill the huge gap between the decline of Rome and the "miraculous" flowering of European civilization. This book takes into account the borrowings emphasized by today's historians, although it is in the context of history as a continuum. The study recognizes that, in the same way as all non-Muslim civilizations borrowed from preceding cultures, so the Muslims borrowed too. However, the Muslims then went on to make their own contributions and created a civilization unlike any known in human history. In turn, other civilizations, especially the nascent civilization of Europe, borrowed ideas and materials from the Islamic civilization.

Islam also produced a continuation in another significant historical context, by supplementing the development of Judaism and Christianity. Thus, it added to the values of these religions and advanced the relationship between the human being and God, between one human being and another, and between the human being and society.

In keeping with the continuum, Islamic civilization provided the foundation of the next dominant civilization, which was that of the West. The West owes far more to Islam and to Muslims than it has so far acknowledged. Describing what Europe was like in those days, Roberts says that the European continent "would long be a cultural importer."[2]

The extensive Islamic segment of the continuum ought to be relevant to the world of the twenty-first century AC, yet many of its contributions, especially in the realm of values, are being ignored. There are parallels between the crises confronting Muslims in the early years of their history and many of the crises that they face in the twenty-first century. How the Muslims of those days overcame challenges is relevant today for both Muslims and non-Muslims. Islam and its civilization have much to offer, since the lessons of its history can also inform those who intend to divert the world from its current course of never-ending conflicts.

Meanings of Islam

This section focuses on what it means to be a Muslim. The religion comprises far more than its five "pillars:" the declaration of faith, the five daily prayers, fasting during the sacred month of Ramadan, paying *the zakah* (welfare tax), and, if economically feasible, making a pilgrimage to the holy cities of Makkah and Madinah. It is more accurate to speak of an Islamic way of life, for, in Islam, there is no separation between religion and the other aspects of life. Pairs of words such as "lay" and "ecclesiastical," "spiritual" and "temporal," and "secular" and "religious" have no equivalent in the world of Islam. A Muslim's life is a single entity.[3] Many non-Muslims as well as Muslims in the twenty-first century unfortunately overlook this reality.

The Islamic way of life, in its totality, was responsible for the creation of Islamic civilization. Islam presents a spiritual way of looking at the world and the quality of life, with depth and seriousness as well as with a sense of wonder. Civilization embodies the way people live, and how they behave toward one another, especially toward the poor, the handicapped, the starving, and the mentally ill. Civilization is how people build communities and encompass all that is of value to its members; it is how people view the world and the universe. Islamic civilization is expressed in these ways.

Islam's origins were simple. It was the first verse revealed to Prophet Muhammad while he meditated in a cave close to the top of the Mountain of Light north of Makkah, in a harsh, unforgiving climate. Not a single event but many, all converging, worked together to sustain Islam. They consisted of a sacred book, known as the Qur'an, which moved and still moves its listeners; a messenger of God, who was and continues to be a model for Muslims; a prophet who was very human; a man who courageously fought wars but preferred peace; a ruler who could have been a king but chose to be simply a leader; a person who was of a noble family, yet treated everyone fairly – men and women, Muslim and non-Muslim, rich and poor, fellow Arabs and foreigners, and people of all colors; an inspired community; a people made aware of their immense potential and fulfilling it; and a religion that proved meaningful to peoples across the earth.

As stated by the late Professor Ismail al-Faruqi, Islam's worldview is progressive with a holistic view of life. This view served as the driving force to create a civilization with far-reaching consequences for humanity.

2

LEARNING AND ISLAMIC
CIVILIZATION

BY EMPHASIZING LEARNING as one of the most important activities, Islam began to fill a chasm that had been widening in the world of the seventh century AC. The major civilizations of Mesopotamia, Egypt, Greece, and Rome had waned and India's had slowed considerably. Although China's civilization flowered during the Tang dynasty, beginning a decade after the appearance of Islam, its influence was restricted to the country's borders until the coming of the Muslims. Europe was in limbo, for its dominant power, Christianity, was impeding progress. During the continent's Dark Ages, Islam's geographic expansion was matched by an intellectual and cultural fervor.

Learning is integral to Islam, and this is clearly stated by Franz Rosenthal in his study of Muslim learning, *Knowledge Triumphant*: "Knowledge is Islam."[1] This viewpoint is understandable, given the first revelation and the Qur'an's emphasis on knowledge. On the Night of Power, a night venerated by Muslims during Ramadan, the cave was filled with the brilliance of light and a voice said to Muhammad, "Read" – that is, "Read aloud." The voice continued, "Read, in the name of your Lord, Who has created man out of a germ-cell. Read and your Lord is the most Bountiful One, Who teaches by the Pen, teaches man that which he knew not" (Qur'an 96:1–5).

The word *ʿilm* (knowledge) occurs in the Qur'an about 750 times, one of the highest word counts in the Text. *ʿIlm* is also one of the most repeated words in the Traditions of the Prophet Muhammad. "Seek knowledge from the cradle to the grave," the Prophet said,

"Seek knowledge even unto China." Although there is an abundance of cognates, especially nouns, in the Semitic languages other than Arabic, ʿ*ilm* is not one of them. It is, therefore, in its Qur'anic emphasis, uniquely Islamic.

The translation of ʿ*ilm* simply as knowledge is highly inadequate. Rosenthal gives twelve major definitions of the word and, in addition, divides these twelve into 107 distinctive definitions as expressed by Muslim scholars. The word is given an additional significance in the first surah of the Qur'an, in the very first verse. It is the root of ʿ*ālamīn*, translated as "the worlds." ʿ*Ālamīn* is literally "that by means of which [one] knows a thing … or that which has been created," – that is, the entire world and, by extension, the cosmos.

Emphasis, in Islam, is on the depth and breadth of knowledge. For example, the significance of the word *ḥikmah*, repeated in various places in the Qur'an, goes beyond its customary translation of simply "wisdom." *Ḥikmah* also means, according to *Lisān al-ʿArab* (an Arabic dictionary), "[conscious] insight into what is most excellent." Depth is further emphasized in the Qur'an (15:75) by the use of another word, *mutawassim*, designating, according to the Muslim scholars Zamakshari and Razi, "one who applies his mind to the study of a thing with a view to understanding its real nature and its inner characteristics."[2]

The Qur'an clearly distinguishes human beings from the rest of creation by their ability to reason. In several places, verse 2:31, for example, where the Qur'an focuses on the creation of Adam, it is explained that "the first human being" was taught names, which Muhammad Asad believes to be the faculty of logical definition and, thus, of "conceptual thinking."[3] Adam received the faculty of rational discrimination. People who possess knowledge are "those who have eyes to see" (Qur'an 3:13), "those endowed with insight" (3:7 and 5:100), and those "endowed with inner certainty" (2:118). Those who have been given knowledge have been given the equivalent of abundant wealth (2:269). Most important, the Qur'an equates knowledge with light (31:20). For every Muslim there is a short prayer in the Qur'an, "My Lord, increase me in knowledge" (20:114).

In two other respects, too, the Qur'an has proved an important stimulus to learning. First, the language is rich in its descriptions of scientific concepts. Second, equally important, is the effect of the language itself on the mind of the listener. Though known widely to scholars, especially those interested in semantics, language as a means of developing the mind is often ignored.

What enhances learning from the language of the Qur'an is the repeated, attentive recitation and listening to the beauty of its words, from a Muslim's childhood to the end of his/her days. Muslim scholars maintain that the Qur'an is not the Qur'an unless it is heard. For this reason, those who recite the Qur'an well are highly esteemed among Muslims. Dr. William Graham was so impressed when he first heard "professional Qur'an reciters" in Cairo that when he had the opportunity in Damascus, he learned to recite the Qur'an himself. He realized then "how vividly alive the sacred text could be for the faithful reciter."[4]

The great importance of classical Arabic, which is the linguistic basis of Islam and its civilization, needs much more emphasis than it has so far received in the West. The quality of the language is clearly evident in the Bedouin tongue, which was also the language of the poets before and after the coming of Islam. Some of the leading poets and writers of the Arab Muslim world lived among the Bedouin or sought them out in the cities to achieve greater proficiency in their use of vocabulary. Al-Jahiz, a renowned Arab writer, joined philologists who went to the outskirts of the city of Basrah to question the Bedouin staying there. The pristine Bedouin language has survived to this day. Muhammad Asad, who lived among the Bedouin, praises this quality and adds that it has helped him appreciate the Qur'an.[5]

During Europe's Middle Ages, Arabic not only dominated the Muslim world but was also present in Europe. Until Latin replaced it, Arabic was used in a number of European universities, as far west as England. The Qur'an was also responsible for an increased interest in learning. In order to understand the revelations recorded in the Qur'an, Muslims scrutinized the words: their definitions, etymology, and connotations, as well as statements, word order, and grammar.

This was done from almost the beginning of Islam when the Qur'an was spread orally. Later, interpreters of Qur'anic statements wrote them down, and these interpretations are still available.

The first Muslim effort at grammar began with the establishment of a school of Arabic at Madinah, as early as the time of the first four Caliphs (11–40/632–661). Ali, the last of these Caliphs, prompted a Muslim scholar to write about the parts of speech. At the end of the first century AH, Ibn Yusuf, the then governor of Iraq, helped establish a grammar school in Basrah. During the next century at this school, Khalil ibn Ahmad made contributions to grammar and was also the first to compile a dictionary of the Arabic language, which was expanded considerably by Ibn Duraid.

The dictionary and basics of Arabic grammar served as a resource for Jewish philology. In the first Hebrew dictionary, written by Saadia ben Joseph, Hebrew words were translated into Arabic. Joseph, Sahl ben Masliah, and David ben Abraham wrote Hebrew grammars, which were based on Arabic grammar, and their works were written in Arabic.

Almost from its inception, the Muslim community considered the ability to read as one of its major needs. Following the first, victorious clash with the pagan Makkans, the Muslims put prisoners to work, teaching the people of Madinah to read and write. In a similar fashion, when forty young Christian scholars were captured during a battle, they were sent to Madinah, also to teach. (The son of one of those young Christians was to become the conqueror of Spain for the Muslims.) Every Muslim child, male and female, learned to read the Qur'an, to recite its verses, and also studied other Islamic texts. The curriculum of the advanced classes included literature, science, and philosophy.

From early on, too, *madāris* (schools of all kinds) were established. Never had there been a society with such a widespread focus on teaching its members to read. Muslim children were reading and writing while in Europe, in the words of Roberts, "kings were normally illiterate,"[6] knowing only how to write their names. Literacy in medieval Europe was the monopoly of the clergy.[7] Muslim

scholars in the early centuries of Islam strongly believed that dili-
gence in learning made a difference to their lives on earth and in the
Hereafter. How they would be treated in life after death, they maintained, depended on their knowledge and piety. Most of the early
rulers of the Muslim world were also highly sophisticated scholars,
who participated in the search for knowledge and made it accessible
to everyone. Books were available to every scholar, regardless of
background, to the extent that the scholars of the Muslim world
included Jews, Christians, and people from other parts of the world.
Words, especially of the sacred books, as well as in works of literature, became so highly regarded that they were recorded in exquisite
calligraphy and decorated with gold and lapis lazuli.

Therefore, learning was the focus of the Muslim community, for
it was encouraged by the Qur'an as well as the teachings and practice
of Prophet Muhammad and his immediate Successors. Furthermore,
Islamic learning flourished hand in hand with the establishment of
the first Muslim community.

3

THE ESTABLISHMENT OF THE FIRST MUSLIM COMMUNITY

THE EARLIEST MUSLIM community was a melioristic society. In other words, the early Muslims changed their way of life in response to revelations of the Qur'an and the behavior of Prophet Muhammad. These elements influenced all areas of life.

The Qur'an emphasizes repeatedly the importance of working in harmony with nature. Islamic expert Seyyed Hossein Nasr states that in Islam there is an "inseparable link between man and nature."[1] "Behold," God says in the Qur'an, "We have willed that all beauty on earth be a means by which we put men to a test" (18:7). One of the "tests" is certainly the manner in which humans treat this beautiful earth. In another verse, the Qur'an points the way: "Walk gently on the earth" (25:63).

Islam insists that this world is not to be denied, but enjoyed. The Qur'an admonishes those who believe otherwise: "Who is there to forbid the beauty which God has brought forth for His creatures...?" (7:32). The Qur'an in fact encourages Muslims to appreciate the world, to savor the blessings of fruit and flowers and of the good things to eat, to be attuned to the rhythms of night and day and the seasons, and to marvel at nature.

Nasr reminds us that the Qur'an makes clear that among the "signs" of God are the "phenomena in the world of nature." Then he goes on to state, "By refusing to separate man and nature completely, Islam has preserved an integral view of the Universe." In one respect, Nasr's message is that people "who live only on the surface of their being," not respecting nature and instead wanting to dominate it, tend toward the destruction of the environment.[2]

Islam gives the human being a high status, too. According to Islam, the human being is not a fallen creature born in sin, nor an outcast because he or she is not of a chosen race. The human being is not caught up in the perpetual cycle of reincarnation, nor a nonentity lost in the mass, nor a creature whose life is absurd or meaningless. The Qur'an describes the human body as a miracle in all its complexity, and one that can acquire divine qualities: "Imbue yourself with divine attributes," the Prophet said. (Qur'an 38:71-72).

In short, God elevated the whole of humankind. The Qur'an states, "We have conferred dignity on the children of Adam" (17:70). Later, it adds, "We have indeed created man in the best of forms" (95:4). As Shabir Akhtar described it, according to Islam, "the saga of human history begins with the 'Rise' rather than the Fall of Man."[3] (Qur'an 2:30).

In essence, Islam focuses on uncovering the true qualities of the human being. A person, the Qur'an emphasizes repeatedly, has dignity and is endowed with what no other creature possesses, namely, the abilities to reason, think creatively, and communicate that reasoning and creativity with the gift of articulation.

The Prophet exemplified this and the other teachings of the Qur'an. His leadership and the Qur'an in fact go together. From the first moment of revelation, his whole life was devoted to the leadership of his community in accordance with Islam. According to Hodgson, "Muhammad seems to have lived a quite simple and modest life without any luxury, by and large accessible and affable with the lowliest, delighting in laughter and in children."[4]

Prophet Muhammad

Muhammad was born in Makkah in 570 AC. From his early years he earned a reputation for being most trustworthy in his personal and business life. He accompanied his guardian uncle on trade caravans, even as far as Syria. His business acumen earned him the position of leading caravans for the widow Khadijah, whom he later married.

He remained devoted to her until her death twenty-five years later.

Muhammad's first revelation, described above, came in 610 AC. He preached to his fellow Makkans, who responded by tormenting him. When the Makkan tribes came together and plotted his death, the Prophet migrated to Yathrib, a city to the north. The event is an important one in Islamic history, for it marks the beginning of the Islamic calendar. It is called Dār al-Hijrah, commonly translated as "the emigration." However, the original definition is the most appropriate: "Turning away from someone familiar or loved, often with the intention of returning."[5]

Yathrib later became known simply as Madinah, the City, from Madinat al-Nabī, the City of the Prophet. There, Prophet Muhammad established the first Muslim community and the first Islamic house of worship. After surviving a number of wars, the Prophet and his people eventually conquered Makkah (with remarkably few casualties), rid the Ka'bah of its idols, and established it as the center of Islam.

When the Prophet purified the Ka'bah of idolatry, he was at the height of his mission. Nevertheless, despite the position he had achieved, he neither wanted, nor sought power. He remained true to what he was – a Prophet of God – from the time of the first revelation. Although the people of Makkah offered him their kingship, wealth, and beautiful women if he would stop preaching, he refused. When they asked his guardian uncle to persuade him, the Prophet said, "I shall not forsake this Cause…not even if they put the sun in my right hand and the moon in my left. I shall still go on…" God asked the Prophet to say to the pagans: "No reward do I ask of you for this [message] other than [that you should] love your fellow-men" (Qur'an 42:23).

Prophet Muhammad was far more than an example to his people. "What made Muhammad so rare a figure in history," says historian Ira Lapidus, "what made him a Prophet, was his ability to convey his vision to people around him so that concepts long known to everyone took on the power to transform other people's lives as they had transformed his."[6] The Muslims were given, to use Hodgson's description, a "vision" that "proved sufficiently potent to ensure that Muslims formed a single great civilization of their own."[7]

Jihad, an activity mentioned in different places in the Qur'an, was the tool to achieve that civilization. The word's closest translation into English is "striving toward a worthy goal." Many Muslims obeyed and continued striving toward improving not only their own lives but also those of others until they achieved a civilization worthy of the name for a thousand years. This book describes their efforts.

The Prophet in fact called for "a greater jihad," explaining it as "the struggle against self." When the Prophet's uncle asked for a gift so that he "might rule men," the Prophet said, "I will give you a greater gift than that, Uncle; for one moment you shall rule yourself." The Sufi Hallaj made a similar response to his servant Ibrahim, who asked for words by which to remember him. "Yourself," Hallaj said. "Unless you enslave it, it will enslave you."[8] Rumi, early on in his *Masnavi* (also written Mathnavi), put it metaphorically. "The idol of yourself," he said, "is the mother of all idols."[9]

Those early Muslims worked with remarkable zeal to establish a viable community. The Qur'an recognized the task for what it was and recommended them to practice jihad, a striving toward a better goal. To emphasize its importance, the Qur'an described it as a greater striving (25:52).

Egalitarianism

Prophet Muhammad was like no other leader of his time in his possession of qualities such as humility, gentleness, kindness, and sensitivity for the feelings of others. The Qur'an, in a number of verses, insists that he was "a mortal man," only a messenger. At home, his wife Aishah said he behaved like an ordinary person. He helped others, including his servants; he went to the market; swept his house; repaired his sandals and clothes; and watered the camels. He actively participated in the life of the first Muslim community in Madinah, sharing meals and labor with the inhabitants. He worked with fellow Muslims in the building of the first mosque. When the time came to excavate a trench to protect Madinah against attack, he did his share of the digging.

In keeping with the Islamic belief in human dignity, Muhammad insisted that there was to be no racism whatsoever in Islam. All human beings were deemed equal, whatever their color. The Prophet had as his close Companions three who were from the three major regions of the world: Bilal from Africa, Salman from Asia, and Suhaib from Europe. The Qur'an states that pilgrims will come to Makkah for the pilgrimage "from every far-away point [on earth]" (22:27). This verse was revealed at a time when the new, small Muslim community had just been established and there were enemies on every side determined to destroy it.

The Prophet emphasized this in his last sermon, insisting, "There is no superiority for an Arab over a non-Arab, nor for a non-Arab over an Arab, neither for a white man over a black man, nor a black man over a white man." It was this "egalitarian quality of Islam," according to Peters, that "[undermined] the old feudal order in the East," thus bringing about a more equitable society wherever it prevailed.[10] Hodgson describes it as "a new system of assuring the security of the weak against the strong."[11] "This deep and strong egalitarianism would characterize the Islamic spirit and inform its religious, political, and even its artistic and literary institutions," says Armstrong in her book, *Muhammad: A Western Attempt to Understand Islam.*[12]

Islam changed the position of women, too. This development was most remarkable for its time, when women were most miserably treated. Arabia was among the worst, since many fathers considered the birth of a baby girl a disgrace and, in many instances, buried her alive. Infanticide is totally forbidden by Islam.

The Prophet made it clear that women were not under the "guardianship" of their husbands. It became customary for women to retain their maiden names upon marriage. A major change was that men were restricted from having innumerable wives. In fact, the Qur'an recommends only one wife as the ideal marital relationship (4:3). Women were given the right to divorce, extremely rare in those days, and the right to alimony (2:241) and child support (2:233), also extremely rare.

Islam was far ahead in another respect, in that a woman had the right to *own* property and wealth and to have control over them. In fact, as Hodgson makes clear, the husband had no access whatsoever to his wife's money and had to support her, their children, and the household from his own funds. Women could also inherit wealth and property, including the exclusive ownership of the dowry she received from her husband.[13] It was not until the passage of the Women's Property Act of 1882 in England that Englishwomen could inherit. In his final sermon, the Prophet noted simply, "You have rights over your wives, and your wives have rights over you."[14] The Prophet's daughter Fatimah and his wife Aishah were noted for their eloquence. These two and Safiyah, the Jewish wife of the Prophet, as well as his granddaughters Zainab and Sukayna, all participated in politics and proved most helpful in resolving matters in the first Muslim community. Women ruled, too, in the Muslim world, not only as queens but also as participants in the affairs of state. The names of many Muslim women are still legendary as outstanding philanthropists. There were Muslim women poets who competed with men in poetry festivals. Muslim women were artists, calligraphers, and musicians, as well as teachers, physicians, and professors.

The Mosque

The center of the Muslim community was, and still is all over the world, the mosque. Its basic structure at this time was simple: on the side facing Makkah there was a small set of steps, and at its side a niche (*minbar*) where the imam led the prayers. The rest of the mosque, whether a cavernous interior or an enormous courtyard, was for the congregation. The later additions, only two in number, consisted of a dome and a minaret from where the *muadhdhin* called the faithful to prayer.

The mosque, from the establishment of the first community, was more than a place for prayer. It was a center of hospitality and, more important to the creation of an Islamic civilization, a center of education. The mosque was the traveler's first stop. Members of the community invited him for meals, and, if he was a learned man, he was asked to give lectures. There are numerous instances of Muslim scholars being retained in a city for months, even years, to educate the community.

The mosque was for a long time an educational institution in the broadest sense. There were lectures for the general public, classes for children, schools for the youth, and lectures for university students. The mosque was the university, the most famous of which is al-Azhar in Cairo, which is more than a thousand years old and the only continuously existing university in the world. Al-Azhar still functions as one of the principal educational institutions of Islam.

The mosque was also a seat of the government in the first Muslim community. The Islamic form of governing is based on consensus (*shūrā*) among members of the community. The Prophet, too, was requested to "take counsel" with his people (Qur'an 3:159). The consensus consisted invariably of what was good for the entire community. Special interest groups and the privileges of a few members of the community were totally ignored.

Taxes and Charity

Islam came closer to fulfilling the ideal of equal rights for all than any other culture at this time. Every person's needs were treated in the same way in the first community. Nowhere is this more clearly evident than in the Muslims' concern for their fellow human beings and especially in their charitable donations. There was certainly the practice of the obligatory payment of a welfare tax. There were other designated charities, too, most of them voluntary, including the major ones at the end of the fasting month of Ramadan and toward the end of the pilgrimage (Hajj). All of these monies were spent on the needy, travelers, the indebted, and scholars, and benefited everyone living in a community, regardless of religion.

Al-Ghazali emphasized a unique characteristic of Muslim charity. A Muslim must give to a fellow Muslim in need, "without his ever asking for it," and without "waiting for him to ask for it." If the needy Muslim "gets to the point of asking for help," then the equilibrium of the community is deeply disturbed.[15]

By contrast, able-bodied non-Muslim men living in Muslim countries had to pay a single tax (*jizyah*), mainly because they did not serve in the army. If they volunteered for military service, they were exempt from the tax. The tax was spent on "protecting" the non-Muslims. There were occasions, in the early history of Islam, where Muslims were unable to provide this protection and they repaid the taxes to the non-Muslim tax-payers. For example, when the Muslims had to retreat from the city of Hims, the commander reimbursed the Christian leaders of the city with the entire amount paid by their community. And when the Byzantines plundered the Copts of Alexandria and the Copts complained they had not been protected, the Muslim commander arranged to compensate them for the losses they had suffered.[16]

Travelers experienced a Middle East hospitality that has become proverbial, for the treatment of a guest went beyond simply welcoming, feeding, and accommodating him. It included protection, even if that guest were a criminal or an enemy. Fukaihah, a Bedouin woman, defended with her life a bandit who had taken refuge in her tent. The second Caliph, Umar, used to give sugar to the poor because he loved sweets.

"Your smiling is charity," the Prophet said. "Your heartening a man to a good deed is charity; your forbidding the forbidden is charity; your showing a man his road in a country where he is lost is charity; and your care for a blind man is charity."[17] Removing a stone from a traveler's path is charity, and so, too, is a kind word. Providing water for the thirsty is considered most meritorious, and this is exemplified by the Prophet when he prevented his men from attacking several enemies who came to the Muslim camp for water.

Perhaps a unique feature of Islamic charity is spending on those who, because of their pursuits, are unable to work to support themselves. These include people devoted to some cause of the faith; those in search of knowledge; those striving to help other people; as well as those who have become physically handicapped in these pursuits.

Perhaps this practice was also the beginning of a community (later, government) granting financial aid to scholars.

The pages of Islamic history attest to the religion's egalitarian character. There are numerous cases of servants becoming lords and, in some instances, rulers in the broadest sense of the word. Numerous great names, especially those of scholars and scientists, came from humble origins, as will be demonstrated in the chapters that follow.

There was a special understanding in that first Muslim community regarding the treatment of animals. All animals, including birds, according to the Qur'an, are creatures like humans, "who live in communities like you" (6:38). Animals are also considered to have an afterlife: "Unto their Sustainer shall they [all] be gathered" (6:38). Zamakshari interprets this statement as meaning that animals will live in the Hereafter with those people who loved them on earth. Toward the end of the Qur'an is yet another verse regarding animals (81:5). On the Day of Judgment "all the beasts will be gathered together," to receive from God, according to Razi, compensation for people's cruelty to them.[18]

The Prophet prevented worshipers from removing a cat and her litter of kittens from a mosque and, instead, had the congregation pray around them. He showed his concern for the well-being of animals in other instances, too. Once, he held up prayers until the people who had just arrived had watered and fed their camels. On another occasion, he pointed out to a man giving a sermon from atop a camel that the animal was not a pulpit. He was also very angry with a group of men who had robbed a bird's nest of its young. And he praised women for being kind to animals, "Good done to an animal has its reward," he said.[19]

Islam expected and expects humans to treat animals and people with dignity and respect. R.V.C. Bodley described an incident he witnessed while he was traveling in an East Asian Muslim country. There was a funeral procession progressing along one of the streets and, as was customary, the mourners were moving toward the front of the bier to carry it for a few steps and then relinquishing it to those waiting in front. A Muslim businessman passing by in a big chauffeured car stopped, shouldered the bier for several steps, then returned to his car and moved on. Bodley had the impression that the businessman did not know the deceased.[20]

There was no need for passers-by to know the deceased. The shouldering of a bier is in itself considered meritorious. However, the thought of gaining merit was far from the minds of the mourners or the businessman, for the latter acted spontaneously, as would any Muslim. It was a Muslim's funeral and that was all that mattered.

Islamic Law

With the expansion of Islam in all directions – east, west, north, and south – there was the need for a common understanding. This need was fulfilled by the establishment of Islamic law, which came to form the foundation of the Islamic civilization.

Four scholars were the original founders of Islamic law. The first, who is also considered by many to be the most eminent and widely respected to this day, was Abu Hanifah (81–150/700–767). He used the Qur'an as the basis of the school of law that bears his name and that is followed by the majority of the Muslim world. Abu Hanifah was diligent in determining which of the Traditions of the Prophet were authentic. He was meticulous in his methodology, sifting every bit of research that came his way. An extraordinary amount of material did reach him, since he had at one time hundreds of scholars working for him and searching through books for data for his attention. His approach to Islamic law was very human. His students themselves became authorities on jurisprudence. When Sultan Alp Arslan built a tomb for Abu Hanifah, he paid tribute to him and also built a school at the side of the tomb.

Abu Hanifah influenced people outside the Muslim community through a Jewish theologian, Anan ben David. According to Sarton, Anan ben David was a Jewish reformer, who in turn stimulated the "development of Jewish thought...for some four centuries."[21] The other three founders of Islamic law were Malik ibn Anas (93–179/712–795), Muhammad ibn Idris al-Shafiʿi (150–204/767–820), and Ahmed ibn Hanbal (164–241/780–855).

Conclusion

This chapter has outlined the development of the Muslim community, from its simple origins to the foundation of a sophisticated administration based on social justice, the endless search for knowledge, a humble awareness of the miracle of God's creation, and the use of it according to God's laws, as exemplified by the life of Prophet Muhammad. The examples described have shown that Islam brought to the world features that were unique and were therefore responsible for its far-reaching and long-enduring influence on a wide range of societies. In the following chapters, these features are explained in greater detail, as well as the changes that occurred in the societies affected as Islam spread across three of the world's continents.

4

THE ISLAMIC WORLD ORDER

THE ISLAMIC SPIRIT was dominant wherever the Muslims went in the world. As a result, relations between the Muslims and the local inhabitants were far different than that which usually existed between the conquerors and the conquered. Within a century of the advent of Islam, the Muslims reached North Africa and Spain in one direction and China and Indonesia in the other. What were the reasons for these successes? Why, long after the battles were over, as much as a hundred years later, were there more conversions to Islam than in the previous decades? Why did the Mongols suddenly convert to Islam, after slaughtering thousands upon thousands of Muslims and destroying great cities, including Baghdad? These are the questions that this chapter will try to answer.

Benevolent Rule

The wars began soon after the Muslim community was established. The Muslims were attacked and they responded – and with a zeal that surprised their enemies. Byzantium and Persia, the two major powers of the time, constantly warred with each other. The Arabs were caught in the middle and, furthermore, used by both as buffers and as allies. As a result, whenever Byzantine and Persia fought, there were heavy Arab casualties.

Byzantium turned against the Arabs simply because the Arabs, inspired by Islam, were emerging from a centuries-long slumber. The Byzantine emperor Heraclius, having defeated the Persians at Nineveh, prepared a new force to march against the Muslims. This was no weak army, which some Western historians insist on giving as the reason for the success of the Muslims. The Byzantine army was very skilled in battle techniques, having had tactical training as well as experience in a number of battles. It had superiority of weapons and numbers and, in addition, an ambulance corps of surgeons and stretcher-bearers. The army had also inherited expertise in the martial arts from the Caesars of Rome. The Byzantine forces far outnumbered the Muslims, as did the Persian army, which was, at around the same time, also preparing to attack the Muslims.[1]

At the battle of Yarmuk, 40,000 Muslims faced 200,000 Byzantine soldiers. In the first major battle in the East, the Persian army under Rustam, a formidable commander, outnumbered the Muslims by six to one. Both major powers had reinforcements available, whereas the Muslims had none. There was a Byzantine fleet off the coast of Palestine to replenish supplies and bring more men to the battle. The Persian forces had a "weapon" far more menacing: they brought in elephants. In the battle for Babylon, thirty-three elephants led the attack.[2] None the less, the Muslims won all the battles. Most remarkable was not only the Muslims' victory itself, but also its extent and the rapidity with which it was gained.

Also significant for the future of the Muslim world was how the peaceable communities behaved toward the Muslims. All the Jews, and many Christians as well (including the Donatists of North Africa), welcomed the Muslims because of the persecution that they had suffered at the hands of the Byzantines.[3] The Roman Empire was brutal enough, but Christian Byzantium, the inheritor of the Roman way of life, especially the military, at times tried to outdo the Caesars. Justinian continued the pogroms against the Jews and the destruction of their synagogues. He also interfered with Judaic worship and urged other rulers to persecute their Jews. A later ruler, Basil II, destroyed Bulgaria. His method of persuading the Bulgarians to surrender was to return to them 15,000 of their countrymen that he had captured and blinded.

The Muslims were fair, for the Prophet had admonished them to "deal gently with people" of other countries. The Muslim commander

Khalid negotiated a just treaty with the people of Damascus, consisting of terms to which the Muslims adhered from that time. The terms were based on what the Prophet and later Abu Bakr, the first Caliph, believed to be the best way for conquerors to behave. "You shall mutilate none," Abu Bakr commanded. "Neither shall you kill [a] child, nor aged man, nor any women. Do not injure the date palm, neither burn it; and do not cut a tree wherein is food for man or beast. Do not slay the flocks or sheep or camels, save for needful sustenance."[4]

The Muslims were consistent, in that they did not destroy the places they conquered, nor did they put the men to death, or enslave the women and children, all of which were customary practices in the wars of those days. To avoid any incidents, the Muslim armies did not even occupy cities. Instead, they built their own tent cities and military garrisons in the vicinity. For a long time, too, no Muslim was permitted even to buy a building or a plot of ground in the communities they had defeated.

"We like your rule," said the Christian people of Hims in Syria after the Muslims freed them from Byzantine rule. "We like your justice, ye Muslims, far better than the cruelty and the tyranny of the old times."[5] The Monophysites of Egypt and Syria welcomed the Muslims, as did the Jacobites and the Copts.[6] When the Muslims conquered North Africa, the Berbers, according to Hitti, "found the new [Muslim] masters more congenial than the old [Byzantine] ones."[7] In India, according to Hodgson, the Buddhists preferred the Muslims.[8]

A noted historian of the Middle Ages, Norman F. Cantor, describes Islam as "a faith which...rapidly appealed to...an enormous number of people." One of his reasons is Islam's "optimistic" nature as a religion.[9] In Jerusalem, the reigning Caliph himself demonstrated the positive nature of Muslim rule. He journeyed to that city in 637 AC because its patriarch Sophronius refused to surrender to anyone but the Muslim ruler. The patriarch had, only a little earlier, given a sermon on "the menace" approaching the Holy City.

When Sophronius went out to meet the Muslim ruler, the person he saw was Umar the Caliph, who was wearing the simple long cloak that he always wore, and riding a horse with a few Muslims accompanying him. Instead of inflicting the horrible massacres on which Sophronius had dwelt in his sermon, Umar offered generous terms, giving security for people, property, and places of worship. Umar then asked to be taken to "the sanctuary of David." The place turned out to be filthy, for the Romans had used it as a dung heap. Umar and his companions cleaned the place and then prayed there.

Visiting the Church of the Holy Sepulcher with the patriarch, Umar noticed that it was time for prayer. Sophronius offered an area in the church where Umar could pray. Umar refused, saying that if he did so, the Church of the Holy Sepulcher would be taken over by the Muslims and converted into a mosque because he had led the way for them to do so. Umar's next action was to reverse the edict of the Christian rulers of Jerusalem. He permitted the Jews to return and, in addition, to pray at the Sacred Wall. According to Paul Johnson, "Islamic rule marked the beginning of Jewish recovery,"[10] and brought a revival of Jewish fortune.[11]

Not only peaceful toward their conquered peoples, the Muslims were also constructive. In Muslim Spain, for example, Amir Abd al-Rahman I developed the city of Cordoba in the eighth century AC, built an aqueduct to bring in fresh water, and added palaces and other buildings as well as gardens. Soon, Muslim travelers and geographers were describing Cordoba as "the Mother of Cities." Its fame, according to Hitti, "penetrated distant Germany, where a Saxon nun styled it 'the jewel of the world.'"[12]

Cities

Some of the garrison towns the Muslims established outside existing cities themselves became cities in their own right. Cairo was founded in this way, as well as Kufah and Basrah. Muslims went on to create other cities, such as Qairawan, Fez, Tunis, Timbuktu, and Baghdad. The creation of new cities was certainly one of the most important determinants in the development of Islamic civilization. Soon, there was the need to establish a place specifically for the expansion of learning. This was Baghdad, the first major Muslim intellectual capital. The Caliph al-Mansur preferred to call his new capital "the City of Peace."[13]

Baghdad was indeed peaceful and, therefore, conducive to intellectual pursuits. It even eclipsed the previous capital, Damascus. Although there was a major center of learning in Madinah, the first center of the Muslim world, it was predominantly religious. Baghdad developed into the greatest center of general education, not only of the Muslim world, but also of Europe and the eastern hemisphere for centuries.

Three out of the four founders of the four schools of Islamic law lived and worked in Baghdad. It was the city that produced the first, and, according to some scholars, the most important Muslim philosopher, al-Kindi. Also founded was the House of Wisdom, perhaps the first institution devoted to intellectual pursuits with an emphasis on the sciences, as well as an institution of higher learning known as the Niẓāmiyah Academy. Both would today be classified as universities.

The Niẓāmiyah's most esteemed professor was al-Ghazali, who, according to Hitti, was "one of the greatest religious thinkers in history."[14] Scholars from all over the world came to Baghdad to study, to contribute, and always to participate in academic discourse. The city housed what was then the biggest hospital, which won the highest praise of people from all over the Muslim world. It also served as a medical school, contributing to major advances in medical knowledge.[15]

Baghdad's fame also rests on other factors. It served as a capital for the Abbasids, the longest-reigning dynasty in Islamic history. The city opened itself to Persian influence and, a little later, to new ideas from both East and West. International trade boomed here. Among the imports were pearls from Oman, paper, ink, silks, and chinaware from China, fine cloth from Egypt, carpets from Merv, elephants, rubies, ebony, and white sandals from India, honey, saffron, salt, and fruit syrups from Isfahan, and cloth from Armenia.

Baghdad also saw changes in political institutions, which became less Islamic and then notorious for their love of luxury and hedonism, practices followed by many Muslim rulers from that time onwards.[16] In 656/1258, the Mongol Hulagu, the grandson of Chingiz Khan, conquered Baghdad. Within a week he had slaughtered 70,000 people and destroyed every major building in the city – the mosques, the palaces, the shrines, the schools, and the libraries. Most of the buildings were burned down, and all the books in the libraries were destroyed and thrown into the river, turning the waters black.

The Muslims created a number of other cities that contributed to and assured the continuation of Islamic civilization after the destruction of Baghdad. The single most important value of these cities was that they became centers of Islamic learning, many of which are still well known today. The most famous of them is Cairo, which had its beginnings in a garrison town during the early Muslim conquests. Cairo gained prestige mainly because of the actions of three rulers. Of the Fatimids, whose capital was Cairo, al-Aziz was one of the most outstanding. He enlarged Cairo with the building of mosques, bridges, palaces, and canals. As a scholar, al-Aziz surrounded himself with other learned men, and he created al-Azhar, the university. His son and successor al-Hakim was inspired by the Abbasid Caliph al-Ma'mun to make the city a center of "science and wisdom."[17]

The second ruler, Salah al-Din (known in the West as Saladin), is still renowned all over the world for his chivalry, good manners, and compassion. On assuming power, he refused to live in the palace, preferring instead a modest mansion and ascetic lifestyle. In addition to the many educational institutions he created in Cairo, Salah al-Din built hospitals, and the Citadel, still one of the most prominent buildings in the city. The third ruler was a member of the Mamluk dynasty: al-Zahir Baybars. Under Baybars and his successors, Cairo became the most distinguished center of Islam. The family's most notable achievements were in architecture, monuments that still retain their splendor.

Another tent encampment that became a famous city, also in North Africa, was Kairouan in Tunisia, founded in 50/670. It was noted as a religious, commercial, and intellectual center. The foundation of Tunis as a capital is among the reasons why the city became a marketplace for grain. It is, nevertheless, still a place of pilgrimage because just outside the city is the tomb of one of the Companions of the Prophet.

A little over a century later, another city rivaled Kairouan's fame.

This was Fez, founded in Morocco in 192 /808 by Idries II. To this city came families fleeing a revolt in Cordoba and from Kairouan. The plan of Fez was unusual, based on mule tracks from the different gates to the markets in the center of the city. That is why no tourist nowadays would venture into the city without a guide. Another unusual feature was the small number of officials governing so large a city, for it had expanded with Jewish immigration from Spain.

Later, with the Spanish Inquisition, the Jewish population of Fez swelled. The city soon achieved fame with its magnificent mosques and universities. Its craftsmanship continues to thrive today, to the marvel of tourists. The founder of one mosque-university, al-Qarawiyyīn, was a pious woman, Fatimah, who had a rich mother. The mosque-university was enlarged, until each of its twenty transepts had twenty columns and the center was under five domes. The structure is so complex that these domes can be seen only from the inside.[18]

Beautification

The Muslims created gardens wherever they went, and filled them with flowers such as jasmine and lilac. These flowers as well as their names are of Persian origin. The word in the Qur'an for Paradise (jannah) also means "garden." The English word "paradise" is derived from the Persian word for an enclosed garden. Another Persian word, gulistan (rose garden), has often been used by Persian and Urdu poets as a synonym for Paradise.

The Qur'anic descriptions of Paradise as green, lush gardens made a deep impression on the Muslims. It is, therefore, easy to understand the enthusiasm with which the Muslim Arabs, and later the Muslims of other regions, took advantage of the presence of water and arable soil to create a touch of paradise on earth. These places were also islands of serenity.[19]

Even before the creation of gardens, the Muslims included hints of Heaven in their artwork. In the first major Muslim building, the Dome of the Rock in Jerusalem (built 72/691), floral decoration abounded and henceforth it was a feature of almost all Muslim

architecture, including mosques, often as a background to calligraphic citations from the Qur'an. This style soon became complex and
formalized and was widely followed in Europe, too, where it was
known as arabesque.[20]

Floral and plant decorations were much more widely depicted in
another, more commonly known Islamic art form: the carpet. These
carpets and rugs were easy to roll up and carry and so became an
essential part of the baggage of every Muslim traveler. The travelers
ventured into the distant parts of the Muslim world and thus transported the designs to the local inhabitants. The creators of these carpets added a sense of infinity to the designs by so arranging them as
to make them seem to extend beyond the physical world. (This topic
is discussed in greater detail in Chapter 13 on the Islamic arts.)

The creation of gardens became an art form, too, which the Arabs
learned from the Persians. When the Arabs settled in Persia, they were
impressed most by the abundance of water – the "fathomless tanks"
and "bottomless pools," – as well as by the exquisite layouts of the
gardens. In planning the building of mosques, the Muslims arranged
for them to be surrounded by gardens.[21]

The emphasis was on balance in gardening as an art form. In addition to the arrangements of the areas of cultivation and the walkways,
there were buildings and pavilions of all kinds, pools of all shapes,
and the merging of the landscape and the streets and the rest of the
city. Many of the features were distinctly Islamic, especially the
domes on the buildings. Decoration on the walls and pillars consisted
of arabesques and thus complemented the plants. The result was a
place of exquisite beauty and, above all, of tranquillity. This quality
is expressed in the Mughal inscription in the Shalimar Gardens of
Kashmir: "If there is a Paradise on earth, it is here, it is here."

Ruling Ideals

Despite their obvious love of beauty, the Muslims did not conquer
for material wealth, although in the process they gained an enormous amount of it. They were happy to have Damascus because
it was one of the world's exceptional intellectual centers. Islam's

emphasis has been primarily on creativity, the chronicling of which has largely been overshadowed by an overwhelming emphasis on the negative aspect of Muslim history. The expansion of Islam has to be seen in the light of what it accomplished, especially in view of the tendency of non-Muslim conquerors at that time to kill, destroy, and enslave. This book could be filled with examples.

Also necessary to keep in mind is that the early wars of Islam were the least destructive of military action; the men, women and children were not killed; the cities were not destroyed; and life in fact improved for most of their inhabitants. The majority of conversions to Islam took place long after the battles were over. Those who persist in believing that Islam was spread by the sword should take account of the most convincing evidence to the contrary, namely, that in countries under Muslim rule, the Muslims were in a minority. According to Albert Hourani, a century after the Muslim conquest, "less than ten percent of the population in Iran and Iraq, Syria and Egypt, Tunisia, and Spain was Muslim," and that it was not until "the end of the fourth Islamic century (9th–10th century AC)...[that] a large part of the population had become Muslim."[22]

The Muslims remained a minority under Muslim governments throughout their rule in countries such as India and Sicily. When the Crusaders reached the Levant, four centuries after the Muslim conquests, Lewis says, "a substantial proportion of the population of these lands, perhaps even a majority, was still Christian."[23]

Bulliet states that conversion took place long after the conquests. In his study, *Conversion to Islam in the Medieval Period*, Bulliet makes an important distinction between those who simply repeated the declaration of faith to become Muslim, and those who underwent "social conversion," which he defines as becoming a member of and identifying with the Muslim community. Bulliet then goes on to chart the social conversions of the newly-conquered territories of Iraq, Iran, Syria, Egypt, Tunisia, and Spain, to demonstrate that there were more conversions as late as a hundred years after the conquests and that the conversions peaked centuries later.[24]

In both the largest Muslim country in the world – Indonesia – and "in China where Arab armies never trod," Philip Curtin reminds us, there were no battles, no conquests, and not even a drop of blood spilled. The Muslims traveled to the Indonesian islands within forty years of the Prophet's death not as warriors but as traders.[25]

Most remarkable is how Islam spread across this region, consisting of around 13,500 islands, all of them miles apart. The people there already had two forms of worship: animistic and Hindu. When Islam arrived, peacefully, almost all the people converted – and of their own free will – except for those on Bali, whose predominantly Hindu religion even today remains undisturbed.

Islam spread in Indonesia slowly at first, with the arrival of Muslim merchants from the shores of India as early as 400 AH (eleventh century AC). Their honesty in particular impressed the Indonesians. About two hundred years later, there were mass conversions owing to the activities of the Sufis. In piety, humility, and selfless service to fellow human beings, the Sufis excelled, and they exemplified Islam as no others did. As a result, Islam and its way of life made a strong impression on the Indonesians. Discussing why Islam proved successful, Woodman says, "The faith was not only a religious belief; it embodied a system of law, a social pattern, a doctrine applied to every aspect of personal behavior."[26] Today, Indonesia is the largest Muslim country in the world.

Support of Non-Muslims

According to the world historian, J.M. Roberts, the Muslims "left the societies they took over by and large undisturbed."[27] From the time of the Prophet, according to Hodgson, non-Muslims "were left to organize their own autonomous life."[28] Islam never regarded either Judaism or Christianity as a false religion.[29] The governments of conquered countries continued, their people went about their lives and, equally important, their business. The Muslim rulers in Baghdad did not disturb the Persians and Jews who were the dominant traders there.[30]

Much later, after a disastrous time in Islamic history – when the

Mongols overran and destroyed a significant part of the Muslim world – those same Mongols converted to Islam voluntarily. Why did they do so? The question has intrigued historians for centuries. From the beginning of the Mongol invasions of the Muslim world, Christians courted them. The Crusaders were the first, insisting on an alliance between them to destroy the Muslims. Then came the Pope and a sizable number of clergy who made every effort to convert the Mongols. The Mongols were genuinely interested in Christian spirituality and they also listened to the Muslims. For decades, there was every indication the Mongols were going to become Christian.

However, discussion alone does not proclaim the reality of a religion. A religion's worth is demonstrated in everyday life, and that was where Islam had an advantage. The Mongols saw how the Muslims lived. Equally important, although the Mongols now had access to a very wide choice of schools for their sons, they sent them to Muslim institutions. They were also impressed with the creativity of the Muslims in their cities, in their architecture, and in their arts. As a result, the Mongols chose Islam. Then, they began competing with other Muslims by supporting education and the arts and in building mosques and schools. Mongol descendants created Islamic civilizations and cultures of their own, such as the Timurid and the Mughal.[31]

The civilized behavior of the Muslims is most clearly evident in their treatment of the Jews. During the early decades of the expansion of the Muslim world, the Christian persecution of Jews persisted. In 694, for example, at the instigation of Egica, king of Spain, Jews were declared slaves and their possessions were confiscated. Therefore, when the Muslims invaded Spain, the Jews fought on the Muslim side. When they fled Christian persecution, they sought refuge in Muslim countries.[32]

Because the Jews knew both the people and the territories of Spain, the Muslims in many instances appointed them to govern their regions. For example, a Jew, Ibn Naghzalah, according to Hitti, "virtually exercised supreme power" over Granada at the beginning of Muslim rule.[33] Abba Eban, in *Heritage: Civilization and the Jews*, has surprised many, especially Muslims, for praising Islam and the Muslims for the fair treatment of the Jews for most of their history. Eban states that the Jews had freedom during Muslim rule. Under the Muslims, Jews achieved "heights of creative energy, of literary grace and aesthetic perfection," as well as "spiritual heights."[34]

In the Muslim world, especially in Jerusalem, Baghdad, Cairo, and Muslim Spain, the Jews retained their own communities, where they lived according to their own laws. They also participated in Muslim life, such as in government and academic institutions, and especially in the sciences as never before in their history.[35] Some served as viziers (prime ministers) to Caliphs and more of them as advisors. One even became a commander of a Muslim army, a position he held for seventeen years. Samuel ibn Naghrela was not only knowledgeable in both Hebrew and Arabic but also a poet and an exceptional scholar of Jewish law.

Jewish scholarship in religion and philosophy achieved some of its most significant advances under Muslim rule. Among the scholars in the East, Saadia ben Joseph gained eminence. An intellectual leader of the Jewish diaspora, he translated the Hebrew Scriptures into Arabic and, in addition, wrote three books on the Hebrew language. Abba Eban describes him as "a great reconciler, balancing the claims of science and religion, of Arabic culture and Jewish belief."[36]

The scholars were mainly clustered around the capitals, although Muslim Spain was the intellectual center of Judaism. Eban describes how the "Jewish cultural flowering" in Muslim Spain far surpassed that of the East.[37] A Jew of Cordoba, Hasdai ibn Shaprut laid the foundations for the development of Jewish culture. When Abd al-Rahman III conquered Cordoba, he appointed Hasdai ibn Shaprut as his counselor, court physician, emissary, and representative at the customs department director's office. The next ruler designated Ibn Shaprut his minister and physician. "It was because of Hasdai's generous activity," Sarton points out, "that the intellectual center of Israel was transferred from the academies of Babylon to Cordoba."[38] Among other Jewish intellectuals in Muslim Spain were Solomon ibn Gabirol, the major Jewish poet of

Spanish Jewry; Moses ibn Ezra, poet as well as philosopher; Judah
ha-Levi, also a poet and a religious philosopher as well as a physician; and Moses ben Maimon, known as Maimonides. Maimonides
was born in Cordoba and had to flee twice – from his home and
from Morocco. Eventually, he settled in Egypt, where he became
a physician to Salah al-Din (Saladin). He wrote a number of works
on Judaic scriptures and philosophy and is still renowned for the
work he wrote in Arabic, *Guide for the Perplexed*, an effort to rec-
oncile reason and religion. When he died, there were three days of
public mourning in Egypt.

Norman Cantor said, "The position of Jews in Muslim Spain...
was more favorable than in any other part of western Europe."[39]
According to Vivian B. Mann, Muslim Spain is for the Jews "synonymous with the 'Golden Age.'"[40] By demonstrating a peaceful attitude
toward the peoples of Muslim lands and allowing the followers of all
religions to develop intellectually, the Muslims had an immeasurable
impact on Jewish and other cultures. In the case of the Jews, Muslim
governance offered a safe haven as well as a stimulating environment
for Jewish cultural and intellectual development.

5

ISLAMIC CIVILIZATION IN EUROPE AND WEST ASIA

THE MUSLIM WORLD expanded even further when the Islamic empire rapidly gained full command of the oceans. For centuries, the Arabs had been traveling in boats and ships, fishing, diving for pearls or coral, and carrying merchandise from one port to another. There is evidence of the Arabs successfully trading with India from long before the Ptolemies. Their success was due primarily to a sound knowledge of the monsoons, for detailed records were kept of the southern Arabian coasts. Both the Arabs and the Indians used sailing ships, known as dhows, at least from the 4th century BC onward. About eight hundred years later, Arab sea trade with India declined because of the emergence of Byzantine and Persian powers on the oceans. Nevertheless, the trade continued, although on a reduced scale.[1]

Geographic and Military Advances

At the time of the first Muslim community, however, the Muslims had no experience of naval warfare. The first attempt — a fleet launched at Bahrain to invade Fars — ended in disaster. The Persians besieged the Muslims, who had to be rescued by land. This disaster prevented the Muslims from building a canal through the Suez isthmus to link the Red Sea with the Mediterranean, an idea suggested by Amru ibn al-ʿAs, the conqueror of Egypt, a decade after the beginning of the Islamic era.

Nevertheless, the Muslims, inspired by the Qur'an, continued to develop their skills in navigation. They added the rudder, which, according to Asimov, the West then encountered during the Crusades. They considerably improved the astrolabe, believed to be the world's oldest scientific instrument, which they acquired from the Greeks.[2] The astrolabe is associated with the Muslim world because the Muslims used it for longer than anyone else. The Muslims added, according to Ronan, ways of "measuring celestial positions, using altitude and azimuth..." ("Azimuth" is of Arabic origin.)[3] Other improvements were made later, so that eventually the Muslims possessed a variety of astrolabes: the linear, the universal, the geared, and the astrolabic clock.

The Muslims also gained the magnetic needle, an instrument that they acquired from the Chinese. In his monumental *History of the Arabs*, Hitti describes how the Muslims used it at sea. The Chinese, he states, discovered "the directive property of the magnetic needle, [but] the Muslims ...were the first [to apply] the needle to navigation."[4] Sarton also makes it clear that the compass was an innovation of the Muslims, although its use was for centuries kept secret for commercial purposes.[5]

The development of Muslim navigation was rapid and there was a well-equipped navy by the time of Uthman, the third Caliph. His admiral, Abdullah ibn Qais Harithi, excelled to the extent that the Byzantines dreaded him. He was killed when Cyprus was taken in 688. Nevertheless, the Muslims went on to further conquests by sea: Rhodes, Crete, Sardinia, and eventually, Spain, Sicily, and southern Italy. Thus, they soon succeeded in controlling all of the Mediterranean.

In one instance, the Europeans benefited from a powerful Muslim navy. Late in the eighth century and well into the ninth century AC, the Vikings devastated England, France, and parts of Spain and Italy. However, when they also attacked the Muslims in Seville, the Muslim navy set upon the Vikings and caused them to suffer many casualties, in both men and ships, driving them back to their homes.[6]

The Muslim ships moved in other directions, too. They arrived at the shores of India and were eventually trading with China. At about the same time, they traded down the east coast of Africa. The person in charge of the fleet was called the *amir* (commander), from which the English word admiral is derived.

At the time of the first naval fleet there was only one shipyard in Egypt. Then the Byzantines attacked the Syrian coast to reach the new Muslim capital, Damascus. This action led to the rebuilding of other shipyards at Akka (Acre) and Sur (Tyre). This in turn led to increased Muslim efforts on the Mediterranean and especially to the continent across, beginning with Gibraltar, being the land closest to Africa.[7]

The name of Gibraltar is derived from the Arabic Jabr Tariq (the Mountain of Tariq). Tariq was the Muslim general who, in 92/711, led the first Muslim forces across the Mediterranean. In the same year, he went on to conquer Malaga, Granada, Cordoba, and Toledo, until he defeated Roderick, the usurper of the Spanish Throne. By 713 AC, Spain was under Muslim control, which lasted until 1492, when the Christians conquered it.

After Spain and Sicily, the Muslims made no further efforts at major conquest and expansion. This is important when judging the ensuing events involving the Muslims in Europe and the distorted views of their history. The Muslims crossed the Pyrenees and advanced into southern France, occupying the Geronne valley. There was only one battle lost, which was at Toulouse.[8]

In 732 AC there occurred a confrontation that has been historically distorted: the Battle of Tours at Poitiers. A small Muslim army, venturing out alone, confronted Charles Martel and the combined forces of the whole of France. The Muslims had overreached their intended territorial goal, a thousand miles from what was to be known as Gibraltar. They were too far from their capital of Damascus. Supplies were low and there was no possibility of reinforcements reaching them. Nevertheless, they fought well and hard. It was a formidable battle, with both sides suffering heavy casualties, and nothing gained by either. Then the Muslim general was killed and the Muslim army received orders to retreat.

The Battle of Tours, which, Western historians assert, stopped the advance of the Muslims and saved the Christians of Europe, was neither "major," nor even a "battle." As the authority David Nicole stated in *The Armies of Islam*, it was "in reality an unsuccessful large-scale Muslim raid." It certainly did not prevent the Muslims from advancing into Europe later.[9]

The Muslim armies, despite the assertions of Western historians, continued their conquests in Europe. From Avignon in 734 and Lyon in south-east France in 743, they moved into Germany and also into Italy and beyond, conquering Sicily in 827, Messina in 834, Castrogiovanni in 859, and Syracuse in 878. The Muslims occupied southern Italy from 882 to 915 AC, venturing as far as Naples and Rome without resistance, although they stopped at the gates of Rome.

Sicily

Apart from Sicily and Spain, the Muslims had no intention of settling in western Europe, because, according to Roberts, they were in fact more interested in trade.[10] This contradicts the constant assertion, especially by some Western scholars, that Europe was in "danger" of being converted to Islam.

The conquest of Sicily began much earlier than that of Spain, the first attempt being made two decades after the Prophet's death, when the Muslims had established a navy. With the support of this sea power, the Muslims defeated the Byzantines at Alexandria. They then turned to Sicily. Nevertheless, the final winning of the island was the last of the series of Muslim conquests of Europe during this early period. A Syracusan rebel approached the Muslims of North Africa for help against the Byzantine governor of Sicily and they responded with an army that conquered the island in 289/902. The Muslims ruled Sicily for a little over two hundred years.

Travelers to Sicily and geographers from elsewhere spoke of a flourishing Islamic civilization. Many of the rulers supported learning, the arts, and agriculture. One traveler, Ibn Hawqal, visited Palermo, the capital of Muslim Sicily, and spoke highly of its religious and educational institutions. The end of the Muslim reign was not the end of Islamic civilization on the island, for under Roger I, Sicily was in all practical ways Islamic. The three official languages were

Latin, Greek, and Arabic. The administration remained in Muslim hands, as did trade and agriculture. Most of the infantry consisted of Muslims. In addition, Muslim scholars and physicians and Eastern philosophers were welcome at the court of Roger I, to the extent that European visitors spoke of him as "an Oriental monarch."[11] The Sicily of Roger I was, according to Hitti, a "Christian–Islamic culture." Hitti adds: "[Arab] genius attained its full fruition [of the finer arts of peace] in a rich outburst of Arab–Norman art and culture."[12]

Sicily continued to be "Muslim" during the reigns of Roger II and Frederick II, the successors to Roger I. Muslim expertise in building ships and sailing them proved advantageous to Roger II. When Muslim rule ended, most of the Muslims remained and continued practicing their professions and skills. Thus it was that those skilled in shipbuilding and sailing built a fleet for Roger II, which according to Hitti "raised Sicily to the position of the leading maritime power in the Mediterranean."[13]

Cultural elements of Islam were present too. Roger II wore Muslim robes decorated with Arabic characters, which made his critics call him the "half-heathen" king. Christians, including the women, also wore Muslim dress. There was a huge demand for these clothes because, Hitti says, "no European felt really well-dressed unless he possessed one such garment." The design of buildings, even churches, borrowed features of Islamic architecture.[14]

Frederick II had an extraordinary relationship with the Muslim world to the east. Muslim rulers were his close friends, especially Sultan al-Kamil Muhammad, the Ayyubid ruler of Egypt, who sent him animals for his menagerie, in particular, a giraffe, "the first to appear in medieval Europe."[15] The Sultan of Damascus sent him a planetarium. However, Frederick II's enthusiasm for almost everything Islamic earned him enemies in Europe. He was, after all, as a ruler of Germany (with Sicily as the "capital" of his government), the Holy Roman Emperor. Nevertheless, the Christians labeled him "the Infidel."[16]

Unfortunately, after the death of William II, Sicilian life was marred by the persecution of Muslims. Battles ensued and the

Muslims were defeated. Many Muslim scholars, writers, and artists fled to neighboring Muslim countries, including the eminent poet Ibn Hamdis, who went first to Tunisia, and then to Muslim Spain.

Nevertheless, as Crespi points out, "The spirit of Islam in Sicily was not extinguished by the defeat of the last Muslims."[17] European scholars continued to travel to Sicily to gain the knowledge inherited from the Muslims. The immense body of Islamic learning was now being translated into Italian. As a result, Mahmud states, "the first language which ousted Arabic as the cultural language of Europe was Italian."[18]

However, there was a greater legacy for Europe from the Muslim rule of Sicily. Frederick established the University of Naples in 1224 AC, where he deposited a large collection of Arabic manuscripts. Copies of the translations of these manuscripts were dispatched to the Universities of Paris and Bologna. When Michael Scot, on the other hand, went to Sicily, he brought the learning of Muslim Spain with him. As a result of these and other Muslim contributions, a significant change began in Europe. In Hitti's words, "This almost modern spirit of investigation, experimentation, and research which characterized the court of Frederick marks the beginning of the Italian Renaissance."[19]

Exploring the World

These ventures into the world led to another major Muslim contribution to geography. It began with the merchants and sailors who wrote narratives and descriptive treatises giving details of the terrains and coasts they traveled as well as outlines of ocean routes. Sulaiman the Merchant, for example, was noted more for the first descriptions the Muslims had of China and of many coastal areas of India than for his trade. The writings of another traveler to China, Ibn Wahb, formed the basis of some of the adventures of Sindbad the Sailor in *A Thousand and One Nights* (more commonly known as *The Arabian Nights*). Among the Muslims, Ibn Fadlan was the first to describe Russia.

There were Jews and Christians, too, who lived in and traveled through Muslim and other countries. Some kept records of their travels. The most eminent of the Jewish travelers was Benjamin of Tudela. He lived in Muslim Spain and traveled across Europe, through Rome, Greece, and Byzantium, then proceeded to cities along the Mediterranean coast, including those of Egypt and Sicily. The descriptions of his travels, the first of their kind in Hebrew, were filled with information on the Jewish communities of the Muslim world and their trade and commerce.

The Christians living there were mostly pilgrims to the Holy Land. Some wrote about their travels and thus Europe gained more information about the Muslim world. Arculf, a bishop of Gaul, traveled to Damascus after his stay in Jerusalem and then to Egypt, where he took particular interest in navigating the Nile and exploring the harbor of Alexandria. Saint Willibard, the first English pilgrim to the Holy Land, also visited Syria after making his pilgrimage. He wrote about his travels and his book proved most valuable to future venturers into Muslim areas because, for example, it provided information on the kind of passports essential for travel in the Muslim world.

Muslim conquests continued into Asia: India, southern Russia, and southwestern China. To communicate with these farther reaches, the Muslims initiated a postal system, for which the Incense Road and other trade routes served as highways. It was under the Abbasids, Harun al-Rashid in particular, that the postal system was made more efficient with Baghdad as its center. "Nine hundred and thirty postal stations were set up…[using] mules and camels…as well as horses," according to James and Thorpe, who add that the Muslims also "developed the pigeon post into a regular airmail system." Initially used for government purposes, the service was soon open to the public for a nominal fee.[20]

James and Thorpe also mention "the first recorded example of parcel post by airmail in history:" Aziz, a North African Caliph, one day craved "tasty cherries grown in Baalbek in Lebanon." His wazir satisfied that craving by having 600 pigeons fly from Baalbek to Cairo, each carrying "a small silk bag" containing a cherry.[21]

These advances and explorations were in keeping with Qur'anic verses and the Hadith (sayings) of the Prophet. Muslims were open to other cultures and, most important, learned from them. Al-Biruni is an excellent example, for he achieved a reputation as an intellectual while still a youth. He was a scholar in every sense, since he was observant, endowed with a critical spirit, eager to learn about the world from books as well as first-hand experience, and skilled as a writer. He was also a true polymath, learning and discovering in various fields, scientific and philosophical, literary and religious. Akbar Ahmed, in *Discovering Islam*, calls him "the first true anthropologist."[22] Al-Biruni was a geographer of Siberia and northern Europe. He was also a physician, astronomer, mathematician, physicist, and historian, in all, one of Islam's most prominent scholars.[23] His sense of wonder led him to uncover things that had been overlooked or ignored so far in the Muslim world.

As part of the court of Mahmud of Ghazna, al-Biruni traveled to India in the late tenth or early eleventh century AC. He was so impressed with the people and culture of India that he stayed there, spending the next twenty years traveling all over the country. He learned Sanskrit so as to read Hindu philosophical works in the original. His aim, al-Biruni stated in his book on India, was to provide an appropriate and accurate description of Hinduism for those who wished to engage in religious discussions. These studies alone took him twelve years. He transmitted Indian learning to the Muslims with his translations of works such as *Sankhaya* [On the Origins and Qualities of Things], and the *Patanjali* [On the Yoga Sutras], and especially with his major work, *Taḥqīq al-Hind* [Facts about India].

The *Taḥqīq al-Hind* is a voluminous, encyclopedic work on India's complex cultures and is available today in English. The work begins with a description of the Hindus and an extensive discussion of their beliefs. It then goes on to cover the literature and sciences of the subcontinent, including geology, geography, astronomy, mathematics, the Hindu calendar, and the laws and legal system. Extremely thorough, it is a work of love for India and its people. Al-Biruni also translated Euclid and Ptolemy into Sanskrit.

Other Muslim travelers achieved prominence with their writings, of whom Ibn Battutah is among the most famous. The others included al-Masudi and Ibn Jubayr. Al-Masudi was a philosopher, historian, and natural scientist. Ibn Jubayr showed great interest in people of different cultures when he made his pilgrimage to Makkah and Madinah and then traveled extensively afterward.

It was from the writings of these travelers that others learned of what life was really like in these foreign locales, not only among Muslims, but also among Jews, Christians, and Hindus. Al-Masudi was so impressed with India that he returned there after traveling in Africa and Central Asia. He believed that in India's past "order and wisdom reigned." He was also an outstanding historian. His history, *Meadows of Gold*, earned him exceptional praise in the West, where he was called "the Herodotus of the Arabs."[24]

Ibn Jubayr traveled through Christian countries, too, and described the harassment of Muslim pilgrims heading for Makkah, which consisted of the capture and sale of Muslim men and women as slaves in the market of Cape St. Mark (Sardinia). In Muslim Damascus, on the other hand, Christians worshiped freely at St Mary's Church. Remarkably, despite the conflict between Muslims and Christians, trade continued even during battles. While the Muslims were laying siege to a fort on the Spice Road, Muslim caravans passed without hindrance through "the land of the Franks."

Ibn Battutah, also an authority on Islamic law, traveled through every Muslim country, and some Christian countries, too, across the Near East, into Asia as far as China, as well as into Europe and Africa. If he covered the same ground today, he would be visiting forty-four countries, covering a distance of 73,000 miles. His travels have additional significance because he undertook them very soon after the Mongols had devastated a significant proportion of the Muslim world. His descriptions of the cities destroyed, especially Baghdad, reveal the extent of the tragedy of the onslaught.[25]

Nevertheless, a major change had already taken place. The Mongols were now Muslim. Ibn Battutah traveled to their capital and from there accompanied the Khan's wife, a Byzantine princess, journeying to visit her family in Constantinople. The guards there took him prisoner. However, the emperor, recognizing Ibn Battutah for the eminent person he was, freed him, commanded everyone to treat him with respect and, in addition, gave him a horse, a saddle, and an umbrella.

Ibn Battutah did not just visit, but also lived for long periods in several countries. He spent eight years in India, functioning as a judge for Sultan ibn Tughluq. Afterward, he visited China and Indonesia before returning home. Nevertheless, his enthusiasm for travel was still strong. He set out again, this time for Muslim Spain and thereafter across the Sahara into West Africa and then through East Africa.

Like Ibn Jubayr, Ibn Battutah was interested in the generosity of the Muslims. His first major experience of giving was during his first journey, in Makkah, during the pilgrimage. From the chief judge of the city to the pilgrims from all over the world, people made an extra effort to see that the needy were taken care of. An outstanding act of charity was the provision of water, since the place was so arid. A very unusual charitable custom caught Ibn Battutah's attention in Damascus. A servant had accidentally dropped his master's Chinese porcelain dish. Immediately, several men approached him and requested him to take the broken pieces to "the custodian of the endowment of utensils."[26] There the servant was given money to buy a similar porcelain dish to replace the original, so that his master would not punish him.

Ibn Battutah finally ended his travels and settled at home in Fez. There, fortunately for the world, he dictated the narrative of his travels. The complete manuscript of his multi-volume *Travels* still exists and has been translated into both Eastern and Western languages. Ibn Battutah was, indeed, one of the most famous travelers in history.

Positive Influence

Wherever it ventured, Islam initiated a milieu of civilized life and discourse. Muslim influence was seen in towns large and small, and all across the world.

Pastoral regions across central Asia became Muslim owing to their proximity to the trade routes. Then Central Asians and Sufis brought Islam to those living away from these routes, until the religion spread both north and east. The Mongols, who, on their own initiative, converted to Islam, brought the religion much farther north and east.

Villages in the Muslim world were therefore not as isolated as those in other parts of the world. The most important contact with the cities was from teachers of religion, who brought other information as well. In another respect, too, religion itself was significant in establishing contact, such as the pilgrimage to Makkah and Madinah, which was always a primary ambition of the Muslims. Those from the villages made every effort to travel to the holy cities and they returned with news gathered from pilgrims from all over the Muslim world. In addition, there were travelers and traders who passed through and brought their news and information. Communication between Muslim villages and the rest of the world has continued to this day.

Islam's conquests were not like those of other empires, for Muslim rule was largely benign. According to Curtin, the empire "was the most dynamic and creative of Rome's and Persia's successors; it was also the principal agency for contact between the discrete cultures" during the height of its civilization.[27]

Muslims helped to enhance life in the countries where they settled. Trade increased. Learning engendered, in addition to its professional benefits, a higher quality of life. In this way, Islam brought forth the potential of the citizens, Muslim as well as non-Muslim, and enriched society wherever Muslims lived and traveled.

6

TRADE

IN AFRICA, MUSLIMS were known as traders and enthusiastic merchants. Except for the very first battles in Egypt and on the Mediterranean fringe in the north, trade and piety took the religion and its followers to sub-Saharan Africa. There, Muslims not only continued trade but also augmented it along the caravan routes and down the east coast. Thus, the Muslims came as partners of the Africans.

This focus contributed to the rise of Islamic civilization worldwide. According to Theodore Zeldin, "The first religion to show any enthusiasm for commerce was Islam."[1] The combination of commercial savvy, religious faith, and cultural openness was a potent force for growth in the Muslim world. Andrew S. Ehrenkreutz calls trade the silent force behind the rise of medieval Islamic civilization. The Islamic conquests, he says, united the two artificial political arenas created by the two major powers, Byzantium and Persia. The Muslims then engendered internal security and, at the same time, improved the commerce on the existing trade routes.[2] Simultaneously, merchants increased the wealth in the conquered areas, especially with the manufacture of the overwhelming number of coins they minted, particularly of gold and silver. According to Robert Fox, "Most prized was gold – the legendary 'Muslim gold,' as it was known throughout medieval Christendom." Hence, the Muslims who settled in different parts of the world brought with them money and investments, and therefore, they also became the new consumers. With their need for food, they extended the economic benefits to the rural areas. The most remarkable aspect of the economic upsurge was that non-Muslims profited from what might best be termed as an enormous enterprise.[3]

Ehrenkreutz believes that as a result of this advantageous economic activity, the Muslim world had a far superior standard of living for all its inhabitants than was prevalent under the Byzantines and Persians, which also led to "the spectacular expansion of Islamic civilization."[4]

Albert Hourani draws attention to another significant factor enhancing Muslim trade. Traders in Muslim countries belonged to the intellectual level of society, and craftsmen were highly respected. Merchants sent their sons to universities to study law, too. "It was not uncommon," Hourani said, "for a man to work both as a teacher and scholar and in trade."[5]

The Arabs had been traders for centuries before the advent of Islam, and one of their most important products was frankincense. Over the millennia, it had been used as incense, as a fumigant, and as medicine by the Ancient Egyptians, Jews, Romans, Chinese, and other people in the East. The harvesting and sale of frankincense had been big business for centuries, if not for thousands of years. It was one of the major products carried on the trade route known as the Incense Road, one of the oldest in the world. Balsam and myrrh were two other products in demand, and, like frankincense, they were harvested from trees in the southern coastal area of the Arabian Peninsula.

The Incense Road ran along the coast of the Peninsula, headed west to Yemen, then north to Jordan. From there it split into two, one route continuing north to Damascus and the other moving west into Egypt. Another route also went north, all the way to Palmyra, where it in turn split into eastern and western routes. An important stopping place on the route was Makkah, the city that would become the most sacred place in Islam. Abraham, taking Hagar and Ishmael with him, is believed to have traveled on the Incense Road to the area that was later known as Makkah. There is a very strong possibility that the Queen of Sheba also took this route when she visited Solomon.

In addition to the spices, the Incense Road carried products from the East, such as gold, silk, and gems, all of which were delivered to the South Arabian port known as Aden. The Incense Road was therefore one of the most coveted areas in history. The Assyrians wanted to conquer it. So did the Greeks and, soon afterward, Alexander. The Romans were almost successful in bypassing the route. The Byzantines succeeded by having their ally, Christian Abyssinia, conquer southern Arabia and thus gain control of the source of the trade. By then, however, the Arab merchants of the area were no longer the rich traders they once were.[6]

The wealth was now in Makkah, which had become an important center of the caravan trade. Later, with the establishment of Islam, the title of the person who led the caravan, "imam," was also applied to the person who led the prayer because both of these people had this in common, that they were guides. Hence, there was derived the use today of the word "imam" as a moral guide.

The Prophet, when young, also traveled on the route to Syria with his uncle and became a trader himself. He was so successful that Khadijah, one of the leading merchants of Makkah, hired him and later married him. The trade retained its prominence and continued along the Incense Road, protected now by an injunction of the Qur'an (106:2), which was strictly adhered to. The route soon became known also as the Pilgrimage Road.

Trade was so important to the Muslims that it was permitted for a Muslim to buy and sell during the pilgrimage, although some other routine pursuits, such as cutting the fingernails and hunting for food, were forbidden. As a result, the city of Makkah also became a peaceful center of international commerce.

Moving into Africa

The earliest trade in Africa, continuing what was already established, was in the eastern part of Sudan and the Horn of Africa, and from the Red Sea ports down the coast and into the interior. Later, trade linked the north with the western bulge of the African continent and expanded the civilizations there, notably Ghana and Mali. Muslims ventured into parts of Africa that very few outsiders had penetrated.

Carts had been used, even in the desert regions, until the introduction of the camel between the second and fifth century AC, although the routes across the Sahara were traversed only sporadically before the Islamic era. However, the coming of the Muslims changed this. According to Philip Curtin, "North Africans regularly crossed the Sahara by about 800 AD," which, he added, showed "the beginnings of Islamic civilization in North Africa."[7] The route itself was extensive, for it ran from the western reaches of the Sahara all the way to the regions of the White Nile on the other side of the continent.[8]

Islam spread with trade until more than half of Africa was Muslim, and the regions of the continent were separated only by language. The northern part of Africa and the Sudan became predominantly Arabic-speaking and was considered largely Arab, while the people in the rest of the continent, as far south as Zanzibar, East Africa, and the Congo, retained their own languages. Owing to the trade, there emerged a new language called Swahili, which was a combination of Bantu and Arabic, and which gained a distinction in its own right. Each area, as a result, had, and still has, its own culture.[9]

Oases on the routes acquired a Near Eastern character with the introduction of the date palm. Muslim trade in these regions led to the creation of additional African civilizations such as Mali, Benin, and Songhai. Mali, in fact, continued to grow until it was an African Muslim empire under Mansa Musa. Mansa Musa, in turn, became a legend, known for his lavish pilgrimage to Makkah with an enormous retinue. He carried 50,000 ounces of gold, most of which he gave away, especially in charity. He brought back scholars with him, who helped improve his economy and assisted in establishing Timbuktu as a center of learning and culture in West Africa, attracting scholars from the other regions of Africa. Timbuktu, on the edge of the Sahara, soon had its own sources of water, for its wells provided water for a city of 40,000 people.[10]

In Benin, the Muslims established a town called Parakou. Meanwhile, on the other side of the continent, in Ethiopia, almost the only merchants permitted to travel to the Highlands dominated by princes were Muslims.[11]

Those early routes were sufficient for trading until the nineteenth century, when increased trade to several additional regions made a new route necessary. The builders of this route were members of a newly-created Sufic order of the Sanusiyya. They participated in the trading and helped to organize it in eastern Libya. Thus, they reestablished unused trade routes and, in addition, created an entirely new trade route across the Sahara.[12]

Muslim religious leaders in Africa soon became known for their "dignity in dress and behavior," to the extent that Christian missionaries also wore Muslim-style dress.[13] The conversions to Islam made an enormous difference to trade. The Africans were soon assimilated and actively participated as traders, moving south, the Nile and its tributaries being used for the transport of the traders and their goods.

Ports on the Mediterranean were developed for trade with Europe: Algiers, Tangier, Sele, Rabat, Tripoli, Misratah, Benghazi, and Darnah. Various caravan routes led to these ports, bringing, among other goods, gold, ivory, salt, dyes, and ostrich feathers from as far away as the Congo.[14]

Nevertheless, Muslim trade did not penetrate the sub-Saharan interior, not even from the coastal areas where the centuries-old trading was now predominantly Muslim. According to Curtin, the Africans discouraged the Muslims from going beyond the coast. However, there was one exception: the Muslims were known to have gone as far as Zimbabwe to mine gold. Down the east coast, the Muslims traded as far south as Kilwa (Tanzania) and Sofala (Mozambique).[15]

How far down the east coast of Africa did the Muslims venture? There is a strong possibility they reached what is today Natal, south of Zululand, in South Africa. In the late 1950s, Muslims living in Durban discovered a cemetery on the bluff across from the docks. The tombstones had inscriptions that appeared to have been written in Arabic, although they were so faded as to be almost indistinct.

Linking East and West

Similar to the early encounter with Africa was the early Muslim contact with China. Many of the Muslim traders who traveled to that country settled there. A battle between Muslim ships and Canton brought one interruption. As a result, Canton was closed to foreign shipping, which then moved to Tonking. About forty years later, Canton was reopened and Muslim trade resumed. Muslim immigration increased and created a sizable Muslim population in China, to the extent that the Emperor of China allowed Muslim judges to decide their legal disputes.[16]

Conversions among the Chinese also multiplied, owing to intermarriage, the exemplary behavior of the Muslims, and honest trade. Muslims continued to make converts in the early Mongol period and created, according to Roberts, "an enduring Islamic minority."[17] Under the later Mongol rulers, Muslims were the only religious group forbidden to preach. However, the Mongols slowly learned to appreciate the Muslims and changed their attitude toward them. The Great Khan at the time of Marco Polo appointed Muslims from Transoxiana to administer Yunan, and thereafter, the number of Chinese Muslims grew significantly. The advent of Islam in China must have been very welcome, for soon afterward, an opera was written about the coming of the Muslims and it continues to be performed today.[18]

The Muslims used another trade route known as the Silk Road, which had begun from China as early as 100 BC to transport silk, the manufacture of which the Chinese kept secret. Recent discoveries date the beginning of the route as far back as the tenth century BC. Not only did the Muslims make full use of the route, but with the help of an agreement between the Abbasid Caliphate and the Tang dynasty, they also made the entire route easy and safe.[19] Baghdad thus became, Sayyid Mahmud writes, "the commercial axis of the east–west trade."[20] According to Curtin, the Jews especially benefited from this trade since they were able to travel to areas in Europe closed to the Muslims.[21]

In addition, the Muslims took advantage of the sea-going trade between Persia and China, which had existed from pre-Islamic times. The Muslim Persians had even established their own settlement on the island of Hainan. On land, the earliest contacts between

the Muslims and the Chinese consisted of Muslim traders settling
within the western borders of China. The Muslims increased trade
in China and were mainly responsible for making the Chinese capital, Ch'ang-an, "one of the most cosmopolitan cities in the world."[22]
In Canton, the Muslim population flourished and expanded to the
extent that the emperor permitted it to have its own judge in Islamic
law.[23]

Soon, there was an increase in trade between the Muslim countries
and China, especially in silk, camphor, musk, and local spices. Commercial life thus benefited both China and the lands under Muslim
rule.[24] China also benefited from the Muslims' knowledge of shipping and navigation. A Muslim, Cheng Ho, helped China become
a sea power by leading Chinese ships in seven expeditions to the
Indonesian islands and, in the other direction, to Egypt, and then
down the coast of Africa to Zanzibar. The primary purpose of these
expeditions was to impress the world with the splendor of China by
giving the finest Chinese crafts to the rulers and the people of the
countries that they visited.[25]

At sea, the Arab Muslims also took advantage of the monsoon
routes to travel to and trade with India (the word "monsoon" is
derived from the Arabic *mawsam*, "season."). Along the northeast
monsoon route, they sailed between Oman and Calicut, while the
southwest monsoon route was used for travel from Aden to Calicut. Both monsoon routes enabled the Muslims, early on, to make
journeys from the Chola region of India, across the Kra Isthmus (in
what is now southern Thailand), around Cochin China, and thence
to China.

There were many examples of the amicable relationship between
merchants and the local communities. According to Curtin "Melaka"
(Malacca) in Malaysia had grown, from a "tiny center of fishing...
into the most important trading city in its region." This trend added
to "the further Islamization of the region." Curtin quotes a para-
graph from Tom Pires's book, *Suma Oriental*, listing the people who
settled there or visited from every part of the world, from as far away
as Cairo.[26]

Muslims also facilitated the link between China and the West, so that merchants could travel safely and easily from the Far East through the Mediterranean to Muslim Spain. Trade had existed in the Mediterranean basin from pre-Islamic times. Curtin points out that although the coming of the Muslims "weakened" the existing unity there, it replaced it with "a new kind of unity that made trade easy." This new trading unity persisted through the centuries, even during times of war, especially the Crusades, and included the Europeans, too. Curtin calls this "a new zone of ecumenical trade."[27]

Curtin points to the Fatimid and Ayyubid periods in Egypt as an example. The Jews participated fully in the commerce and joined the Egyptian Muslims in their trade with India. Christian ships called at Muslim ports. There was a legal representative for foreign merchants, assisting them in collecting debts, storing goods, arranging lodgings, and transferring money.[28]

Within the Muslim world, increased trading led to the creation of new towns. There were initially open-air markets in a central area, where farmers and others met to sell their products once a week. These places soon became settlements, then towns, and some of them cities. As entirely new habitations, they were subject to no tribe and hence developed into what they were meant to be – peaceful trade centers. Other people such as artisans and craftsmen followed and the trade extended beyond the immediate area. There emerged, in Hourani's words, "a chain of great cities running from one end of the world of Islam to the other," from Spain to North Africa to Egypt and Syria, to Makkah and Madinah, to Iraq, Iran, and India.[29]

Within seventy years of the Prophet's death, Muslim merchants had reached the Indonesian islands and brought back spices. Later, according to Asimov, the Muslims introduced these spices to Europe and the Europeans learned for the first time that food could be tasty and could also be preserved with condiments other than salt. The Western words for some of the spices are derived directly from the Arabic or from Arabic through other languages, among them caraway, carob, cumin, saffron, and tarragon.[30] Other words in the Western trade vocabulary derived from Muslim trade include amber, damask, jar, lemon, orange, marzipan, muslin, satin, sherbet, sofa, spinach, syrup, talc, traffic, tariff, risk, tare, caliber, ream, and magazine.[31]

Honest Dealers

One of the reasons for the success of Muslim merchants was the common principle of honesty. The Qur'an insists on honesty in several places. Verse 26:182-183 contains two admonitions to the merchants: to weigh with a true balance in all their dealings and not to "deprive people of what is rightfully theirs." The Prophet emphasized these admonitions. Mustafa al-Maraghi, a Grand Shaikh of al-Azhar, who was known throughout the Muslim world as an eminent theologian, concluded one of his finest sermons with a conversation between a Muslim and the Prophet. "What is faith?" the man asked. The Prophet answered, "Sincerity." "And what is conviction?" The Prophet answered, "Honest dealing."[32]

This "honest dealing" led to the invention of the check ("cheque" in British English). The origin of the word "check" given by the compilers of Western dictionaries is open to question. They trace it to the Persian word for king, shah, As it is used in chess, shah matt means "the king is dead," which the etymologists believe is the origin of the phrase "check mate" in chess. How is it possible to confuse the words for the death of a king with a word denoting a request to a bank to pay money? There does not seem to be any logical basis for their conclusion.

There is unanimity among scholars that the Arabic shakk, used early in the Muslim world, meant precisely what check (or cheque) means today.[33] James and Thorpe point out that the Muslims "developed a sophisticated banking network."[34] There were head offices of these banks in Baghdad and branches in other cities in the Muslim world. In addition to currency and checks, the banks handled letters of credit.

Curtin, describing the advantages of the honesty of Muslim traders, says that "this pattern of Islam spreading first to a local commercial class and only afterward to society at large can be found historically on the frontiers of Islam from Senegal to the Philippines."[35] The Indonesians, too, were impressed with the honesty of the Muslim merchants, many of whom came from the Arab countries, although most were from India, and also from China. Some of the Muslim merchants settled in the coastal areas of the islands, learned the local language, and married the local women, and these settlements became communities.

Yet, despite their affluence, the Muslims did not consider themselves privileged and thus did not isolate themselves from the rest of the people, for they worked in harmony with their non-Muslim neighbors. Mahmud singles out Gujarati and Bengali Muslim merchants as the most influential in bringing Islam to the inhabitants of the coast of Sumatra and other islands, from where Islam spread into the interior.[36]

An additional reason for the positive attitude of the Easterners toward Muslims came from an unusual source, namely, the colonists of Europe. The Portuguese, especially, were not only bent on trade but also on spreading Christianity, more often with violence. China, which had excellent trade relations with the Muslims, did not know how to handle these violent traders. Worse, the Portuguese (and later, the Dutch) insisted on intervening in local affairs. Such intervention in Indonesia, according to Lapidus, "stimulated the acceptance of Islam."[37] Islam, in fact, became the dominant religion of Indonesia and has remained so ever since.

In their ventures to other parts of the world, the Muslims certainly did not destroy as they went, and instead preserved in their entirety the communities that they conquered. They went on to "conquer" the local people with the way they helped the economy. By contrast, non-Muslim governments actually discouraged commerce, especially in China and Europe. It was not until the seventeenth century that the European governments realized trade was "a direct asset to the state."[38] For example, the Venetians at the edge of the Balkans, in Fox's description, realized that "agriculture became more attractive commercially through the introduction of new crops like maize, adopted from their traditional enemy, the Turks." Fox adds that to this day, the area is lush in the spring and summer "with the squares and columns of the Turkish Grain (Gran Turco)."[39]

Thriving Trade Network

What facilitated all the trade, for the first time in the history of the world, was a single community radiating from the center of Islam, from the Near East to China in one direction and, in the other, across the northern half of Africa into Europe. It covered most of the eastern hemisphere. If this fact appears startling, it must be remembered that the area of the Indian subcontinent alone is as large as that of Europe. Routes and roads linked even remote parts of the Muslim world. There were also thriving seaports. Those that existed before Islam were enlarged and in many instances rebuilt, and, in addition, new ones were created. Hourani described this Islamic area as "a single empire ... an economic unit important ... because it linked together two great sea basins of the civilized world, those of the Mediterranean and the Indian Ocean."[40]

Muslim Spain was an outstanding model of what Islam had to offer. Abd al-Rahman III worked diligently toward making a prosperous civilization in the West, and it was during his reign that Cordoba emerged as the richest city in Europe. Sarton described it as "one of the great centers of civilization."[41] One-third of the Caliph's budget, for example, was spent on improving irrigation with the construction of new watering systems. Hence, Muslim Spain became the most developed region in Europe. These are the major reasons why Crespi labeled the rule of Abd al-Rahman III "the golden age of Muslim Spain."[42]

Spain continued to improve its trade. Several books on agronomy were published to help farmers. There was also a prosperous textile industry, one of its products being an exquisite kind of silk that became known as Spanish silk. Tanning leather achieved such a level of refinement that "cordovan" is still used to describe the soft, supple leather that was originally produced in Muslim Spain.

Nevertheless, Europe was slow to benefit from the proximity of this Muslim country. Perhaps the neighboring Christian countries, because of their animosity toward Islam, acted as too strong a barrier. Later, almost all the energy of the Christians was devoted to the conquest of Andalusia.

During the ensuing battles in Spain, too much was destroyed, especially whatever trade there existed between the Muslim and Christian areas. However, the Christians did profit from the conquests. Among the treasures they captured from the Muslims were libraries containing thousands of books, which were then translated into Latin. This did not result in the immediate spread of Muslim learning into Europe, for the Church kept its Latin translations. When it finally did come, the Renaissance of Europe emerged from another direction, with enormous help from Islamic civilization.

Often ignored in histories is the extent to which Muslim trade improved the continent of Europe, by helping it to change from a conglomeration of small, feudal pockets into a vast area of international trade. This, together with the learning that Europe acquired from Islam, helped create the Renaissance of Europe.[43] Campbell, too, says that the Renaissance sprang from Islam because the Muslims introduced to the West, then facilitated the study of much of what they had preserved from the Greeks.[44]

As already pointed out, the West received the immense riches of Muslim learning from Muslim Spain and Sicily, not from the Crusades. However, the Crusaders certainly grew rich from trade. They bought the artistic products of Muslim goldsmiths and lapidarists to be used as reliquaries in churches. Later, when the Crusaders settled in Muslim areas, they preferred to concentrate on trade instead of fighting battles, and took advantage of the products from the East brought there by the Muslims. These products, especially sugar, were in demand all over Europe.

After the Fifth Crusade, Egypt was the focal point of trade with Europe, owing to the interest of the financiers of Venice and Genoa. With the enormous increase in trade, Marseilles in France, was emerging as the leading port for the goods from the East. Banks were established in the cities of Europe, and they did business with the banks of Syria, later appointing trade commissioners in that part of the Muslim world. The first gold coins minted in Italy were called Byzantine Saranecentus and were inscribed in Arabic.[45]

The trade with the Muslim world also initiated an awakening of Europe's need to explore beyond its continent. This occurrence is clearer when seen from another perspective. For centuries, trade was wholly one-sided: the East, including China, had almost everything to offer to Europe, but Europe had nothing to exchange – no products, no knowledge, no sciences, no technology. There were times when Europe offered slaves. The only other means of exchange were precious metals, such as silver, followed by gold. Even these proved insufficient at times. In the nineteenth century, in desperation, Britain forced opium upon China as a means of exchange for products.

The Europeans also grew rich from trade with the Muslim world. Since they had the monopoly of goods from the eastern lands, the Muslims are invariably described as deriving huge profits from it. What is overlooked is that the Europeans, too, made an enormous amount of money from Muslim trade. The Portuguese, the very people who complained of "extortionate prices" on the part of the Muslims, went on to realize "a thousand-percent profit" on their cargo in Lisbon.[46]

There is, however, a significant difference in the way the Muslims traded in those days, compared with the Europeans. The Muslims respected the rights of local people to the ownership of their lands, whereas the Europeans simply took the land by force and used the local people as cheap labor. Many Europeans acquired monopolies, some from the Muslims, others by force.

Venice was one of the former. Since the other Italian city-states, Genoa and Pisa, had gained from the Crusades, the Muslims did not want to do business with them. As a result, Venice profited from the Muslims' decision and achieved its famous growth and status. Genoa later contributed crews for Muslim ships. Other European countries acquired enormous wealth in trading with the East, the Portuguese and the Dutch, in particular, and afterward, the British. The British are believed to have extracted from India one hundred thousand pounds for every pound that they invested there. India indeed contributed to British wealth and power.[47] Roberts refers to an unnamed British viceroy as saying, "As long as we rule India, we are the greatest power in the world. If we lose it, we shall drop straightaway to a third-rate power."[48]

The trade with Europe was soon extended to the Scandinavian countries. Evidence of that commerce appeared with the discovery in northern Europe in the twentieth century of millions of coins from Muslim countries. There was an additional difference in the way the Muslims did business in Europe. Although in most instances the trade was directly between the Europeans and the Muslims, the Jews also acted as middlemen for the Muslims. Europe was rigidly feudalistic at that time, with only two classes of people: the aristocracy and the rest of the population, including skilled workers. The Jews introduced the banking system from the Muslim world into Europe, which is the primary reason why they as a group became associated with money. Jewish traders and bankers created the middle class in the West.[49]

Through Sicily, to southern Italy, and then through central and northern Italy, Muslim trade and culture traveled to the rest of Europe. The dinar of the Muslim world, for example, was recognized currency in Italy. Muslim scholars, artisans, craftsmen, and artists continued to work in Sicily after the Normans conquered the area, for their knowledge and skills were still in demand, primarily from royalty and the nobility.[50] Although products such as robes were made for Christians, they carried inscriptions in Arabic as part of the decoration. Italians learned from the Muslims and started producing their own silks, other textiles, glassware, and crafts. They also learned about the arts, architecture, sciences, and literature. "Dante's ideas of the other world," says Hitti, "...certainly appear to have been of Oriental origin."[51]

Thus the achievements of Islamic civilization in Europe and Asia stemmed from the Islamic principles of cooperation, honesty, and welfare for all concerned. In particular, Muslim innovation in collecting and transporting important products created networks of trade and transportation that would remain for centuries.

7

AGRICULTURE AND TECHNOLOGY

AGRICULTURE WAS A central element of Muslim trade and another determining factor in the economic and cultural expansion of the Muslim world. Very little of this history is known to the West owing to distorted and stereotyped notions of the world of Islam, such as the idea that Arab lands were only arid and its people had little knowledge of cultivating the earth. Andrew M. Watson, in *Agricultural Innovation in the Early Islamic World*, rejects these notions and instead conveys a surprising picture to the contrary. Not only were Muslims very knowledgeable, but they also helped expand available agricultural products and introduced some new ones, including alfalfa (the word is derived from Arabic).

Watson gives the following reasons. Muslims, he said, were "unusually receptive to all that is new," for they had the "capacity to absorb and transmit." They also implemented some worthwhile changes that increased agricultural output and hence strengthened the economy. The innovations included the introduction of higher-yielding new crops, the improvement of the varieties of existing crops by more specialized land use, and the upgrading of irrigation systems. The major effects were in the production of fruit, vegetables, rice, grains, sugar cane, palms, and cotton.[1]

Food Products

Fruits included orange, lemon, lime, banana, watermelon, and mango. The citrus fruit originated in Burma and was cultivated in the neighboring countries of China, India, and Malaysia. Banana and mango also came from this region and watermelon from eastern equatorial Africa. Some citrus was known as far as the eastern Mediterranean. The Muslims took fruit into more countries and farther west into Spain. The cultivation of oranges, among other fruit, in the Americas came originally from Muslim Spain. The banana was also known in the eastern Mediterranean, including Egypt, before Islam. Muslims took the banana on a more direct route to the West through North Africa and into Spain.[2]

The watermelon was carried to the East in pre-Islamic times before the Muslims introduced it to the West. From East Africa its cultivation spread north into Egypt and the Holy Land, then east to India, where it was developed into the large, sweet watermelon as it is known today. The Muslims cultivated the Indian variety of watermelon, and initially used the dried fruit and its seeds as medicine. Later, it became a fresh fruit crop and as such was grown in Egypt and the Maghreb and then in other parts of the Muslim world.[3] The mango tree had a limited diffusion. It was transported from India to Oman in the Gulf and from there to southern Iraq and much later to East Africa.

The Muslims were also responsible for the cultivation of three vegetables beyond their places of origin: spinach, eggplant (also known as aubergine or *brinjal*), and artichoke. By the time the Muslims had reached northwest India, where spinach was domesticated, it was also being grown as far east as China. The Muslims brought it west. Eggplant already existed in China, where it was most likely native, and in Persia during pre-Islamic times. From Persia the Muslims took it to Egypt, across North Africa and to Spain. The artichoke, on the other hand, was carried east by the Muslims from North Africa and also into Spain.[4]

Muslims contributed to the widespread cultivation of other food products. An important cereal for the Near East (and much later for other parts of the world, too) was hard wheat, used for the making of couscous and, when finely ground, for flat round bread and spaghetti, macaroni, and other pastas. The origin of its cultivation began and the route it followed is not documented. In recorded history, however, wheat has always been associated with the Arab world, from where the Muslims took it to Central Asia, Abyssinia, the Maghreb, and Spain. These new environments resulted in new varieties. There is also a strong possibility that spaghetti and other pasta were brought to Italy by the Muslims.[5] According to Watson, an Italian fourteenth-century book on foods described all kinds of pasta as *tria* and a four-teenth-century Catalan book labeled noodles as *aletria*. Both words "are clearly borrowed from the Arabic *itriya*," which refers to a kind of pasta. *Itriya*, Watson adds, "has a long history in the languages of the Near East."[6]

Another valuable agricultural product was sorghum, also known as the great millet, which was in greater demand. Sorghum could be grown under drought conditions and in poor soil and hence was cultivated more cheaply than other cereals. It also had other uses. Its stalks and seeds were used as cattle and poultry fodder, and some of the varieties were used to make thatch, baskets, brushes, and brooms. Sorghum originated in East Africa and was quite widespread by Islamic times. The Muslims found a new variety developed in India and transferred it to the western areas of the Muslim world, thus completing a circle in the distribution of this cereal: from East Africa, it had gone to India, and from India, the Muslims took the new variety to East Africa.[7]

The cultivation of rice (from the Arabic *ruzz*), on the other hand, depended heavily on the availability of abundant water. In pre-Islamic times it had come from China and India to the eastern Mediterranean although it was not grown widely. With the coming of Islam, rice was extended, beginning with the areas around the Tigris and the Euphrates, to the extent that it became a staple diet among the Muslims. The Muslims also brought rice into Africa, although there is linguistic evidence that it had been introduced earlier into East Africa, to which it had been carried across the ocean from India.[8]

Even more restricted in where they can be grown were coconuts and dates, two more products that the Muslims carried westward. The coconut came from India, but the dates were already a staple in the desert regions from long before Islam. The Muslims contributed to its cultivation by developing new varieties until there were several hundred. The Middle East and North Africa are still famous for their dates. Those grown in southern California, some of which are the best dates available in the West, were brought directly from Arab countries.

The strongest linguistic evidence of Muslims transporting an agricultural product to the West is the origin of the word "sugar," which is derived from the Arabic *sukkar*. Surprisingly, until the spread of Islam it was restricted to eastern Asia. After the Muslims discovered it, however, its spread was rapid, though cultivated only in the Muslim world, including Spain and Sicily. Nevertheless, the cultivation of sugar in those two countries ended soon after the Muslims were expelled from there.

Natural Resources and Cultivation Methods

The origin and spread of cotton have a more complicated history. Although the word itself comes from the Arabic, where it originated is not known. Botanists have traced cotton growing wild in areas as far apart as the valley of the upper Nile, southwest Africa, and in the Indus valley of the region now known as Pakistan. Where it was cultivated is more certain: in the Indus valley of the Mohenjo-Daro civilization about 2,000 BC. In India at the beginning of the Christian Era, cotton made into fabric was part of the international trade. Cotton goods were sold in northeast Africa and, two centuries later, in Egypt and China. Its cultivation afterward was restricted to areas providing the climate it required: long warm seasons in countries such as India, Malaysia, and China.

A new variety of cotton adapted to a cooler climate and requiring a shorter growing season was eventually developed. Cotton became a most popular and important textile under the Muslims. It had a very wide cultivation in nearly every Muslim country, as well as in non-Muslim countries in Europe, spreading from Muslim Spain into France, Germany, Italy, and England. Its distribution grew into a major trade, with a wharf in Baghdad built specifically for the cotton business.

The cotton industry was developed in the Muslim world. A book by Ibn al-Mubarrid describes ten types of cotton weavers and several kinds of linen, rug, carpet, canvas, and sack weavers. The major demand was for fine cotton. Trade in all kinds of cotton became so important that in Egypt alone, according to Janet Abu-Lughod, "Textiles constituted the second industry that linked rural production to the 'industrial' economy."[9] Centuries later, the Ottoman Turks developed an industry in Gaza, producing a different kind of cotton fabric, which became known as "gauze," named after Gaza.[10]

The Muslims carried agricultural products and methods of cultivation into Muslim Spain. The variety and abundance of fruit, especially, rapidly became of major trade value. It was more than sufficient for local consumption and was exported to Muslim and non-Muslim regions, such as Makkah, Alexandria, Damascus, Baghdad, and Central Asia as well as Constantinople and India. The trade made an enormous difference to the people of Andalusia, Muslim and non-Muslim, and to the economy as a whole. "This agricultural development," Hitti says, "was one of the glories of Muslim Spain and one of the Arabs' lasting gifts to the land."[11]

Why the Success?

All the agricultural products existed in Asia and Africa for centuries before the coming of Islam. Why then did the advent of this particular religion make all the difference in their variety and distribution? Why did the Muslim world diffuse them to a great many other parts of the world? The answer is simple. Islam is dynamic: it is outgoing, positive, meliorist, and concerned about people. It has engendered development within the individual, the community, and the world. It has also endowed Muslims with a spirit that people can be helped and that the world can be improved.

A comparison with the earlier civilizations puts this into proper perspective. The centuries of the Mesopotamian, Egyptian, Indian, and Chinese civilizations were devoted to growth rather than expansion. Greece had too brief a golden age, and a major internal conflict — the Peloponnesian war — prevented its ideas from being disseminated abroad until after the coming of Islam, when the Muslims did it for the Greeks. Rome was the first civilization to benefit from

Greece. However, inheriting ideas is different from putting them into practice.

The Romans were more obsessed with power than with people. The picture that comes to mind when one thinks of the civilization of Rome is a centurion standing straight, gleaming metal weighing him down: a metal helmet, a metal vest, a metal shield, and a heavy metal sword. Yes, they did build cities, about which they learned much from the Greeks. Nevertheless, the cities, even Rome and especially those in the farther reaches of the empire, had to be manned by the military forces. It was as though the military forces were propping up the only civilized parts of its world, namely, the urban areas. Therefore, when the empire declined, it left many of the people in the outlying areas helpless.

The fall of Rome devastated parts of Europe. According to Abu-Lughod, the people had been so rigidly controlled that when they were left on their own, far too many of them simply did not know how to proceed in many circumstances. The Church was of no help to these people. The attitude of the Christians is especially evident in what they did to the new agricultural products after the Muslims were expelled from Europe in the Middle Ages. Many of the products the Muslims had cultivated were abandoned.[12] Watson notes that the Christians lacked "skills, incentives, favorable attitudes, and receptive institutions." He gives a telling example. Frederic II of Sicily had to send to Tyre for experts in sugar production, and Jaime II of Aragon turned to Sicily in an effort to reintroduce sugar and cotton into the lands he had conquered. He did not succeed.[13]

There are many other significant reasons for the Muslim contribution to agriculture. Watson provides an excellent discussion in the later chapters of his book. Islam was not restricted to a single region of the world but extended across the three continents of Africa, Asia, and Europe, and "Muslim scholars were unique in their extensive knowledge" of these areas, much of it gained from direct experience. Watson gives as another reason that the Muslims also had a fondness for travel, such as to Makkah to perform the pilgrimage. Yet there was also much freedom to move from one place to another. Even the ordinary people and the poor moved around and they carried with them seeds, live plants, roots, cuttings, implements, and expertise in the cultivation of individual plants.

In addition, Watson states, the Muslim government facilitated the movement of both people and products with its laws, common currency, and weights and measures, as well as with a network of roads, caravan routes, extensive areas where the caravans could rest for days, if necessary, and ports. Agriculture was big business, too, helped no doubt by the cosmopolitan character of cities and towns. Word soon spread when there appeared a new product or a new way of preparing foods, and so cookbooks were published. Non-food agricultural products were also in demand. Cotton fabric, for example, proved comfortable to wear in hot climates. The Muslims manufactured other textiles, too, such as muslin, sarsanet, damask, taffeta, and tabby. All these names are derived from Arabic.[14]

Technology and Engineering

There was also the development of technology. Watson devotes a chapter of his book to irrigation, and al-Hassan and Hill give further details in their excellent study, *Islamic Technology*. When writing about technology, as with other fields, the tendency among Western scholars, as has already been mentioned earlier in this book, has been to insist that the Muslims acquired almost all their knowledge from previous civilizations. "In our studies we have followed in the footsteps of our predecessors," Abu al-Faraj Abd Allah ibn al-Tayyib has said.

Al-Hassan and Hill point to the work by the Banu Musa brothers, *Kitāb al-Ḥiyal* (The Book of Ingenious Devices), which demonstrates significant improvements over the technology the Muslims inherited from the Greeks. Al-Hassan and Hill add that "out of the hundred devices described in [this book], about seventy were of their own design."[15] James and Thorpe describe the Banu Musa brothers as "pioneers in an extraordinary renaissance of high-tech engineering in the medieval Islamic world."[16]

The principles on which these machines were based consisted of sound engineering. Novelty and practicality were demonstrated in a number of inventions. Muslim engineers were fond of adding extraordinary parts to simple clock mechanisms until they were more marvels than utilitarian objects. An outstanding example was a water clock that the Caliph Harun al-Rashid sent as a gift to Charlemagne. James and Thorpe describe the clock as consisting of two enormous vessels "that gradually filled when the moon was waxing, then emptied as it waned." In their book, James and Thorpe emphasize "the brilliant technological achievements of the golden age of Islamic engineering during the Middle Ages.[17]

In irrigation and other uses of water, for example, methods had existed for millennia before Islam. However, Muslim engineers improved most of them and added inventions of their own. According to al-Hassan and Hill, for example, al-Jazari invented the "first known instance of the use of a crank as part of [a] machine." Even when Muslim engineers produced devices considered unimportant, "the ideas and components embodied in the devices are relevant to the development of modern machine technology."[18]

The Muslims extended the existing underground conduits that transported subterranean water. "The greatest expansion," James and Thorpe state, was in Iran during the medieval Islamic period, and is "still a mainstay of modern Iranian agriculture."[19] The Muslims also went beyond existing methods for bringing up water from lower levels to the areas of cultivation. One of the machines they invented ran smoother than those already in existence and, much more important, increased the output fourfold. Though water wheels had been used for grinding corn, the Muslims were the first to use water power in industry. Consequently, the use of animal power was largely eliminated, to be replaced with machines using water power. These machines made efficient use of pumps that the Muslims had invented, one of them having six cylinders driven by water power. Large mills were built on the banks of the Tigris and Euphrates, from Mosul to Baghdad, and the production for each mill was approximately ten tons a day.

Nowadays, windmills are mainly associated with only one country in Europe and that is the Netherlands. However, al-Hassan and Hill quote Joseph Needham, the outstanding authority on Chinese science and technology, who points out that the history of windmills really begins with Islamic culture and in Iran,[20] and that Europe possibly adopted them from Muslim Spain. Al-Hassan and Hill leave no doubt that windmills were already established in the Muslim world by the third century AH (ninth century AC). Many other technological advances helped facilitate production and trade. The building of roads, bridges, dams, ships, ports, industrial plants, and mills, each in its own way contributed to the cultivation or manufacture of food and products. Advances in the sciences, chemistry, and metallurgy in particular, enhanced the processes.

Distillation, Glassmaking, and More

Chemistry was used in the manufacture of products and the process itself was also of value. In the example of alcohol, the word is derived from Arabic, which is understandable since Muslims were the first to discover a means of making it. This discovery required a thorough knowledge of, and extensive experience in the art of distillation. A Muslim scientist, Jabir, also discovered that alcohol was flammable and therefore could be used in some laboratory and other experiments as well as in industries. Muslims wrote books of recipes describing different uses of alcohol, which were appropriated without any acknowledgment of the sources by Western scholars such as Adelard of Bath, Roger Bacon, and Albertus Magnus.[21]

Distillation was of immense value in the refinement of petroleum. Western history begins with Western oil companies traveling to Near Eastern countries, discovering oil, and tapping oil wells. Yet the Muslims had established the petroleum industry in the region a thousand years earlier. The Baku oils were in commercial use during the early Islamic period and the crude oil springs in Darband were in production in 272/885. James and Thorpe cite Marco Polo visiting the Baku wells and reporting that "a hundred shiploads might be taken from it at one time." Oil was also produced in Iraq, Egypt, and Persia. There was a single Arabic word – *naft* – for crude oil and refined oil. The distinction was made between the two by calling them black *naft* and white *naft*. The oil was used mostly for domestic lighting.[22] Muslims also developed more efficient techniques in the manufacture of glass. "With the rise of Islamic civilization," al-Hassan and Hill state, "the early glass industry underwent a renaissance." By the third century AH (ninth century AC), there were glass factories in Iraq, Syria, Iran, North Africa, and Spain. The glass made in Samarra early in the period was of the highest quality.[23]

Among the materials for the making of glass were two that the Muslims especially used. One was ashes, made from a Syrian herb known as saltwort, and the other manganese dioxide to clarify the glass. The Muslims applied a number of decorations such as mosaic, molded patterns, blobs, ribs, ripples, indentations, luster, and enameling. The finest examples of embossed, enameled, and gilt glass are the mosque lamps, many of which are displayed in, among other places, the Museum of Islamic Art in Cairo, and the Metropolitan Museum of Art in New York.

In addition to the glassware now considered an art form, a wider variety of Islamic ceramics is exhibited in many museums throughout the world. Here, too, the Muslims made innovative additions to glazes already available, especially in the creation of a white, almost semi-transparent finish to the surface, and tin and other metallic glazes to add luster to the pottery.

Syria continued to manufacture glass products through the centuries until Venice started making its own in the thirteenth century AC. During the Crusades, the Christians gave Venice the secrets of Syrian glass-making, which the Venetians themselves kept secret to maintain a monopoly in the glass trade in Europe.

Both distillation and an increase in the manufacture of small glass containers added refinement to perfume, another product, which, though linked with the East for centuries, became more closely associated with the Muslim world. Shakespeare refers to "the perfumes of Arabia" in *Macbeth*. The most prominent of the fragrances is musk because it is found in Paradise. The Prophet was fond of it and other fragrances.

Another perfume related to Heaven is essence of roses. As pointed out in Chapter 4, a synonym of Paradise is *gulistan* (a rose garden). Sa'di used the word as a title for his renowned book of poetry. When a friend gathered fragrant flowers, Sa'di said that he was going to create a rose garden that would last far longer than any of the flowers around him. In Sa'di's native Iran, a place known as Jur was devoted to the cultivation of, and was famous for, the attar (essence) of red roses and rose water. There are records of 30,000 bottles of the attar of roses from Jur delivered to a Caliph in Baghdad. Today, guests in some parts of the Muslim world are greeted with rose water, and in mosques special festivities are celebrated with the sprinkling of rose water over the congregation. The pure attar of roses, preferred by Muslims, is one of the most expensive of flower essences.

Ibn Sina (known in the West as Avicenna), one of the world's greatest physicians, was the first to derive the attar of flowers from distillation. He is said to have experimented with "the rose of a hundred petals." Other Muslims continued to experiment until there were one hundred and seven methods and recipes, as described in a treatise by the scientist al-Kindi. Perfumes were manufactured in Damascus, at several centers in Iran, and later in Muslim Spain.[24] Shapur and its valley in Iran "produced ten world-famous varieties of perfumed oils...extracted from the violet, water-lily, narcissus, palm flower, white lily, myrtle, sweet marjoram, lemon, and orange flowers." The trade in perfumes was at first largely in the Muslim world and then it was extended to India and China.[25]

There is still a thriving perfume industry in the Muslim world. Muslims prefer the "local" essences because they do not contain alcohol. In my travels in the Near East, I came across shops that sold nothing but perfumes, their shelves filled with large, tall glass bottles of each kind of essence. In these shops, the preparation of perfumes is considered an art. The seller discusses the needs of a customer at length before mixing the most appropriate fragrances for him or her. A Muslim will apply attar to his clothes before going to a mosque for congregational or festive prayers.

These and other products came to be associated with Muslim and Arab trade. Over history, there were changes in the nature of what was transported and sold. Although the trade route retained the name "Silk Road," this particular route eventually no longer carried silk from China. Silk was now being manufactured in the Muslim world and was part of an increasing production of all kinds of textiles. Areas became famous for the kind of fabric they manufactured. Attab, a district of Baghdad, was the first to produce a striped fabric that came to be known as *attabi*. It was later "imitated by the Arabs in Spain...under the trade name tabi," and sold in France, Italy, and other parts of Europe.[26] The term, Hitti reminds us, survives as "tabby" to describe "streaked or marked cats." Another city, Kufa, was noted for silk head coverings; hence, *kūfiyyah* is now a generic name for the head cloth worn by the Arabs.[27]

All kinds of fabrics were woven and converted into textile products in both town and village homes. The home thus became a part of international trade. All that were needed were a loom and skill in weaving and in making products such as brocade, tapestry, sofa (derived from the Arabic *suffa*), cushion covers, and carpets, for which the Muslim world is still renowned.

Carpets were for centuries an exclusive home industry. Remarkably enough, high standards in quality and design were maintained. Caliphs purchased carpets from the same sources as did Muslims from all other walks of life, the only difference between the carpets of the rich and those of other social classes being the size. The former were far bigger and, in many instances, had more decorations. A carpet made especially for al-Mustaʿin's mother had woven into it threads of gold portraying birds, whose eyes consisted of rubies and other precious stones.[28]

In all, the Muslim empire exerted a massive influence over the commercial lives of Europeans, Africans, Arabs, and Asians for many centuries. Muslim success in spreading religion and culture set the stage for economic expansion. Friendliness in trade dealings allowed Muslim techniques, products, and language to penetrate various areas of the world.

8

FLOWERING OF ISLAMIC LEARNING

AS THE MUSLIM community grew, so did its acquisition of knowledge, and its efforts gained momentum during the finest century of the Abbasid Caliphate, especially under the Caliphs Harun al-Rashid and his son and successor al-Ma'mun, both of whom contributed greatly to the advancement of Islamic civilization. This was the time when Muslims began writing books, primarily on the Qur'an and other religious subjects. Ibn Ishaq's biography of the Prophet, rewritten by Ibn Hisham, is considered the oldest historical work in the Muslim world. The second oldest is *Futūḥ Miṣr*, a history of the conquests of Egypt and the regions westward, by Ibn Abd al-Hakam.

The period saw the greatest number of translations into Arabic of works from various nations. The first translations from Greek into Arabic were commissioned by the Umayyad prince, Khalid ibn Yazid ibn Muawiyah long before the end of the first century AH, for he was interested in Greek philosophy and science. The initial major program of translations was implemented by the second Abbasid Caliph, al-Mansur, founder of Baghdad.[1] Himself a devotee of learning, al-Mansur arranged to have books translated from Syriac, Persian, and Greek into Arabic. The most popular of these was (and still is) *Kalīlah wa Dimnah*, translated by Ibn Muqaffa from a Persian version of an Indian Sanskrit original. His translation was fortunate because both the Persian and the Sanskrit versions were lost. Hence, all subsequent translations into other languages, Asian and European, including Icelandic, had to be made from the Arabic.[2]

Of immense help was the existence of institutions of learning, especially libraries, at Jundishapur in Iran. The history of these institutions begins in Roman times with the famous library at Alexandria, founded by Alexander and maintained as a royal library from the third century BC by Ptolemy rulers. Western scholars insist that Muslims destroyed the library. However, an authority on medieval history, Hugh Kennedy, points out that this myth was "long ago consigned to the garbage can by serious historians."[3] The library was in fact burned down twice, though not by Muslims: first in 48 AC by Julius Caesar, and then, after it was rebuilt and restocked, a second time in 389 AC at the insistence of Theodosius, the Christian emperor. Although many important Greek works were destroyed in these fires, a few survived. The Nestorians rescued these few and, together with other books available, hid them from harm. These volumes eventually found their way to Jundishapur.

Another Christian emperor, Justinian, closed the schools of philosophy in both Athens and Alexandria, so the Nestorians of these schools moved first to Syria, and then to Persia. There, they were welcomed and settled in Jundishapur. When the Muslims conquered Persia, they extended protection to the Nestorians and, owing to their esteem for learning, preserved the works available in the Jundishapur libraries. In return, the Nestorians were of valuable help to the Muslims in translating Greek works into Arabic.

Housing the collections of Greek books in Jundishapur and elsewhere in the Muslim world helped considerably in preserving them, because more destruction followed centuries later in Constantinople. According to Asimov, "it was the last place in the world where the full corpus of Greek literature existed. He described how Enrico Doge of Venice diverted the Fourth Crusade and moved it against Constantinople. When the Crusaders sacked the city, almost the entire corpus of Greek literature was destroyed.[4] Greek works in their Arabized versions eventually reached Latin Europe, reawakening interest in not only Aristotle but also Greek texts.[5] There are two other misconceptions, almost a chorus among Western historians, which need to be rectified here. One is that by borrowing from Greece, the

Muslims were really borrowing from the West. The other is that the texts translated into Arabic were not made from the original Greek. It should be remembered, however, that at the time of the translations, there was no West to speak of. "The idea of classical Greece," Roberts states, was "a creation of later ages rather than that of the Greeks themselves."[6] It was centuries afterward that, as Hodgson notes, the West "retroactively" appropriated Greek history. Hodgson adds that Greek, as well as Syriac and Persian, "cultural elements...formed the ancestral traditions of most of the Muslim population."[7]

William McNeill also says that "Archaic Greece" derived much of its learning from the Orient, one example being Thales of Miletus, the founder of Greek philosophy. Oriental ideas, McNeill adds, "infiltrated...the old heartland of Hellenism."[8] Roberts quotes a German scholar who says that when neo-Platonic philosophy appeared, Asoka, the Buddhist king of India, sent missionaries to Macedonia, Cyprus, and Egypt.[9]

Muslims had access, Western scholars also assert, only to "inferior" Syriac editions of Greek works. The efforts of the Banu Musa brothers brought more accurate translations from the original Greek, for they employed a Nestorian physician, Hunain ibn Ishaq, to collect Greek manuscripts and translate them. However, Ibn Ishaq went even further. He procured good Greek manuscripts, collated them, compared them with existing Syriac and Arabic versions, and then translated the originals with the care of a most devoted scholar. Centuries later, when these works were translated from Arabic into Latin, Cantor said, "it was amazing how accurate were the final versions."[10]

Abbasid Caliphate

The story of the three Abbasid Caliphs is one of coincidence or perhaps fate. On a night like no other in Islamic history, one Caliph died, another succeeded him, and a third was born. Al-Mahdi died; Harun al-Rashid assumed the throne, and al-Ma'mun was born.

Harun al-Rashid is more famous for three reasons. He was the first of the Caliphs to become a world statesman. During his Caliphate, Baghdad achieved the magnificence that earned it the distinction of being the heart of the Golden Age of Islam. He was so popular that he became the most widely-known Caliph all over the world as a legendary figure in *A Thousand and One Nights* (commonly known as *The Arabian Nights*). Al-Rashid's depiction in the *Nights* is in one respect authentic,[11] in that he did disguise himself and roam the streets of Baghdad to see how his people were faring.

What is far less known is the extent of his love of learning, which particularly benefited his son al-Ma'mun, the next Caliph. Harun made every effort to see that his son was educated by the best teachers. The most learned of these was Imam Malik, the founder of one of the four schools of Islamic law and the author of its major compendium, one of the four basic law books of Islam. Imam Malik lived in Madinah at the time of Harun al-Rashid so the Caliph invited him to Baghdad to teach his two sons. Imam Malik refused, declaring, "People go in search of learning. Learning does not go in search of people." Harun al-Rashid agreed and accompanied his two sons to Madinah and, with them, attended Imam Malik's lectures.

As a result of studying under teachers such as Imam Malik, al-Rashid's successor al-Ma'mun excelled in law, literature, philosophy, rhetoric, and the sciences. His learning did not end with his schooling, for when he was governor of Merv, he learned from people from different parts of the world who gathered there, including Buddhists, Persians, and Turks. Therefore, it is not surprising that when he became Caliph, he founded the House of Wisdom in Baghdad, which attracted scholars from many parts of the world.[12]

This House became the center of more translations from Greek, Syrian, Persian, and Sanskrit works. Al-Ma'mun made every effort to obtain manuscripts from the Byzantines by sending a deputy to Emperor Leon the Armenian. The Caliph had the help of the sons of Musa, also known as the Three Brothers, who, in addition to making valuable contributions to mathematics and astronomy, paid out of their own funds the salaries of several translators from Greek.[13] The House of Wisdom had a research center as well as an astronomy observatory. Al-Ma'mun built another observatory near Damascus. The quest for learning at this institution was overwhelmingly superior and gave the Muslims the status of the real standard-bearers of civilization at that time.[14]

The rulers in those days were also scholars with a high level of sophistication. They participated in the quest for knowledge and, equally important, made it accessible to any Muslim and to other scholars from the non-Muslim world. Books were available to every scholar, regardless of background.

As a side note, what was considerably useful to the Muslim scholars was the introduction of coffee into the Muslim world. According to James and Thorpe, coffee originated in Ethiopia and was taken from there to southern Arabia. Muslim scholars in Makkah and al-Azhar and other universities were among the first to use it because coffee helped keep them awake late into the night. "Muslim pilgrims," James and Thorpe state, "spread the habit to every corner of the Muslim world." The earliest recorded Western discovery of coffee was by Gianfranceso Morosini, an envoy from Venice to Turkey. He described it as "a black liquid…extracted from a seed which they call cavee, and which they say has the quality of keeping a man awake."[15] The first coffee house in Europe was opened in Paris in 1643.

Al-Hakim created another, bigger institution over two centuries later, which was known as the Abode of Wisdom. This designation is synonymous with al-Ma'mun's, although it was understood to mean the House of Science, for that was the main subject of study at this university, although all subjects were included. According to al-Hassan and Hill, the House of Wisdom offered its research facilities and lectures "free to the public, who were provided with ink, pens, and paper."[16]

Before the end of the first century AH, there was considerable progress in many areas of learning. Ibn Abad recorded the first code of law and Abu al-Aswad the first Arabic grammar, initiating research into these topics. In the succeeding years there was a flowering of knowledge, in archaeology, for example, as demonstrated in the works of Ibn Duraid, al-Hamdani and Abu al-Faraj al-Isfahani, and history in the works of al-Tabari and al-Masudi.

Women, too, excelled in acquiring knowledge: Qur'anic studies, theology, law, the arts (especially poetry and music), and medicine.

The immediate need was for midwives, although women went further and studied other branches of medicine. In some sources, there is mention of them practicing as surgeons and teaching "in Salerno and other Italian cities."[17]

The wives of the Caliphs competed with one another in the writing of poetry. One poem, written by Maysuna, wife of Muawiyah, proved very effective. In it she expressed her longing and love for the rough life of the desert, preferring it to marble palaces, and called her husband "a fat lout in purple." The Caliph heard of the poem and sent her back to the desert.[18]

Another wife of a Caliph – the mother of the famous Harun al-Rashid – rejected both music and poetry and, instead, attended a religious school. As a result, she gained eminence and power, both politically and economically, for she was the richest woman of her time and the mother of two Caliphs. On the day of her funeral, it rained and her son Harun al-Rashid led the funeral procession, walking barefoot in the mud. Women from outside the courts were also exceptional. Shuhda, during the Abbasid Caliphate, was one of the foremost authorities on the Traditions of the Prophet. Another, Amat al-Wahid, studied law under her father, a Baghdad judge, and became an eminent judge in her own right.[19]

The most famous woman of the Abbasid period, known today simply as Rabiah, preferred to seek knowledge of a totally different kind, that of the transcendental. During her lifetime, Baghdad was built and developed. However, her concerns were far from that city and its glories and hedonism. As a Sufi, she lived in Basra, where she was born, and her possessions were meager, consisting of a jug, a mat, and a brick for her pillow.[20]

Numerous other Muslim women achieved prestige in learning and other fields. A.M.A. Shustery lists them in his study of Islamic culture: among them were 17 rulers and administrators, 9 orators, 4 who built mosques and other public institutions, 42 theologians and traditionists, 23 musicians, and 76 poets. There were also many others, unnamed, including physicians.[21]

The abundance of research and writing is more than adequately demonstrated in *The Fihrist of al-Nadim*, whose English subtitle is *A Tenth-Century Survey of Muslim Culture*, the most comprehensive listing of thousands of books and interesting details about the authors. However, the *Fihrist* is far more than a bibliography, since it is a record of a highly intelligent mind responding to the immense wealth of knowledge available to him and other Muslims. All the works cited, the author makes clear, are written in Arabic by Arabs and non-Arabs. The subjects dealt with – in the order of discussion – are languages, writings, scriptures, the Qur'an, grammar and philology, history, essays, biography, genealogy, poetry, theology, jurisprudence and tradition, philosophy and the sciences (logic, mathematics, music, astronomy, engineering and medicine), magic and fables, sects and creeds, and alchemy.

Ibn Abi Yaqub al-Nadim (d. 385/995) was fortunate to have a father who was a bookseller and whose shop was well stocked and certainly one of the largest in Baghdad. Al-Nadim must have devoted his life to the study of books. Evidently, his mentors were the three people that he describes in his book as the most "avaricious for learning": al-Jahiz, Ibn Khaqan, and Ibn Ishaq al-Qadi. Al-Jahiz read a book from beginning to end soon after he received it. Al-Fath always had a book with him, which he read in every spare moment, even while walking. Ibn Ishaq was always reading a book whenever al-Nadim visited him, or selecting the next book to read.

A significant fact the *Fihrist* affirms is one that its author does not discuss: in addition to the overwhelming abundance of books in libraries, there were vast collections in the homes of individuals. Books were a vital part of their lives. The best example cited in many texts is that of al-Sahib in Abbad, who refused to take a more lucrative post as vizier to a Samanid ruler because it meant transporting his enormous library, which he estimated would need four hundred camels. Al-Hakam II of Muslim Spain had four hundred thousand books in his library. That he read a great many of them is demonstrated by the annotations he made in the books' margins.

For any scholar who came to the *Fihrist* three hundred years or more after it was published in 938 AC, there was considerable disappointment. As pointed out earlier, almost all the books cited by al-Nadim were lost when the Mongols destroyed Baghdad in 656/1258 and the contents of entire libraries were thrown into the Tigris, turning the waters black. Although a few of the books were available in other cities, of all the titles in the *Fihrist*, only one in a thousand survived.[22]

Yet before then, numerous Arabic books had already been translated into Latin. At the same time, there were far more books, still not translated, which were of considerable value to the West. For those who wanted to read the originals, especially during al-Nadim's lifetime in the tenth century AC, the first Arabic–Latin dictionary became available.

The use of this dictionary was most likely limited to ecclesiastical institutions, since the Church monopolized learning at the time and monks were required to know Arabic so that they could translate Islamic works into Latin. However, some of the translations were poor. The monks overcame one difficulty by simply adopting the many Arabic words with no Latin equivalents, which is how they eventually became part of the English vocabulary.

Later, with the establishment of universities in the West, there were courses on Arabic as well as in Arabic. Frederick II, for example, founded the University of Naples in 1224 AC, "the first in Europe to be established by a definite charter" and "in it he deposited a large collection of Arabic manuscripts." One of the students at the University of Naples was Thomas Aquinas.[23]

The use of Arabic as a medium of instruction at Western universities was a continuation of what had already been available to scholars from the West, particularly in the Muslim learning center of Cordoba. Western scholars were by then emerging on their own, moving away from Church-controlled learning institutions. Even though the Church highly disapproved of what they did, these scholars attended institutions in Muslim Cordoba. The primary reason is given by Roberts: "For [centuries], no science, no school in the West could match those of Arab Spain."[24]

The West also borrowed other practices from Muslim institutions, among which, especially practiced in Andalusia, were "dialectic tournaments" called "disputations." A more accurate description of these events would be seminars. According to Campbell, this Muslim custom also led to the Western modern practice of demanding theses and dissertations from aspirants to university honors.[25]

Another means of acquiring knowledge also spread to the West. In the Muslim world, students heard of and sought eminent scholars in different cities, some traveling from Muslim Spain all the way to China, as well as from one part of the Muslim world to the other. Europe adopted this practice from Islam: when universities were established in the West, a European scholar would travel to several cities in quest of the knowledge of his specialty.

During the tenth century AC, another change was already in progress. Literary and scholarly works were no longer written in Arabic alone, for Persian was regaining its earlier status. Though almost exactly the same language it had been in pre-Islamic Persia, Iranian Persian had absorbed numerous Arabic words, as did many other languages in predominantly Muslim countries. The importance of the "new" Persian language and the literature in which it was used was demonstrated in the publication of *Lughat-i-Fars* (Lexicon of Persian) by Ali Ibn Ahmad.[26]

Learning by Experience

The Muslims also very highly respected learning from experience in almost every area of life, from providing medical treatment to dyeing cloth, working in metal, practicing law, meting out justice, to participating in a mystical devotion to God. Muslim scholars did not ignore arts and crafts. "Unlike the Greeks," Carlton S. Coon states, "[the Muslims] did not consider the techniques of the artisan class unworthy of mention."[27]

Muslims throughout Islamic history exemplified the importance of experience in every facet of life. A few kept records or employed others to write for them. The efforts of most of the others remained unwritten, although much information was handed down verbally. This has been consistently overlooked by too many scholars of later times, who have based many of their conclusions solely on the basis of records available.

Higher learning in the Muslim world, as pointed out earlier, was to be found among the colonnades of the mosques. There were very few assigned books as such, for the knowledgeable masters themselves were living textbooks. Their students took copious notes and memorized them. As a result, only the names of those intellectual giants whose students acknowledged them in writing have survived.

An exemplar of learning and experience is Imam al-Ghazali (known as Algazel in the West), also the greatest scholar of Islamic theology. His father was a vendor of yarns, nevertheless, although illiterate, he recognized the value of education. A friend helped al-Ghazali and his brother acquire an education. From his home in Tus, al-Ghazali traveled to Jarjan to study under Abu Nasar Ismaili, who was a notable scholar there. He journeyed to other cities also to benefit from prominent learned men.

On one of these journeys, al-Ghazali was robbed of everything he had, including all the copious notes he had taken during lectures. He implored the leader of the robbers at least to return these notes. The leader laughed and questioned an education that relied solely on what was recorded on paper. For al-Ghazali this was a turning point. From that time, he committed learning to memory and in the process discovered the prodigious extent of his memory. This subsequently led him to concentrate on and expand his understanding of available scholarship and to submit it to scrutiny and analysis.

There were more institutions of higher learning at the time. Al-Azhar University in Cairo had been in existence for over a hundred years, having already established academic traditions still being practiced today, especially in the West. Among them are the distinction between undergraduate and graduate work and the wearing of black caps and gowns. Alfred Guillaume writes that the origin of the baccalaureate is most likely the Arabic phrase applied to graduates of a university: *bibaqq alriwaya* (the right to teach on the authority of another).[28] Salah al-Din (Saladin) also established more institutions of higher learning in Palestine and Syria.

Two other universities in Nishapur and Baghdad, which soon gained a reputation as high as that of al-Azhar, were founded by Nizam al-Mulk, a vizier of the first of the Seljuks. He himself was learned in Islamic law and was known for his love of education, to the extent that even in the twentieth century new schools in the Muslim world are often named after him.

Al-Ghazali traveled to Nishapur to study Islamic law, where he achieved prominence in his studies so that Nizam al-Mulk appointed him professor of law at the university in Baghdad. He also joined the legal profession and there, too, proved highly successful. Nevertheless, he was not satisfied with his success in these cities. He was filled with doubts, particularly regarding the authority of the senses as well as the authority of reason. Lacking certainty, he felt incomplete. He renounced his post and books and lifestyle and set out on a quest that was to take him to Makkah, Madinah, Damascus, Jerusalem, and Hebron.

In Damascus, al-Ghazali secluded himself and devoted his time to prayer, contemplation, and mysticism. He left Damascus because he came across a lecturer quoting at length from the books he had written. Fearing that he would be recognized and given all kinds of honors, thus fueling his pride, he moved on to Jerusalem. At Abraham's tomb in Hebron, he resolved not to be obliged to royalty and not to participate in needless discussions.

"It became clear to me," al-Ghazali wrote, "that the mystics were men who had real religious experiences, not just men of words." He thus became a Sufi and experienced mysticism for himself. This experience ended his doubts and led him to certainty. With this certainty, he wrote what has since become known as a work second in importance only to the Qur'an and the Hadith – *The Revival of the Religious Sciences* – which earned him titles such as "the Renewer of Religion" and "the Proof of Islam."[29]

Al-Ghazali was highly critical, too, of the deviations from the moral teachings of Islam by almost everyone, including philanthropists and social workers, the ruling classes, the theologians, and the rulers themselves. People were now practicing charity, he said, because they wanted renown, not from a love of humanity. The morals of the subjects as well as the ruling classes had deteriorated. The religious leaders had sold their consciences in their lust for power. Aware of how hedonistic the rulers had become, al-Ghazali recognized the right of the Muslims to correct their rulers.[30]

Al-Ghazali, more than any other Muslim scholar, explored the farthest reaches of both knowledge and experience, and hence demonstrated that learning was relevant to far more than what was encompassed by the intellect. Every living thing and everything else on earth and in the universe, big or small, come under the purview of everyone who wishes to know more about them. Nearly everything is knowable. The exception is what the Qur'an describes as the unseen, although a minute part of that can be experienced.[31] Al-Ghazali's ultimate idea of knowledge is a demanding, but idealistic one to keep in mind.

Study of History

Another major intellectual was Ibn Khaldun, the founder of sociology, who is accorded a most distinguished status in history. Pointing out that "history had, in principle, been the ultimate reality" for Muslim scholars, Hodgson adds that Ibn Khaldun "developed a new, historically oriented kind of political science" as well as "the essentials of economics and money theory."[32] M. Saeed Sheikh describes Ibn Khaldun's approach as "the scientific method of historical research."[33] Ibn Khaldun's major work, the *Muqaddimah* (the *Prologue* to his multi-volume *Universal History*) is nowadays required reading for history Ph.D. candidates at many Western universities.

Sarton, on the other hand, recognizes Ibn Khaldun as "the greatest philosopher of man's experience" and "the founder of the philosophy of history."[34] Arnold Toynbee describes his *Muqaddimah* as a philosophy of history that is undoubtedly the greatest work of its kind that has ever been created by any mind in any time or place.[35] Hodgson describes him as "the last great" philosopher of the Andalusian tradition.[36] Ibn Khaldun himself professed to be a philosopher, emphasizing that the history he was writing, especially his introduction to it, was in his own words "a branch" of philosophy.[37]

Ibn Khaldun's ideas were new, including his use, as the central thesis of his *Muqaddimah*, of a pre-Islamic word ʿaṣabiyyah (cohesion), which primarily described, according to Shaukat Ali, "unity of purpose, oneness of thought and action, dynamic leadership, and social and economic cohesion in a tribe."[38] Ibn Khaldun extended the definition to be applicable to the whole of society. The reason why Ibn Khaldun continued to uphold nomads as examples of ʿaṣabiyyah was their need to maintain unity or perish. Urban life, on the other hand, was prone to disintegration for the following reasons: an overwhelming propensity for luxury and comfort, emphasis on material wealth, injustice, corruption, neglect of the less fortunate, and disregard of the dangers of aggression from both outside and within.[39]

All of this is at the heart of Ibn Khaldun's philosophy of history as summarized by Chejne: "Society [has] cycles of growth from primitive to sedentary patterns, and finally to a highly sophisticated urban structure characterized by a level of luxury that ultimately leads to its decay and downfall."[40] Of course, Ibn Khaldun's philosophy is far more complex. It is enhanced by a detailed and incisive analysis of every facet of society: religious, political, economic, psychological, historic, geographic, and educational. One has to marvel at the insights provided by Ibn Khaldun: rulers who take the wrong road, sycophancy in court, the lengths to which people go to gain power, the major advantages of religion, the value of labor, the economic disasters due to oppression, the effects of food, the environment, the air, and the essentials of society, including the simplest of arts and crafts. The *Muqaddimah* is in itself a veritable education, and its study is to engage with a brilliant mind.

The *Universal History* is an enormous work, consisting of seven volumes. Ibn Khaldun's perspective was vast, from the Creation to the events of the previous years. It included events from Biblical, Persian, Greek, and Roman times, as well as the history of the Arabs from their earliest days to their impending loss of Muslim Spain and defeat after defeat at the hands of the Mongols. It is not surprising, therefore, that Ibn Khaldun felt pessimistic that people would learn from history. Hodgson states that Ibn Khaldun thus became convinced "that Ibn Rushd was right after all: one cannot reform society at will."[41]

What was considerably worthwhile to scholars like al-Ghazali and Ibn Khaldun was the continuing accumulation of books, which were rare items before Islam. The little writing that existed was done mainly on leather, dried stems of palm leaves, bones, and flat white stones. Only important documents were written on parchment, the best of which was made of gazelle hide. However, after the conquest of Egypt, papyrus readily became available to the Muslims.

Another major contribution of Islamic civilization to the West came in the early eighth century AC, seventy-one years after the establishment of the Muslim community. This was the discovery of writing paper from China. It was of a high quality, made from vegetable fiber or linen or hemp cloth. The Muslims employed the Chinese to produce the paper until they learned the technique themselves. Within a hundred years, Baghdad was producing vast amounts in a paper-mill. Soon there were mills in Egypt, Morocco, Spain, and Sicily, producing all kinds of paper, white as well as various other colors. France learned to make paper from Muslim Spain and Italy from Muslim Sicily.[42]

Wisdom from India

Muslims continually turned to India, even though the vast wisdom of India, in its scriptures and literature, was almost totally oral. The Hindus shared the knowledge stored in their memories with the Muslims who came to India in quest of learning. There is the significant example of al-Biruni, discussed in Chapter 5, whose love of Indian wisdom was unparalleled and who acquired much knowledge from Hindu sages.

According to Hitti, "India acted as an early source of inspiration, especially in wisdom literature."[43] Ismail al-Faruqi says that the Muslims turned to India before the end of the first century AH, and adds, "Sindi scholars were responsible for introducing Sanskrit knowledge and wisdom into the Near East." Later, the Muslims also learned medicine, pharmacology, astronomy, and mathematics from India.

One contribution from India was among the most important of any other civilization, which the Muslims acquired and eventually gave to the West. The zero, together with the Indian numbers, are more widely known as Arabic numerals because the West learned them from Arab Muslims. Al-Faruqi states that there were several numerical systems prevailing in India, which the Muslims combined into two. They used both, although only one of these, the "Ghubari," according to al-Faruqi, "was adopted by the West." Al-Faruqi then singles out the most important Muslim invention, which was the symbol for zero. The Indians had no such symbol, for they used a blank space to designate it. Another name for the zero, "cipher," the West borrowed from the Arabic ṣifr.[44]

The genius of Islamic civilization is demonstrated in the way it utilized the learning it acquired from other cultures, created an intellectual milieu of its own, and made its own contributions to the knowledge of the world. Intellectual activity was the one constant throughout Islamic civilization, regardless of political or other conflict. In fact, the pursuit of knowledge among Muslims, and including non-Muslims, reached heights no one else achieved during the Middle Ages.

9

THE SCIENCES

WHEN MUSLIMS ASKED Prophet Muhammad to perform miracles like those of the earlier prophets, God requested them to look at their surroundings and themselves, because in the natural world there were miracles upon miracles and the greatest of all miracles was the human being. "Go all over the earth and behold how [wondrously] He has created [man] in the first instance" (Qur'an 29:20). The Qur'an states it simply in a number of other verses, each time adding that these are signs for "all who are endowed with insight" (Qur'an 3:190), "for people who use their reason" (Qur'an 2:164).

Almost an entire surah (91) requests close observation of the sun and the moon, the sky, "the earth and all its expanse" (91:6), and the human self. In another surah, God makes it clear that He has displayed His wonders "before you" (30:24).

The works of the famous Muslim poet, Rumi, are also full of praise of the natural world. He singles out the bee as a recipient of the gift of "wit" from God and the silkworm for its special skill. He admonishes his readers: "How long do you regard mere form, O form-worshippers," adding that "if the form were all that made man," the Prophet and his worst enemy "would be upon a par." Rumi affirms what the Qur'an wants the Muslims to do, that is, to maintain a constant sense of wonder. [1]

The Muslims did observe, closely and carefully. They saw how the plants came forth, even in the desert after a rare rainstorm. They observed the sky at night, when even in the cities the stars were bright and low, glittering on an enormous inverted dark blue dome.

There are also passages in the Qur'an that must have intrigued those who contemplated the wonders of the universe and the earth. Among them are several references to water. God's "throne was over the waters" (11:7). The earth is "one single entity" and God "made out of water every living thing" (21:30), and, in a separate passage, God "created all animals out of water" (24:45). A verse describes two kinds of water, one fresh and the other "salty and bitter" (25:53), and adds that "out of this water [He] has created man" (25:54).

Other verses are intriguing, too, especially Qur'an (41:11), which portrays the skies as "smoke" (gaseous matter, perhaps?), where God "applied His design" and willed the earth into being. Yet another verse reminds people "how much is hidden from them" (34:9), with the implication that there are things beyond their perception or experience.

At the same time, the Qur'an draws attention to the temporal nature of God's creation, including the human being, by repeating a word not fully understood: *taqdīr*, which means "measure" or "potency." The *Concordance* of the Qur'an lists 131 verses where the derivations of *qadar* appear in five different categories. Each of these categories, in turn, has its own nuances, almost all of which emphasize God's power. In addition, many of the verses state that God has given the things He created a particular measure (Qur'an 54:49, 25:2 and other verses). *Taqdīr* is, therefore, the law of calculating that measure throughout the world. That it means both "measure" and "potency" gives it an additional significance: *taqdīr* balances the extremes of quantity and quality, at the same time neglecting neither.

This law, since it continues to function, is understandable if it is considered in terms of today's knowledge. As Muhammad Rashid Rida pointed out in the late 1940s, when the Qur'an speaks of a time allotted to people, as it does in (10:98), it refers to "their natural life-span."[2] It is one of the laws of Nature that, to use the Qur'anic description, everything has its appointed term. It is demonstrated in the different lifespans of different creatures as determined by biologists: three years for a mouse, for instance, 30 years for a cow, 100 to 150 years for a turtle. The potency of things is expressed in figures, for example, horsepower, volts, roentgen, velocity, etc.[3]

Islam did not oppose scientific research; on the contrary, the Qur'an provides every encouragment. Because the Muslims relied most heavily on observations of the world around them, they accomplished far, far more than Greek science. Aristotle might have insisted that to study the world around us from a scientific perspective, a person must observe. However, the "sciences" of the Greeks were largely in the hands of the philosophers, who preferred theory and speculation, resulting in endless dialog, and hence the products of the mind were considered more important than the reality around them.

The Greek Comparison

Many Greek scholars did observe and made lasting contributions to the sciences. The first major Greek scientist, Thales, who learned geometry from Egypt and astronomy from Babylon, went out in search of what the world was made of and came to the conclusion that the primary element was water. Pythagoras, in addition to his contribution to geometry, stated that the earth was not flat but round. Democritus's description of matter is today accepted as scientific fact: that it was composed of tiny particles, which he called atoms. It was Aristotle who laid the greatest emphasis on observation, thus initiating a truly scientific approach. He focused largely on classification. One of his students, Theophrastus, stated that Aristotle wrote a botany treatise classifying 550 plants. Nevertheless, most of the Greeks refused to accept new scientific findings, for they strongly adhered to their religion, consisting of myths and legends. For example, a philosopher who contradicted myth by saying that the sun was "a red-hot disc" was banished. There are some scholars nowadays, according to Roberts, who believe that Greek rationality stood in the way of scientific progress because of the insistence on "logic and abstract deduction rather than the observation of nature."[4] An example Roberts gives is that of Aristarchus of Samos, whose contention that the earth moved around the sun was rejected because it contradicted Aristotelian physics.[5] The Muslims were particularly impressed with Ptolemy, an astronomer and mathematician of those times, who was not Greek, but Roman. He is noted for his theory that the earth was the center of the universe. When Copernicus corrected Ptolemy over thirteen centuries later, the Church prosecuted all who supported him, including another great scientist, Galileo.[6]

Ptolemy used the works of previous astronomers, together with his own observations, in the compilation of his major work, *He Mathematika Syntaxis* (The Mathematical Collection), which was later renamed *Ho Megas Astronomos* (The Great Astronomer). It is possible that this most valuable contribution to astronomy would have been lost had it not been for the Muslims. One or more copies had been housed in the Alexandria Library. After the first burning of the library, scholars decided to rescue many of the remaining books, which they removed and hid. There was only one copy of Ptolemy's work and it was taken to Jundishapur in Persia, to be kept safe in the library of a monastery there. Around the middle of the eighth century AC, when the Muslims explored the library, they discovered Ptolemy's work together with a vast number of other Greek books on philosophy and the sciences. With the help of the Nestorians of the monastery, who were guardians of the library, all of them were translated into Arabic. Consequently, the Muslims learned of and from the great astronomer.

Ptolemy's work deals with the solar system and the universe and includes a catalog of 1,022 stars and their position in the night sky. For the Muslims, this information extended their knowledge of the universe and helped them identify the stars when they discoursed on the heavens. *Ho Megas Astronomos* proved so valuable to the Muslims that, instead of retaining the original title, even though it contained the word *megas* (great), they gave it the superior Latin label of *megiste*, Arabicized into *Almagest* (The Majestic [Book]), a title which is still used today, even in the West – a tribute the Muslims paid to Ptolemy.[7]

Sciences historian Colin A. Ronan notes that after Ptolemy in the second century AC, Greek science largely stagnated.[8] Western physicists have criticized Muslim astronomers for too rigid an adherence to Ptolemy and his geocentric theory, and for not seeing his errors. This criticism comes from hindsight, from the vantage point of the twentieth and twenty-first centuries, after centuries of other major discoveries in astronomy. In any case, when Copernicus generated his heliocentric theory, he was reluctant to make it public because the Church was rigid in its adherence to the geocentric theory, which it believed to be in accordance with the Bible. For decades after Copernicus, Christians were far more tenacious in rejecting the sun as the center of the universe, and even burned people to death for saying so. The Muslims, on the other hand, definitely knew of the heliocentric theory around the tenth century AC, since al-Biruni mentions it.[9] Unlike the Bible, the Qur'an certainly does not contradict the reality of the universe or the earth. Indeed, early Muslim scholars had already concluded that the earth was round, basing their interpretation on a description given in the Qur'an. Meanwhile, Europeans refused to accept this fact well into the Renaissance, insisting that the earth was flat.

Muslim scholars responded to Ptolemy and developed important research of their own. Al-Battani, considered one of the greatest Muslim astronomers, made changes in Ptolemy's calculations of the orbits of the moon and some of the planets.[10] Al-Battani also made a valuable contribution to spherical trigonometry, creating a formula with "no equivalent in Ptolemy."[11] Other Muslim astronomers modified Ptolemy's theories and "on occasion criticized him explicitly." Muslim physicist Ibn al-Haytham wrote *Doubts Regarding Ptolemy*, warning, "God did not make scholars impervious to error." Even after the Mongol destruction of Baghdad, there were new astronomical tables compiled, including one by Nasir al-Din al-Tusi in an observatory built by Hulagu Khan, the destroyer of Baghdad. Other Muslim astronomers in the East "perfected the sphere of Ptolemy."[12]

At the other end of the Muslim world, Muslim Spain rejected Ptolemy outright, both Muslim and Jewish astronomers turning instead to Aristotle's works. Jabir ibn Aflah was one of the major critics of Ptolemy, to whose works he made emendations of his own.[13] Muslim astronomers made corrections to Ptolemy's planetary model so as to conform to the tables in almanacs that the Muslims compiled based on observation, and admitting the existence of other planetary systems.[14] This directly contradicts the contentions of physicists such as Timothy Ferris, who criticizes Muslim scientists for adhering too strongly to Ptolemy.[15]

The most outstanding Muslim physicist, al-Haytham, rejected Ptolemy's explanations of irregular planetary motions. A Muslim astronomer of Cordoba, al-Bitruji, went further in considering Ptolemy's "interpretations of planetary motions...to be no more than mathematical constructions."[16] Al-Bitruji's contribution, Hitti says, "marks the culmination of the Muslim anti-Ptolemy movement."[17] Also relatively unknown is that Muslims learned more about astronomy and mathematics from sources other than Greece. Most of that knowledge came from India. A scholar from that country, Manka, introduced to Caliph al-Mansur and other learned Muslims at his court a work known as *Siddhanta*, which dealt with astronomy based on a Hindu system. The Muslims also acquired from the Hindus the knowledge of mathematics, which is discussed below. Muslims, in fact, called mathematics "the Indian science." Another source was Iran, as recorded in a Pahlavi text known simply as "Astronomical Table of the King." It was translated into Arabic, was preferred by Muslim astronomers, and used as a reference in Muslim Spain.

The Abbasid and Ummayad Eras

There is little documentary evidence available to evaluate the scientific contributions made during the Ummayad era. Nevertheless, at the beginning of Islam, the Arabs had already become aware of the sciences, especially medicine, for Greek medical books had been translated into Syriac at Jundishapur. The Prophet knew of "the first scientifically-trained medical man in Arabia," al-Harith ibn Kalada, "an elder contemporary of the Prophet." Then, with the high regard they had for learning, the Muslims during their conquests preserved the Byzantine and Persian scientific institutions. Jundishapur became a science center for the Muslim world, and its scholars came to Damascus, the Ummayad capital. Thus were the beginnings of Islamic learning established during the Ummayad Caliphate.[18]

Whatever the condition of the sciences during the Umayyad era, there is no doubt that Islamic science, which dominated the world for centuries, flowered when the Abbasids began their rule. Learning of all kinds gained its initial momentum under the second Abbasid Caliph, al-Mansur, the founder of Baghdad. The creation of this city was, some historians believe, the beginning of an entirely new society.

Examined within the context of its culture and its times, that beginning turned out to be a major achievement. Scholars from India, the Byzantine empire, and Persia were gathering not only in Baghdad, but also in Basra and Kufa, to learn from the Muslims. All of the scholarly materials – the discussions and the texts – were in a language that had never before been used for the sciences. Everything had to be translated into Arabic before it could be interpreted, which in turn led to new terminologies and, more important, to greater creativity.[19]

Names of some of the Muslims who made contributions to science were either not recorded or were lost. Yet before the Muslims knew of Greek geometry, they were able to calculate circumferences with a *pi* that was "much more accurate than that of the Greeks."[20]

In astronomy, there is much more evidence of the names of Muslim scientists being obliterated because these names were either Latinized or entirely replaced. William J. Kaufmann, III, an authority on astronomy, says, "Many of the brightest stars in the sky have Arabic names." Kaufmann gives as an example the names of the stars that outline the Big Dipper, one of the most prominent features of the night sky. The "seven brightest stars" of the Big Dipper are named Alkaid, Mizar, Alioth, Megrez, Dubhe, Pheebe, and Marak. The Arabic origin of these Latinized names is still just recognizable. However, the names of almost all the others are not. Although over 850 stars had Muslim names, most of them have been Latinized or replaced. For example, the brightest star in the Librae constellation is now called Alpha Librae, although it was known for centuries by its Muslim name, Zeben al-Ganubi.[21]

There are records of scientific activity at the beginning of the Abbasid era, consisting mainly of small advances in astronomy and,

concomitantly, mathematics. The emphasis on these areas is understandable. The Muslim world was vast at the time, extending from
the Atlantic to the Pacific across the eastern hemisphere. The direction of Makkah had to be determined and prayer times calculated
in different regions, so the need for accuracy in these calculations
persisted for several centuries.

Scientific studies gained momentum and the libraries were of considerable help here. The library that was part of Caliph al-Hakim's
House of Wisdom surpassed all others, for all the sciences were represented there. Much later, another library in Cairo was noted for its
size, consisting of forty store rooms containing books on all branches
of science.

Around one hundred AH, the Muslims discovered the Greek
astrolabe, believed to be the world's oldest scientific instrument. It
has come to be associated with the Muslim world, since the Muslims
used it the longest. The earliest mention of the astrolabe that has survived is that of Simplicios, a Greek philosopher, whose works were
written in the early part of the sixth century AC. Around the same
time, another accurate description was published by John Philoponus.
Approximately thirty years later, Seberus Sebokht, a Syrian bishop,
wrote a full treatise based on Greek sources.

Western scholars believe that the astrolabe described by Philipo-
nus was that used by astronomers for well over a thousand years. Islamic sources, on the other hand, describe improvements made by
Muslims, including, as pointed out by Ronan, the "measuring [of]
celestial positions, using altitude and azimuth...a specifically Arabian system." Ronan notes that the word "azimuth" is of Arabic origin.
Abu Mansur al-Khwarizmi described another effort to increase the
efficiency of the astrolabe. About a century later, Ali ibn Khalaf and
Ibn Yunus (the latter known in the West as Azarquiel) made other
improvements.[22]

Ibrahim al-Fazari (d. 796 or 806 AC) was the first Muslim to construct an astrolabe. A hundred years later, Hamid ibn Ali and Ali
ibn Musa gained eminence as the finest makers of the instrument.
Al-Zarqali (1028–1087 AC) invented an improved astrolabe that was

named after him in Latin, *saphaca Arzechelis* (from the name given to the new version, *safiḥah*). In addition, al-Biruni mentions an astrolabe based on the heliocentric theory, made by Abu Saʿid al-Sijzi, a Persian astronomer and mathematician (c. 945–c. 1020 AC).

The astrolabe was the most complex of the instruments the Muslims used in their astronomy studies. They developed a variety of astrolabes, among which were the linear, universal, geared, and those known as astrolabic clocks. Other instruments included the quadrant, the armillary sphere, the diopter, the torquetum, the equatorium, compasses, and sundials.[23]

Alchemy

Less than a century and a half after the advent of Islam there appeared the beginnings of Muslim science. The name that stands out in this period is that of Jabir ibn Hayyan (d. 803 AC). Though a Sabian, he was part of the Muslim world as well as the Muslim community of scholars and scientists in Baghdad. He is known in the West as Geber the alchemist.[24]

Jabir was a true alchemist (from the Arabic *al-kīmyā'*) in the philosophical sense, for he was interested most in "the purification of the soul."[25] Although the popular notion of alchemy is the transmutation of base metals into gold, it is more accurately a speculative philosophy focusing on the metaphysical and, as described in the *Encyclopaedia Britannica*, the attempt "to discover the relationship of man to the cosmos and to exploit that relationship to his benefit."[26]

Nevertheless, alchemy is also the beginning of the science of chemistry (the word "chemistry" has its origin in the word "alchemy"). Alchemy, to use Ronan's words, "stimulated a careful study of metals and minerals."[27] Jabir is famous for his books on alchemy, which clearly describe the philosophy. However, he is also an excellent example of an alchemist becoming a scientist, for he amended the Greek ideas and methods of practicing alchemy. The Greeks believed that all metals were the same and therefore any metal could be transmuted into another. The Greek procedure consisted of endless discussion and theorizing. Jabir had a laboratory and experimented with metals and other chemical substances. He was thus one of the major founders of modern chemistry. His descriptions of laboratory procedures are sound demonstrations of experimental work in chemistry.[28] Among the descriptions Jabir gives of his work are the purification of chemical compounds, the refinement of metals, the preparation of steel and various other chemical substances, the dyeing of cloth and leather, and the making of acids. The strongest acid then known was vinegar, which Jabir distilled and produced the stronger acetic acid. This achievement was significant in a larger context, because previously, the only way to induce a chemical change was with heat. A stronger acid proved to be another means of creating chemical changes, especially after the use of heat. Jabir was meticulous in adhering to the scientific method. For example, he classified metals into three kinds: volatile "spirits," malleable metals, and non-malleable substances. He was above all an excellent practitioner.[29]

From Jabir's works, the Arabic technical terms he used were adopted directly into European languages. Among them are alkali, antimony, alembic (for the upper section of a distillation vessel), ludal (for the lower section), realgar (arsenic disulfade), and a word not currently used in English – "tutia" (zinc oxide). Jabir quite possibly discovered a new chemical substance, sal-ammoniac, since the Greeks did not know of its existence and he was the first to mention it. Jabir also explored the possibility of solving one of the major problems alchemists set for themselves, which was to find a substance that would cure all diseases and prolong life. Because the experiments for such a substance almost always required some kind of dry powder, the word for it became established as "elixir," an Arabic word meaning "the dry one."[30]

Jabir's books were the most important in alchemy and chemistry, not to be equaled in Europe until the sixteenth century AC, when Italian and German scientists began to excel in these areas. Until then, Jabir's Latinized name Geber maintained its eminence in Europe. The prestige attached to Geber's name was such that in 1300 AC, over five hundred years after Jabir's death, an unknown scientist discovered sulfuric acid and to have his discovery readily accepted, he used the name Geber as the discoverer.[31]

According to Meyerhof, Jabir's "influence can be traced through-out the historical course of European alchemy and chemistry."[32] Yet Jabir's work on alchemy (and hence in chemistry) became known in Europe after the work of a Muslim scholar who was born more than a century after Jabir: Abu Bakr Muhammad ibn Zakaria al-Razi, known in the West as Rhazes (c. 254–313 or 323/854–925 or 935). Perhaps al-Razi was far more famous than Geber since he was one of the great physicians of the Middle Ages. Or perhaps because he was, as Sarton describes him, "a genuine chemist." He wrote books on chemistry, which also described chemical apparatus, and in addition, he tried to classify mineral substances. Equally important, he made an effort to apply his knowledge of chemistry to his medical practice.[33] His major work on this science, *Kitāb al-Asrār* (The Book of Secrets), was translated into Latin by "the eminent translator" Gerard of Cremona around 1187 and was the outstanding "source of chemical knowledge until superseded in the fourteenth century" by Jabir's works. Roger Bacon quoted from it.[34] Al-Razi was a true scientist in that he insisted on working on "what could be proved by experiment."[35]

The study of chemistry continued among the Muslims for centuries, though not as a separate discipline. It was of considerably more value in the treatment of diseases and, therefore, research in chemistry was pursued as part of pharmacology. This is clearly evident in the most outstanding medical works of the Middle Ages, such as Ibn Sina's *Canon* and *Book of Healing*. In these books, Ibn Sina provided classifications of minerals and speculated on how they were formed.[36] However, since pharmacology is part of the medical sciences, it is discussed in further detail in Chapter 10. Another area, botany, considered more important as a medical science rather than purely a natural science, is also covered in that chapter.

Mathematics and Astronomy

Sarton chooses the renowned mathematician Muhammad ibn Musa al-Khwarizmi to represent the first half of the ninth century AC. The word "algorithm" (a set of mathematical rules) is derived from his name.[37] The algorithm proved particularly useful when it became the basis of the computer, for "[a]ll computer programs," Ferris says, "are algorithms."[38] According to Sarton, al-Khwarizmi "influenced mathematical thought to a greater extent than any other medieval writer."[39] His description of algebra gave this branch of mathematics its name (from the Arabic *aljabr*). Al-Khwarizmi distinguished algebra from geometry.

His other contributions to mathematics include geometric solutions, degree measurements, and trigonometric tables. Adelard of Bath translated these tables into Latin earlier than the Renaissance, in 1126 AC. The same book contained other tables also translated at the same time, which were concerned with astronomy and which Sarton believes to be "the first Muslim tables." Al-Khwarizmi was an astronomer as well.[40]

Thabit ibn Qurra, a mathematician/astronomer who followed al-Khwarizmi, was not a Muslim, though he was a member of Caliph al-Ma'mun's academy in Baghdad. He belonged to a Hellenistic group at Harran, a city that under a previous Caliph had a school of philosophy and medicine at its center. Thabit ibn Qurra gained for his group the designation of Sabeans because the Sabeans were recognized under Islam as a religion based on divine revelation.

Thabit's contributions, in addition to some improved translations, particularly those of the works of Euclid, included new propositions and a worthwhile commentary on the postulates and axioms of Euclid covering geometry, mechanics, and irrationals. His is the first known work on the shadows of the sundial. His book on the balance was translated into Latin. Among his observations in astronomy, which he recorded faithfully, were his efforts to determine the altitude of the sun and the length of the solar year.[41] Thabit's legacy in the annals of Islamic science was a son Sinan, two grandsons Thabit and Ibrahim, and a great-grandson Abu al-Faraj, all of whom achieved distinction as scientists and translators.

Owing to the efforts of astronomers, a sound knowledge of the night sky made an enormous difference to travelers, who needed to know the positions of the constellations and the movements of the bright stars to establish the route to follow and to calculate the time. The moon, too, had a significant role in the lives of the Arabs, which explains the importance of the lunar calendar. The Arabs demarcated twenty-eight successive groups of stars known as "lunar stages." The position of the moon against these stages revealed the season of the year. The annual rising of specific stars marked the agricultural seasons.[42]

Another major mathematician/astronomer hardly mentioned in Western histories of science, even though he may be one of the greatest Muslim mathematicians, is Abu al-Wafa (940–998 AC).[43] His major contributions to mathematics were geometric constructions and trigonometry. The trigonometry in existence at the time was from the Greeks, who considered it "a solely theoretical art."[44] On the other hand, the Muslims, according to Carra de Vaux, were "unquestionably the inventors of plane and spherical geometry, which did not, strictly speaking, exist among the Greeks."[45]

Many of Abu al-Wafa's accomplishments are too technical to be detailed here. His studies in geometry included parabolas and the volume of the paraboloid. He solved geometric problems, including one concerning a polyhedron, with one opening of the compass. He introduced the secant and the tangent in trigonometry. There is a strong possibility that the spherical trigonometry introduced to the Chinese by Kuo Shou-Ching was derived from Abu al-Wafa.[46]

Abu al-Wafa also worked on the Arabic translation of Ptolemy's *Almagest*, though one already existed. However, the earlier version was considered to be unsatisfactory, so Abu al-Wafa improved the text. Both mathematics and astronomy led the two Banu Musa brothers to determine the circumference of the earth. They observed the altitude of the Pole Star (the North Star), measured it from northern and southern vantage points, and used trigonometry to arrive at 24,000 miles, which was "the real figure." James and Thorpe point out that the Banu Musa brothers were also "pioneers in an extraordinary renaissance of high-tech engineering in the medieval Islamic world."[47]

One great mathematician/astronomer is very well known in both East and West as a great poet – Omar Khayyam, or, more accurately, Umar al-Khayyam (1048–1131 AC). He acquired the best education then available and at his university met Nizam al-Mulk, who later became Grand Vizier to the Seljuks. Although al-Khayyam preferred the pursuit of poetry, he accepted the invitation of both his friend Nizam al-Mulk and the Seljuk sultan to take charge of the observatory in Isfahan. He maintained a scholarly interest in mathematics, astronomy and, much less known, medicine, so that he was also known as the Healer.

One of al-Khayyam's duties at the observatory was court astrologer, a duty that he performed reluctantly because he did not believe in astrology. Nevertheless, his fame rests on the outstanding work he did in mathematics and astronomy, his book on algebra, for example, being far in advance of not only the Greeks, but also al-Khwarizmi. Among the additions al-Khayyam made to al-Khwarizmi's work in algebra were cubic equations (al-Khwarizmi dealt only with the quadratic), a classification of equations, and solutions to cubic and quadratic equations with the help of conic sections. His method of solving equations of the third degree, Meyerhof says, "marks a stage in the advance of this branch of mathematics."[48] Khayyam's original books on mathematics were believed lost and available only in translations. However, they were recently discovered in Iran and published there. Nizam al-Mulk also asked al-Khayyam and Abd al-Rahman Hazini to head a team of mathematicians/astronomers to improve the accuracy of the Persian solar calendar. Al-Khayyam succeeded to the extent that his calendar was far more accurate than the Gregorian.[49] As to what extent, accounts differ. According to Ronan, al-Khayyam's calendar "would have been in error by no more than one day in 5,000 years."[50] Muslims also invented mechanical calendars, some equipped with elaborate gears. James and Thorpe give as an outstanding example a geared calendar devised by Abu Saʿid al-Sijzi, which "recorded the moon's phases and the movement of the sun against the signs of the zodiac."[51]

In those days, mathematics and astronomy were studied together, as though they constituted a single entity. Among the contemporaries of al-Khwarizmi, there were outstanding mathematicians and astronomers as well as specialists in both fields. The following are among those who made important contributions. Sahl al-Tabari

(c. 838–c. 870 AC), a Persian-Jewish astronomer and physician, was the first to translate Ptolemy's *Almagest* into Arabic. Habash al-Hasib (d. c. 870 AC), astronomer, was the first to devise the method of calculating time by means of an altitude. The outstanding astronomer of the ninth century AC was al-Farghani. His book, known in the West as *Elements of Astronomy*, is not a translation of the original Arabic title, which was *Book on Celestial Motions and the Complete Science of the Stars*. It was translated into Latin in the twelfth century AC and was considerably influential for the next three hundred years.

In Muslim Spain, too, valuable astronomical work was passed on to the West, especially in the compilation of astronomical tables. Ibn Saʿid, a historian who was noted for a concise universal history, was also a keen observer of the night sky. His compilation of his numerous observations and those of others were used by al-Zarqali (1028–1087 AC) to establish new tables, later known as the Toledan tables, which became authoritative in western Europe. Al-Zarqali introduced these tables with a complex trigonometrical discussion. He was one of the leading scientists of al-Andalus, as was al-Majriti (d. 1007 or 1008 AC).[52]

From Muslim Spain, the West learned that the earth was a sphere. Hitti writes that the Muslims kept this fact alive, and singled out al-Balansi of Valencia as an "exponent" of this doctrine. This knowledge appeared in a Latin publication of 1410 AC. From this work, Hitti adds, Columbus learned that at least the top part of the earth was round.[53]

Muslim scientists are difficult to classify according to their specializations. True to the spirit of "Islamic Man," they ranged widely, not only in the sciences, but in other areas as well. An example from the period under discussion is al–Kindi (801–873 AC). He was, like many Muslim scholars, a polymath. Many of his works dealt with philosophy, earning him the title "the Philosopher of the Arabs." Al-Kindi also wrote books on mathematics, physics, pharmacology, and geography. According to Sarton, his book on geometrics and physiological optics influenced, among others, Roger Bacon and Witelo. His Muslim treatise on Arab music is the earliest surviving work. Al-Kindi was, in addition, an exceptional physicist.[54]

Al-Kindi is most frequently mentioned when physics in Islamic history is discussed. His 265 works included 33 treatises on physics alone, for example, on meteorology, specific weight, tides, optics, music, and especially the reflection of light. Most notable among these is *On Optics*, of which there appears to remain only the Latin translation made by Gerard of Cremona, who also translated most of al-Kindi's other books. *On Optics* influenced Roger Bacon, Witelo, John Pecham, and other scientists in the West. Incidentally, al-Kindi was among the first of a growing chorus that insisted gold could be acquired only from mining and not from processing base metals in the laboratory.[55]

The major Muslim contribution to physics was the work of Abu Ali al-Hasan ibn al-Haytham (965–c. 1039 AC), known in the West as Alhazen. Colin Ronan described Ibn al-Haytham as "the greatest Islamic physicist."[56] Referring to Ibn al-Haytham, Meyerhof says, "The glory of Muslim science is in the field of optics," adding that the Muslim physicist "outshone [the mathematical ability] of Euclid and Ptolemy."[57] A biography lists around 200 works by him on a range of subjects including medicine, optics, mathematics, physics, and philosophy.

Ibn al-Haytham trained as a physician in Basra, the city of his birth, and Baghdad. However, he soon became interested in other scientific fields. Early on in his career, in Cairo, he accepted a challenge from the Fatimid Caliph al-Hakim in an area about which he knew little or nothing: it was the task of controlling the annual floods caused by the Nile. He failed.

When Ibn al-Haytham started seriously observing the nature of light and of the human eye, his genius emerged. He was fascinated with the play of light on all kinds of objects, with colors, how the light changed during different parts of the day, with reflections, as well as with the refractions of light rays through air and water and the way certain phenomena created optical llusions. Nevertheless, it was not observation alone that led to discoveries but also experimentation, which was now common practice among Muslim scientists.

Ibn al-Haytham's investigations led him to refute the theory of both Euclid and Ptolemy, that the eye sends out visual rays to an object;

those visual rays return to the eye with the image of the object; and this is how the eye sees. He demonstrated that rays of light come to the eye from the object, a discovery wrongly attributed to Leonardo da Vinci. As a result, in John William Draper's words, Ibn al-Haytham "was the first to correct the Greek misconceptions as to the nature of vision."[58] Ibn al-Haytham's further experiments revealed that images register on the retina and are conveyed to the brain along optic nerves.

Ibn al-Haytham extended his observations to the effect of the atmosphere on the way the light falls on the earth. The greater the density of the atmosphere, the greater was its effect on light. What is more, the atmosphere created optical illusions. The position of stars, for example, appeared closer to the zenith than their actual position. He made experiments with starlight and rainbows. Ibn al-Haytham's major work on optics, *Kitāb al-Manāẓir*, whose original no longer exists, was translated into Latin and published in 1572. The book influenced the development of optics in the Middle Ages, including scientists such as Witelo, Roger Bacon, Leonardo da Vinci, and Johann Kepler. His other treatises focused on the causes of rainbows, halos, and eclipses. Not wanting to look directly at the sun during an eclipse, Ibn al-Haytham made a small hole in the shutters of his windows and watched the image thrown on the wall across from the windows. Whether or not he invented the camera obscura, this is its first description on record.[59]

One of Ibn al-Haytham's significant works is *On the Burning Glass*. In Meyerhof's words, "The work exhibits a profound and accurate conception of the nature of focusing, magnifying, and inversion of the image, and of formation of rings and colors by experiments." The magnifying lenses of his theory were not made until three centuries later in Italy.[60]

Al-Biruni, mentioned several times already, made other contributions to the sciences, most of them little known. His work in geology is an example. What al-Biruni learned from Hindu sources regarding the cycles of time made him investigate geological history. He succeeded in determining specific gravities with a precision quite remarkable for his time. His writings on astronomy resulted from observations made with instruments produced by himself. Al-Biruni wrote texts on pharmacology, botany, gravity, the earth sciences, physics, and mathematics.

The majority of the Muslim scientists, in their own modest way, spent their lives advancing Islamic science in worthwhile pursuits such as translation, study from others — both Muslims and non-Muslims — instruction, and writing books, many of them an integration of earlier findings and new discoveries. Most of these books were translated into Latin.

These men were accomplished polymaths, among whom one of the most eminent was Nasir al-Din Tusi (1201–1274 AC). Most remarkably, he lived during the turmoil of the Mongol invasions and their most devastating destruction of the Muslim countries. For Nasir al-Din, however, the Mongol Khan Hulagu turned out to be a life-saver. Nasir al-Din had gained fame as an astrologer and thereby drew the attention of the Assassins. One of their governors captured him and sent him to the citadel of Almut, their stronghold in the Caucasus Mountains. The fortress had proved to be most formidable against conquest for almost two hundred years until Hulagu captured it. It is probable that Nasir al-Din revealed the secrets of the fortress to the invading Mongols. Hulagu freed Nasir al-Din, who became his trusted advisor and remained with the Mongols until his death.

Nasir al-Din's outstanding knowledge of astronomy led Hulagu to commission him to build an observatory in Maraghah in Iran. The observatory soon became famous internationally for its outstanding library, astronomers, and the best scientific instruments. The Muslims were perfectionists in the making of these tools. There were special instruments, too, in particular, those made of rings of equatorial armillaries, both solsticial and elliptical. One that was most widely used was a set of five elliptical rings marked in degrees and minutes. These were among the instruments that the Europeans used as models when they began to construct their own. Alfonso of Castile, for example, made use of them when he wanted to build the finest armillary sphere, as did Regiomontanus, during the Renaissance, who wanted "to reconstruct the elliptical of Ptolemy."[61]

For Nasir al-Din, the observatory was the means to prove his own worth, which in turn led to valuable contributions and fame in the field of astronomy. He spent twelve years compiling a new set of planetary tables, the Ziji Ilkhani. He also worked at length on a comprehensive book of astronomy that assimilated all known concepts of the time. The importance of the book, known in short as the *Tazkira*, is evident in the number of languages, both eastern and western, into which it was translated and the number of commentaries it produced, including one in Turkish. Nasir al-Din was forthright in his criticism of Ptolemy and made many corrections in the *Almagest*, which paved the way for the Copernician Reform.[62]

Nasir al-Din made other contributions in mathematics, especially in geometry and trigonometry. Here, too, he wrote a comprehensive study of what was known in the field of mathematics at the time, in sixteen volumes, four of them covering the Islamic period. His own achievement he recorded in *The Treatise on the Quadrilateral*, a respected work on spherical trigonometry.[63]

Nasir al-Din went on to write three treatises on optics, two on music, one on medicine, two on logic, and others on mineralogy, geography, geodesy, philosophy, theology, and ethics. He was indeed a true polymath and a major contributor to science.

Geography

The Muslim world's scientific contributions helped to distinguish the Muslim Middle Ages in many other disciplines. In the Muslim world, geography as a science began with al-Ma'mun's creation of the House of Wisdom in 215/830. The discipline perhaps began as an accumulation of descriptions from travelers. Or, scholars may have discovered that existing materials gave them a picture of the world with which the Muslims were becoming acquainted. Perhaps it was a Greek text that pointed the way to the science. The oldest known work on geography in Arabic was written by an Iranian named Ibn Khurdabeh, who lived in the third/ninth century.[64]

Ptolemy's *Guide to Geography*, one of the works translated from Greek into Arabic, in addition to introducing the Muslims to the science of geography, induced them to investigate the regions of the earth for themselves. As a result, the Muslim scholars were the first to correct in the *Guide* many errors that were due, of course, to the limited knowledge of the Greeks at the time. Al-Khwarizmi, a mathematician, revised Ptolemy's work, improved it, and published it with new maps under the title *The Face of the Earth*.

Later, the Muslim polymath who did the most to correct Ptolemy was al-Biruni. He noted several locations in Ptolemy's calculations that had been misplaced, owing primarily to the inaccurate distances used to calculate longitude and latitude. Al-Biruni proceeded to determine accurately the latitudes and longitudes. He made geodetic measurements, and then raised the question of whether the earth rotates around its axis, a question he was unable to or did not answer.[65]

Al-Biruni and his predecessor al-Masudi were the two great geographers of their time. They dominated their centuries, al-Masudi in the tenth AC and al-Biruni in the eleventh AC. The tenth century AC saw the flowering of geography, and Sarton cites several distinguished Muslim geographers (and travelers) of that period. They and their important contributions include the following.

Ibn Sarafyun was primarily interested in the earth's areas covered by water. His work focused on the seas, islands, lakes, and rivers of the world. Ibn Rusta compiled an encyclopedia of "The Very Precious Things," a significant portion of which dealt with geography. Abu Zaid was an editor of the writings of many other travelers, some of whom are known from Abu Zaid's compilations. One example was Ibn Wahb, who visited China in 257/870 and whose writings rivaled and predated those of Marco Polo.[66] Al-Hamdani was a geographer as well as an archeologist and his most important work was a geography of Arabia. Abu Dulaf was fortunate to accompany an Indian prince on his travels, and wrote of his own exploration of Tibet. These geographers and travelers enhanced the knowledge of the world and, in addition, continued to create maps as they became acquainted with individual terrains. Many of the maps were now produced in color. Al-Biruni stood alone in the eleventh century AC as the world's outstanding geographer.

Geography at the time approached a high status in the western regions of the Muslim world, with many geographers, too numerous to discuss here, living in al-Andalus. Nevertheless, two of them – al-Bakri and al-Idrisi – became famous outside Spain. Al-Bakri elevated geographical writing to a new height in al-Andalus,[67] for he was a poet, historian, philologist, botanist, and geographer. His first work was a geographical dictionary. The second was a more ambitious multi-volumed history and geography, where he also described political entities and people, Muslim and non-Muslim, in some unflattering terms. Part of the work could be considered economic geography, dealing with trade, industry, and natural resources.

Al-Idrisi, a prominent geographer and cartographer of the Middle Ages, came from Spain, yet achieved distinction elsewhere.[68] His patron was the Christian king, Roger II of Sicily. Roger II, wanting to replace the Greek and Arab maps then available with a more accurate version, commissioned al-Idrisi to lead a team to produce updated copies "with features to be shown in relief and the whole to be engraved in silver."[69] Al-Idrisi created a silver planisphere and, in addition, wrote *Roger's Book*, also titled *The Delight of Him Who Desires to Journey Through the Climates*. Sarton describes the book as "the most elaborate description of the world of medieval times."[70] Its distinction from the works of other Muslim geographers was that it also contained details of many Christian countries. Al-Idrisi later wrote another geographical tome, this time for William I – *Pleasure of Men and Delight of Souls* – which contained far more information than his first book.

Al-Idrisi's work was unusual in several respects. He drew upon his own travel and experiences. Not content with the books on geography already available to him, he relied heavily on a group of geographers who surveyed regions.[71] Unusually for those times, his works were filled with an abundance of maps.

About fifty years later, there emerged another outstanding geographer known in his early life simply as Yaqut, changed to Yaqub. He was later known as al-Hamawi, because the merchant who rescued him from servitude and educated him was from Hama.

Sarton states that Yaqut was "the most eminent Greek of his time," a Muslim convert who was both a geographic encyclopedist and an explorer.[72] Although Yaqut wrote other books, his *magnum opus* was *Mujam al-Buldan*, a geographical dictionary on which he worked for more than a decade. In addition to information about places all over the Muslim world, it contained information on history and ethnography and short biographies of learned men as well as grammatical discussions.

At about the time of Yaqut, there appeared route guides to help travelers of all kinds, especially those making pilgrimages to Makkah. Soon, there were guide books for Muslim pilgrims with stage-by-stage itineraries and useful notes on cities.[73] Possibly the very first travel guides, these books were of immense help to students wandering across the Muslim world to learn from different sages.

Muslim scholars traveled to learn geographic facts at first hand, and they also relied on descriptions brought back by other travelers. Muslims and non-Muslims traveled easily across the eastern part of the Muslim world except during the Mongol onslaught. Travel resumed soon afterward, owing to a major change among the Mongols. They converted to Islam voluntarily and, following a few decades of Mongol conquests, maintained peace.

Overall, travel continued without interruption, especially in places that the Mongols never reached. Some travelers wrote of their journeys, one of whom, in particular, achieved wide fame for the quality of his work. He was Evliya Çelebi, a Turk, who spent forty years traveling in Ottoman Turkey as well as other parts of Europe. When he returned home, he spent what were to be the final three years of his life writing about his journeys and produced a *Book of Travel* consisting of ten volumes.

The resumption of the ease of travel also meant that scholars could move freely from one part of the Muslim world to another. The entire Muslim world constituted a university, fulfilling the tenet that learning is required of all Muslims and that they should travel in search of knowledge. This requirement determined the direction of Islamic civilization and its salient traits.

Clearly Islamic sciences developed owing to the civilization's openness to the achievements of other civilizations, especially the sciences of Persia, India, and ancient Greece. The translation movement encouraged by Muslim rulers played a significant role in this regard. In addition, the advances in Islamic sciences influenced the Renaissance. The story of the development of Islamic sciences, especially medicine, requires a close scrutiny, and it is therefore the subject of Chapter 10.

10

MEDICINE

WHEN WRITERS WISH to denigrate the standard of Western medical practice in the Middle Ages or elevate that of the Muslims, they give case histories drawn from records of those times. A chapter on medicine in an illustrated history of the medieval period (Madden, Thomas F., ed., *Crusades: The Illustrated History*, Duncan Baird, 2004) begins with two events during the Crusades. A Christian soldier was wounded in the leg and a Muslim physician took care of him, bandaged the leg, and sent him back to his camp. There, a Christian physician took one look at the leg and amputated it. The soldier died. In the other case, a Christian king had a stomach ache, was examined by a Muslim doctor, and was told he should rest for the night. A Christian doctor reversed the advice and gave the king medication. The king's condition worsened and before the night was over, he was dead.

Usamah ibn Munqidh, born in 1095, when the Crusades began, narrated two other incidents, illustrating what the Christians of Europe knew at the time. In his *Book of Reflections*, he described two cases remarkably similar to those described above, although with a difference. The man with a wounded leg was not a soldier but "a man" and the patient suffering from a stomach disorder was a woman. The Arab physician treating both was Usama's uncle, Thabit. The other details remain the same: both patients died because of erroneous medical treatment.

Usamah then described two cures by Christian physicians on the other side. In the first case, the patient was Bernard, a treasurer to a Christian count. A horse kicked him on the leg, the leg became infected, and was treated with ointments. A Frankish physician cleaned off the ointments and washed the leg with very strong vinegar. The other patient was a Muslim youth whose neck was afflicted with scrofula. The young man accompanied his father to Antioch on business. A physician, also a Frank, noticed the scrofula and was willing to give the father a recipe to cure it, provided the father did not sell the cure but share it instead. The father agreed. The Christian physician's method worked and the youth's neck was soon normal.

Medical Communities and Experts

Medical expertise in those days was not one-sided, since, like today, medical news traveled quickly. At the beginning of Islam, the four countries that excelled in medicine were China, India, Greece, and Persia, owing to Persia's most advanced learning center at Jundishapur, where Greek scholars had been given refuge, had settled, and flourished. Khusraw Anusharwan, the patron of these scholars, sent his own physician, Burzuya, to India to bring back books on medicine as well as Indian physicians. However, there were certainly perceived cures of all kinds everywhere, particularly herbal and folk remedies.

Jundishapur contributed physicians to the Arab and Persian world. Al-Harith ibn Kalada, one of the first known physicians in the early years of Islam and a contemporary of the Prophet, acquired his medical training there. Ibn Kalada's system for good health is as valid today as it was during his time: moderation in eating. He said it was harmful to eat when one was already satisfied. Prophet Muhammad and Ibn Kalada were on amiable terms and the Prophet sent him people who were ill. The Prophet also knew Ibn Abi, who was a surgeon. Another contemporary of the Prophet, Paul of Aegina, was in demand in the Arab world because of his skills in obstetrics and surgery.

The Prophet himself gave some common sense advice regarding illnesses, for example, the use of honey, cauterization of wounds, and cupping (still used in China today). Implicitly recognizing the dangers of infection, he warned Muslims against visiting an area where there was an epidemic. He also recommended visiting the sick and heartening them. He gave other advice, largely regarding healthy eating habits and hygiene.

Though no records indicate it, Muslims must have derived more medical knowledge from the Greeks, at least as early as the time of the second Ummayad Caliph, when the first translations under Islam were made from Greek and Coptic into Arabic. Some of these translations were philosophical. Nevertheless, as Shakespeare reminds us, "there was never yet philosopher that could endure the tooth-ache patiently."[1] Although many Muslim physicians were also philosophers, in their communities they were most in demand for their medical expertise.

There are records of medical practitioners at the beginning of the Umayyad Caliphate. Ibn Uthal was physician to the first Umayyad Caliph. Another doctor was Abu al-Hakam, who lived to the age of one hundred. His son Hakam was known to have successfully treated a severe arterial hemorrhage. Hakam's son Isa, also a skilled physician, wrote what must have been the Muslim world's first book on medicine, although not even a fragment has survived. Another medical practitioner from that early period whose name is recorded in history books as treating ophthalmia was a Bedouin woman called Zaynab.

In 148/765, the second Abbasid Caliph, al-Mansur, was unable to find a physician in Baghdad to cure what was ailing him. He sent to Jundishapur for Jurjis, son of Bakht-Yishu, who cured him and stayed with him for some years. Jurjis performed another service, which benefited all Muslims, in translating medical works into Arabic, the first on record. Jurjis's son was also a doctor, serving at the hospital in Jundishapur. From that time, the Bukht-Yishus were among the leading physicians for over 250 years, six generations in all. The last was Jibrail.

Jibrail was not among the "keepers" of medical knowledge at Jundishapur, where the physicians were reluctant to share their knowledge with outsiders. Since the works of Galen and Hippocrates were translated only into Syriac at the time, future physicians had to rely on these scholars, who did not hesitate to turn away students or eject them from their classes. Nevertheless, one of the students,

Hunain ibn Ishaq (809–873 AC), was determined to study, in particular, to master Greek. When he had achieved his aim, he was welcomed back by Jibrail ibn Bukht-Yishu to Jundishapur, where the master who had ejected the determined student sought to be reconciled with him.

Hunain excelled as a physician. Caliph al-Mutawakkil heard of him and invited him to Baghdad. He first asked Hunain for an effective poison to eliminate an enemy, offering a reward if Hunain agreed, or death if he did not. Hunain refused. The Caliph then revealed that he had been testing Hunain and appointed him court physician.

Despite the demands of the court, Hunain found time to translate Greek works into Arabic. As mentioned in Chapter 8, he was meticulous in his translations, collating different texts and matching a text as closely to the original as possible. He trained one of his students, Isa ibn Yahya, to help him with the translation. Together, they were responsible for thoroughly reviewing the entire canon of Galen and then rendering these works and those of Hippocrates into Arabic, translations far superior to any produced earlier.

Hunain did not rest with translations, for he wrote about a hundred works of his own, most of which dealt with medicine. Three of his books were most influential in both the Muslim world and elsewhere. *Medical Questions* was an introduction to medicine. The other two were "Ten Dissertations on the Eye," and "Questions on the Eye." "Ten Dissertations" was the first known work on the anatomy of the eye.

Hunain also taught, and one of his students who contributed to medicine was Isa ibn Ali, a Christian also known as Jesu Haly. Many of his accomplishments were overshadowed by the more famous, so his name is seldom mentioned in the histories of medicine except in his specialty. Ibn Ali was an outstanding ophthalmologist and his expertise in this area was demonstrated in a mostly original book, for in addition to ophthalmic anatomy and physiology, it dealt with the external diseases of the eye. It was a comprehensive work covering 130 eye diseases and 143 medications. The entire original text still exists and constitutes the oldest Arabic work on ophthalmology. [2]

A contemporary of Hunain was al-Kindi, more noted as a philosopher than as a physician. Of the two hundred works he wrote, twenty-two were medical. One of his special interests was in the preparation and dosage of medications, to which he devoted an entire volume, for his aim was to determine accurate prescriptions.

Training and Practice

In the Abbasid era, all scholars gained some medical knowledge and, as a result, most of them were polymaths. The atmosphere was conducive to learning and the scholars were highly esteemed. The quest for knowledge reached the Caliph's harems, where among the residents was a lady called Tawaddud. She was challenged by the Caliph, Harun al-Rashid, to answer questions put to her by experts, especially one on medicine. She successfully answered all of the questions and, in addition, put to the authorities questions that they were unable to answer.

Examinations were then commonplace. "To the Arabians," Campbell states, "we owe the introduction of the idea of the legal control of qualifying examinations for admission to the medical profession."[3] The examination on medicine included, in addition to diagnoses, pathology, dietetics, and hygiene. Distinction was made between an ordinary headache, migraine, and a hangover. There were Arabic words for, among others, catarrh, elephantiasis, vertigo, sea-sickness, and craving for a drink. "Arabic," according to Browne, "is on the whole well adapted for providing a suitable technical terminology, which, in fact, it has done for the whole Muslim world."[4]

In the early ninth century AC, Baghdad had 860 licensed physicians and many hospitals and schools.[5] About fifty years later, the first major book on medicine in Arabic was published, written by Ali ibn Rabban (838–870 AC), a physician to the Abbasid Caliph al-Mutawakkil. Ali must have had the knowledge of his time, for he called his book *Firdous al-Ḥikmah* [Paradise of Wisdom]. This was also the first major work that went beyond recording what was gleaned from the Greeks and, in addition, credited Arab and other sources. Although the book discussed philosophy, psychology, and other sciences, it mainly covered medicine. Ali acknowledged his debt to Hippocrates, Aristotle, and Galen, yet he also credited Yuhanna ibn Masawayh and Hunain ibn Ishaq. He included a summary of the medicine of India. The book's table of contents reads as though it were a textbook of today. One of Ali ibn Rabban's students was al-Razi, recognized as the greatest of all Muslim physicians, to be discussed below.

Soon, there were too many medical practitioners, some of whom were not necessarily qualified, for they had not taken the examination. Caliph al-Muqtadir insisted that the physicians of his realm, about 860, be examined, and he appointed Sinan ibn Thabit the examiner. Only doctors who had achieved a high reputation were exempt. One of those taking the examination was a dignified elderly gentleman, whom Ibn Thabit treated with respect. The elderly gentleman revealed that he had had no teacher and, not being able to read, had not learned from the medical texts available. Nevertheless, he had some knowledge, so Sinan permitted him to continue practicing as long as he did not treat beyond what he knew. The next day a young man presented himself before Sinan. In response to Sinan's question regarding where he learned medicine, the young man said that he learned from his father. Who was his father? It was the old man of the day before. Sinan let him also practice, as long as he followed the advice given by his father.

Major Medical Figures

An important period in the history of Islamic medicine covered three great physicians, writers of major texts, and philosophers: al-Razi, al-Majusi, and Ibn Sina.

Abu Bakr Muhammad ibn Zakaria al-Razi (Rhazes) was born in Rayy, near modern Tehran, in 236/850. His work signaled the maturity of Arabian medicine, his most significant contribution being to distinguish smallpox from measles.[6] Al-Razi's studies included mathematics, philosophy, astronomy, and medicine. Two of his works sound familiar today: One focuses on the "division of labor," emphasizing "cooperation" and "mutual assistance." The other deals with the "pleasure–pain theory:" the more pain one experiences, the more intense is the pleasure experienced after that pain.[7]

Al-Razi studied medicine under Hunain ibn Ishaq and also gained an abundance of practical experience at the hospitals where he visited and practiced, thus earning the title of "The Experienced" among many others. One of his unusual habits, which proved valuable in his career and in the writing of his books, was that he always talked at length with and learned from the older pharmacists and dispensers of drugs in the different hospitals. His services to rulers were unusual, too, for instead of working directly for them, he served in hospitals. The laboratory apparatus that he used for his chemical experiments was unknown to the ancients. Al-Razi was made director of the hospital in Rayy, then, as his reputation spread, also of the new and biggest hospital in Baghdad. Even before the hospital was built, he was consulted on where it should be located. He arranged for pieces of meat to be hung in different parts of the city and chose the area where the meat showed the least decomposition. Muslim physicians were aware of the effect of environment on health. The "Paradise of Wisdom" states that the physician "must know what food and drink and nutriment is suitable for every climate."[8]

Al-Razi's reputation also prevented him from settling in one place, for many rulers summoned him to serve them. How long he stayed in any particular area depended on the whims of these rulers or the current political situation. However, al-Razi always returned to Rayy, where he spent his declining years, suffering from a cataract. Some said that his eyes became affected because he spent too much time studying. He died in Rayy in 313/925.

Al-Razi made meticulous notes on every disease he encountered, the remedies he prescribed, and the results of the treatment. These notes proved a valuable asset to his written works, for he produced more than two hundred books, half of them on medicine. Among his early works was a ten-volume treatise on Greek medicine. Then he proceeded to make his own contributions in areas such as gynecology, obstetrics, ophthalmology, and common diseases of the East such as bladder and kidney stones. One of his exceptional books was on children's diseases, for which he was given the title "Father of Pediatrics." Al-Razi also made a highly significant addition to medications, being the first to introduce chemical preparations into the practice of medicine.[9]

His fame became more widespread for his treatise on smallpox, for it contained the first accurate description of the disease and its symptoms, and it is still valid today. The book became one of the earliest and most widely published texts in Europe, reprinted more than forty times, well into the nineteenth century. Dr. Max Neuberger, a German authority on the history of medicine, ranks it "high in importance in the history of epidemiology,"[10] and Hitti states that it "served to establish al-Razi's reputation as one of the keenest original thinkers and the greatest clinicians not only of Islam but of the Middle Ages."[11] In his next and most important work, al-Razi was more inclusive, encompassing the state of knowledge of medicine at the time. This was *Kitāb al-Ḥāwī* (The Comprehensive Book) in twenty-one volumes, a veritable medical encyclopedia that took him fifteen years to complete. It was so huge that only a few copies were made. According to Max Meyerhof, its extensive contents include all the Greek, Syrian, Arabic, Persian, and Indian authors for each disease, his own opinion and experiences, and "many striking examples of his clinical insight."[12] Al-Razi excelled as a clinical observer.[13] The Latin translation of *Kitāb al-Ḥāwī* was completed in 1279 under the title *Liber Continens*. From 1486 it was reprinted many times. Meyerhof believes that "its influence on European medicine was thus very considerable."[14]

Al-Razi also wrote about the "psychological" aspect of medicine, part of which might be considered psychosomatic. In doing so, he touched on matters many doctors dare not discuss today: why even skilful physicians cannot heal all diseases; why frightened patients easily forsake even the skilled physician; why people prefer quacks and charlatans to skilled physicians; and why ignorant physicians, laymen, and women have more success than learned medical men. His books on the other sciences in which he worked – physics, astronomy, and mathematics – have been lost, although descriptions of some of his work still exist. Al-Razi divided the world into animal, vegetable, and mineral, a division still in use today. One of the challenges he confronted was to determine specific gravity by means of a hydrostatic balance. He is also known to have worked on matter, motion, time, and space.

A contemporary of al-Razi who also gained fame was Yuhanna ibn Masawayh. He was a physician to Harun al-Rashid and head of the medical school in Baghdad. Al-Razi mentioned Ibn Masawayh's books on medicine in his writings, although these books no longer exist. Not as famous as either al-Razi or the other eminent Muslim physician Ibn Sina was Ali ibn al-Abbas al-Majusi, known in the West as Haly Abbas. Very little of his life is known, except that he studied under an Iranian professor and then continued to study on his own, mastering first the works of the ancients and then those of his predecessors. At the request of the Amir, Adhad al-Dowlah Fana Khusraw, he wrote *Kitāb al-Mālikī* (The Royal Book), consisting of twenty discourses totaling around 400,000 words. Its finest pages are those devoted to dietetics and medications. There is also original material on the capillary system and evidence that babies do not emerge by themselves but are pushed out by the muscular contractions of the womb.[15] The section on anatomy was the sole source in Europe for a century,[16] until it was superseded by other more accurate descriptions in other works.

The major advantage of *Kitāb al-Mālikī* was that it was concise and readily available, which also made it a favorite among students. Al-Razi's major work was voluminous and not many copies were made, whereas *Kitāb al-Mālikī* was easily published and therefore widely distributed. More than a compilation of medical knowledge, the book also provided critiques of Hippocrates, Galen, and contemporaries. Al-Majusi was also critical of al-Razi regarding the size and cost of his work for students to buy. His concern for students led him to advise them on gaining experience. Al-Majusi counseled them at length to visit hospitals regularly, pay attention to the conditions prevailing there, and frequently discuss with the patients their symptoms and progress.

The most highly recognized of Muslim scholars and a prominent medieval philosopher was Abu Ali al-Husayn ibn Sina (Avicenna) because he excelled in two areas, philosophy and medicine. For his work in philosophy, he was known as the "Second Teacher," that is, second to Aristotle. As a student, Ibn Sina surpassed his teachers and continued his studies without guidance. He read almost every book in the Imperial Library in Bukhara, including, in his own words, "books whose titles were not known to most people and other books I have never come across since." His ultimate objective was as lofty as his learning. As he noted, his goal was "the perfecting of the human soul." He started writing when he was twenty-one, averaging about fifty pages a day, and produced 238 works.[17] With Ibn Sina, Muslim medicine reached the pinnacle of its achievements. He started studying medicine at the age of sixteen and found the task complex though not difficult. His teacher, Ibn Nuh al-Qumri, was himself an outstanding physician. More remarkable is the fact that by the age of eighteen, Ibn Sina was already practicing medicine and, even more extraordinary, he was already famous by then. Ibn Sina was summoned by the ruler, Nuh ibn Mansur, who was duly impressed and, in return, permitted Ibn Sina free use of his library. Ibn Sina did more than read the books, for by the age of twenty-one, he had written an encyclopedia of all the sciences except mathematics.

Ibn Sina led an adventurous life. As his fame spread much more widely, other, more powerful rulers demanded him as their personal physician. He evaded kidnapping by one king, was the victim of an army mutiny, and imprisoned by the ruler that he had cured of colic (Ibn Sina's specialty). When the colic returned, the ruler freed Ibn Sina so that the famous physician could heal him again. His enemies, many denying that he was a sincere Muslim, did not spare him after his death. He died at the age of 58, unable to treat himself successfully.

Ibn Sina's eminence in medical history rests on his masterpiece, *al-Qānūn fī al-Ṭibb* (The Canon of Medicine), known in the West as simply *The Canon*, in five volumes, around a million words. It encompassed the medical knowledge of his time and, in addition, medical discoveries of his own and more material on medications.

His original work included further discoveries in the nature of contagious diseases and advice on the prevention of disease. Ibn Sina described in detail 760 drugs to be used in the treatment of both acute and chronic diseases.

Ibn Sina is recognized as the first to describe the preparation and properties of sulfuric acid and alcohol. He recommended wine as the best dressing for wounds. In addition, he gave a fairly accurate description of diabetes, including the fact that the urine of the diabetic was sweet. In addition, he distinguished between mediastinitis and pleurisy, recognized the infectiousness of tuberculosis, and the transmission of epidemics by land and water.

The *Canon* was the most popular medical text in the East and the West, where it was published in many European languages. Dr. William Osler, Canadian professor of the history of medicine, describes it as "a medical Bible for a longer period than any other work."[18] The section on surgery is said to have influenced a number of outstanding European physicians.

The *Canon* was more than an encyclopedia of medicine, for it was based on philosophy and logic. For example, the volume on drugs is arranged alphabetically and the volume on diseases deals with the body from head to toe. Each topic in turn is subdivided, a methodology Meyerhof believes to be "in part responsible for the mania for subdivision which affected Western scholasticism."[19]

There is an abundance of praise for the *Canon* among scholars in both East and West. Ibn Sina's work changed medical history, for it enabled the knowledge that Muslims had acquired and developed to be much more widely known than any other work. The Latin translation of the *Canon* was for centuries the medical textbook of the West. As mentioned in Chapter 9, Ibn Sina was also an expert on geology, which was just as important a legacy as his work in medicine. His treatise on minerals was the main source of the geological ideas of Christian encyclopaedists of the thirteenth century.[20] "His wonderful description of the origin of mountains," says Garrison, "...fully entitles him to be called the 'Father of Geology.'"[21] Ibn Sina's works had considerable influence in Europe, and formed the principal reading of Christian scholars.[22]

Psychological Medicine

The Muslims also practiced another branch of medicine that al-Razi himself described as *al-ʿilāj al-nafsānī* (psychotherapy). There are records of several cases in which al-Razi, Ibn Sina, and other physicians applied this type of medical treatment. One of al-Razi's cases had a surprising prelude. He was requested to cure Amir Mansur of Transoxiana of severe arthritis of the joints that had rendered him prostrate and puzzled all the physicians that the Amir had consulted. On the way to the Amir's palace, al-Razi and his group had to cross the Oxus. He looked at the huge expanse of the swift waters that had to be crossed and at the small boat available for the crossing. Feeling apprehensive, he refused to board the boat. The Amir's messengers, in obedience to their ruler, bound al-Razi and placed him in the boat. When they reached the other side, al-Razi showed no anger, but instead, revealed why he had been reluctant to board the boat. Had he done so on his own and been drowned, he explained, people would have remarked that he was a fool to have risked his life. However, since he had been forcibly carried into the boat, they would not have blamed him.

Although al-Razi treated the Amir with various methods, he was not successful. Finally, he decided on a different, highly unorthodox approach. For this, he said to the Amir, he required the ruler's best horse and best mule. The next day, riding that horse and leading the mule, al-Razi accompanied the Amir to the hottest room in a bathhouse outside the city. Al-Razi subjected the Amir to hot showers and a medication he had prepared. Then he left the Amir alone, put on his clothes and returned with a knife. He confronted the Amir with accusations of wanting him drowned and threatened to kill him. The Amir in a rage jumped to his feet. Al-Razi ran out, jumped on the horse and with his servant on the mule, rode back home. The Amir was delighted that he was able to move his legs. However, having threatened the Amir with a knife, al-Razi refused to return to accept a reward and sent back the horse and the mule with a letter explaining why he had to resort to the unorthodox treatment. Nevertheless, the Amir sent him his reward. Another similar case, treated by an unnamed physician, tells of a woman with swollen joints who was also cured with the use of "shock" treatment.

Ibn Sina related the following incident and discussed its significance. A young relative of the ruler of Jurjan lay listlessly in bed, suffering from a malady that had no physical cause. Since his doctors failed to arrive at a diagnosis, Ibn Sina was summoned to give his opinion. He examined the patient and decided on an elaborate procedure. He asked someone who knew the region to call out the name of every town while Ibn Sina held the patient's pulse. At the name of a certain town, the pulse quickened. Ibn Sina then sent for someone who knew all the streets in that town to call out their names. Again there was a quickening of the pulse at the name of a certain street. The next request was for a man who knew every house in that street and the procedure was repeated. This time there was more of a quickening of the pulse at the mention of a specific house. The patient was in love with a young woman in that house, Ibn Sina declared. The diagnosis turned out to be accurate and a marriage cured the patient of overly pining for her.

Another case that Ibn Sina treated but did not record concerned a prince who declared that he was a cow and insisted he be killed "so that a good stew may be prepared from [his] flesh." He refused to eat. Ibn Sina agreed to treat him and sent a message that a butcher was on his way to slaughter him. Ibn Sina entered the patient's room with a butcher's knife. He had the patient bound, then said that he was too thin and ought to be fattened. The patient complied with the order and started eating again. His strength returned and he was soon cured of his delusion. The person who recorded this case added that, to resort to this kind of a treatment, a physician ought to be possessed of "pre-eminent intelligence, perfect science, and unerring acumen."[23] Ibn Sina's *Canon* also explains the method of psychotherapy in general terms.[24]

Many other Muslim physicians who followed Ibn Sina, though not as famous as the most prominent, nevertheless, in one way or another added to the progress of Islamic medicine. One example was Ibn Jazla, who was born in Baghdad about a hundred years after Ibn Sina and died in 1100 AC. He wrote two books on medicine, which were also admired for their excellent Arabic calligraphy.

Physician Abd al-Latif was born in Baghdad. He taught medicine and philosophy in Damascus, Aleppo, and Cairo. He also wrote 166 works, many of which were medical. Salah al-Din (Saladin) invited him to Egypt, where he also met Maimonides. One of Abd al-Latif's books details his experiences in Egypt.

Abd al-Latif's contemporary was Ibn Abi Usaybia. He was born and educated in Damascus, and then migrated to Cairo, where he was a hospital physician. Ibn Abi Usaybia was the first historian of Islamic medicine. His *Lives of the Physicians* consists of biographies of only the most famous and was useful to Western historians, too. Another of Abd al-Latif's contemporaries was Ibn al-Nafis of Damascus. He achieved prominence for having written a worthwhile commentary on Ibn Sina's *Qānūn*, valuable enough to be translated into Latin.

Medical Achievement in the West

There were medical advances in the western reaches of the Muslim world, too. During the early centuries of Muslim Spain, scholars aspiring to become physicians traveled to Baghdad and other cities, including Cairo and Damascus, and as far as Iran, to acquire knowledge and experience at universities and hospitals. Al-Maqqari compiled a list of the Andalusian scholars traveling east. Despite conflicts and differences in politics and among rulers, life at the non-government level proceeded according to the tenets of Islam established at the time of the Prophet – those of a universal community. Travel, especially in search of knowledge, persisted regardless of who ruled or where. [25]

Later, Muslim Spain established its own universities, especially in Cordoba, and so there was little need to travel east. Nevertheless, some continued to do so. The universities of the East and West differed. In the East, Jews participated freely in the intellectual pursuits of Muslim society. However, in Spain, they played a far greater role, especially in the academic world, excelling in both medicine and philosophy. Hasdai ibn Shaprut, one of Muslim Spain's first eminent physicians, was a Jew. In addition, in Andalusia, more Christians participated in this field.

The medical schools and hospitals in Muslim Spain improved in quality. As a result, around the sixth century AH (twelfth century AC), the quest for medical knowledge grew in the other direction, from the East to Andalusia. This further facilitated the flow of Muslim expertise into the rest of Europe.

Writings on medicine started soon after the Muslims settled in Spain. One of the early texts was that of Arib ibn Sa‘d, who was a court physician to the Andalusian Caliphs Abd al-Rahman III and al-Hakam II. He wrote a book on gynecology, the hygiene of infants and pregnant women, and obstetrics. Abu al-Qasim al-Zahrawi (936–1013 AC), known in the West as Abulcasis, was one of the most noted of Muslim Spain's physicians for his original contributions to surgery. He was also the physician to Abd al-Rahman III and al-Hakam II. Other than that, very little is known about his life. He was famous, especially in Europe, for his book on surgery, encompassing what was known in his time. This text had a long, appealing title whose basic meaning was "an aid to him who is not equal to long treatises." It was the first medical work to contain diagrams of surgical instruments.

The book itself does not share the title's modesty. It is filled with al-Zahrawi's original contributions including the cauterization of wounds, the crushing of a stone inside a bladder, and the necessity of vivisection and dissection.[26] The different methods of cauterization are well illustrated. There is also a description of ophthalmic and dental surgical operations and the Arab methods of treating wounds.[27] One section discusses fractures and paralysis due to spinal injuries. Another chapter focuses on obstetrics and describes an obstetric posture currently known in the West as Walcher's position. The work is also the first to offer the treatment of deformities of the mouth and dental arches. An attractive feature of this medical treatise is the number of illustrations of surgical instruments, giving today's scholars a clear picture of the devices used in Europe in the Middle Ages. Another, lesser-known, work by al-Zahrawi deals with pharmaceutical preparations derived from minerals, plants, and animals and is considered an early example of the use of chemistry in medicine.

Al-Zahrawi's influence on the medicine of Europe was considerable in another respect, for he wrote very clearly and presented his material methodically. This so impressed Western scholars that it increased their interest in the medical knowledge of the Muslims, and thus al-Zahrawi helped to raise the status of surgery in Christian Europe.[28]

Another Andalusian court physician, Ibn Zuhr, maintained an equally high standard in original work in medicine. Ibn Zuhr, Latinized into Avenzoar, devoted his learning and life to medicine alone, unlike other physicians of his time, who acquired knowledge in other disciplines. He started early by learning from his father, who was a skilled physician. Ibn Zuhr achieved fame in both Spain and North Africa. He died at an early age.

Ibn Zuhr, too, wrote a number of works. His most outstanding contribution, to which he devoted an entire volume, was on medicine and diet and the therapeutical advantages of combining the two. He recorded his astute observations in detail and even kept meticulous records of himself, including details of an abscess with which he was afflicted. His description of the itch mite is said to be the first, although Hitti states that he was anticipated by Ahmad al-Tabari two hundred years earlier. His top priority in the training of physicians was experience.[29]

The most famous of Andalusia's Muslim scholars was Ibn Rushd, known in the West as Averroes. He was recognized as a philosopher and his influence in the West is primarily in this area. However, he was an accomplished jurist as well as a physician, practicing as a judge in both Seville and Cordoba. Andalusian biographers emphasize this aspect of his career, especially since he drew on his experiences as a judge and wrote extensively on law.

Completeness was the first principle governing Ibn Rushd's work. He spent sixteen years in the writing of an encyclopedic tome on medicine. He has the distinction of describing an unusual feature of smallpox, namely, that those who survived the disease were immune to it. Perhaps this knowledge led eventually to the development of vaccinations. His description of the retina demonstrates that he fully knew its workings. Ibn Rushd's contribution to pharmacology is also phenomenal. His works in this area became a standard reference in Europe throughout the Middle Ages, and their influence was so great that it is still evident in today's pharmacopoeias.[30]

A contemporary of Ibn Rushd, who was equally famous in the West for both philosophy and medicine, was known by three names: Abu Imran ibn Maymun in Arabic, Mosheh ben Maimon in Hebrew, and Maimonides in Latin, the last still used today. He was, like Ibn Rushd, prominent more as a philosopher than as a physician. His medical education was derived from al-Razi, Ibn Sina, and Ibn Zuhr. He, too, depended heavily on observation for additional knowledge, and his written work on medicine includes original contributions. For example, he described an improved method of circumcision, and mentioned constipation as a cause of hemorrhoids, for which he prescribed a largely vegetarian light diet. Diet as well as personal hygiene were the focus of the *Book of Counsel*, which he wrote in Arabic for Sultan al-Afdal, and which was later translated into Hebrew by Rabbi Moses ben Samuel ben Tibbon. In another work, Maimonides focused on the poisons of reptiles and their antidotes. Another major work consisted of a translation of Ibn Sina's *Canon* into Hebrew.[31] Maimonides turned to medicine later in life out of necessity. Although he preferred philosophy, he was unable to continue working in that discipline in Cordoba, owing to the new, intolerant Almohad Muslim ruler there. He fled to Fez, then to Palestine, and finally migrated to Cairo, where he settled. The fortune his entire family had invested in the jewelry trade of his brother David was lost in a shipwreck that also took the life of David himself. Maimonides became a practicing doctor and prospered. He was the personal physician of Salah al-Din al-Ayyubi (known as Saladin in the West). During the Crusades, his fame crossed enemy lines and reached King Richard of England, who in turn wanted Maimonides as his own physician. However, Maimonides refused this offer. The synagogue in Cairo named after Maimonides was and continues to be visited nowadays by ailing Jews, who spend a night there in search of a cure.

The contributions of the most noted physicians of the Muslim world have survived because they wrote about their discoveries and their books were widely distributed in both the East and the West. Other names are now known only from their books. There are also those who might have advanced medicine whose names were not recorded, yet whose findings nevertheless helped considerably in the development of this field.

Biology and Medicines

The study of plants among the Muslims had a curious beginning. Writers, especially poets, wanted to explain their metaphoric references to flowers, trees, and other plants, particularly those beyond the experience of their readers, so they described them in detail. Therefore, by the time scientists and physicians became interested in botany, the descriptions of many plants were already available.

Zoology, the other major branch of biology, had its beginnings in what today might be termed the veterinary sciences. There must have been, as in the other areas of medicine, local practitioners with knowledge of animal diseases and their cures. The first recorded study in the Islamic period is that of Abd al-Malik ibn Quraib al-Asmaʿi (740–828 AC). He wrote several works, with individual texts dealing with camels, horses, and sheep, another devoted to wild animals, and one on the human body. His writings demonstrated that the Arabs already had a considerable knowledge of human anatomy.[32] Veterinary medicine as a distinct discipline began soon afterward. A work on horsemanship by Abu Yusuf Yaqub ibn Akhi Hizam, stable master to Caliph al-Mutadid (829–902 AC), contained the rudiments of veterinary science.

The discoverers of a great many medications remain unknown, from the person who discovered some efficacious herbs in a forest to the person experimenting in a laboratory. Their contributions are nevertheless known collectively as Greek, Indian, Persian or, from our period, Islamic. A prominent example is Yunani (derived from

Ionian) medicine, which is still widely practiced in India. The findings, however, were too precious to be ignored. They were collected and published in volumes compiled by those who concentrated on the pharmaceutical aspect of medicine.

One of the most outstanding compilations is known only in its Latin version, since the original Arabic sources have been completely lost. An unknown person who called himself Mesue compiled the text. An outstanding feature of this work is the section on purgatives, which are classified into three different kinds: laxatives (tamarinds, figs, prunes, cassia), mild purgatives (senna, aloes, rhubarb), and drastic purgatives (jalap, scammony, colocynth).[33]

Ibn Serabi, Ibn al-Wafid of Toledo, and Ibn al-Baytar were three scholars from Andalusia who devoted most of their research specifically to medications. Other than their written work, very little is known about them. Ibn Serabi, also known as Serapion Junior, and ibn al-Wafid of Toledo each wrote books on pharmaceuticals. Ibn al-Baytar wrote a more extensive work on the same subject. He was born in Muslim Spain and died in Damascus around 646/1248. He devoted a major part of his life to studying medicinal plants in Greece, Egypt, and Asia Minor. What he learned from these countries and from the works of others, and what he himself discovered, he recorded in the most complete text on medications used in the Muslim world. He described about 1,400 medicaments, of which three hundred were considered new for his time.

Muslims were also responsible for various methods of preparing medications. Equally important, they introduced into their practice medicines discovered from either their own investigations or their discoveries during travels. In addition, the Muslims invented the pharmacy and developed skills in preparing medications in the form of syrups, juleps, alcohol (all Arabic terms), and tragacanth. ("Tragacanth" is, according to the *Random House Dictionary*, a gummifier: used to impart firmness to pills and lozenges.)

One of the supplies of the pharmacy was an unusual item that proves Muslim physicians utilized anesthesia by inhalation. This was the "soporific sponge." It was soaked with soporifics that induced insensibility to pain. It was then dried and stored until it was needed, when it was dampened and placed against the nostrils and mouth. Campbell believes that the sponge enabled Muslim surgeons to perform surgeries more efficiently. The sponge was first used in the West when Theodoric of Bologna acquired it from the Muslims and introduced it into Europe.[34]

Edward Browne writes that both Arab and non-Arab Muslims made the largest contribution to the body of scientific doctrine that they inherited from the Greeks regarding chemistry and *materia medica*.[35]

There were soon pharmacies all over the Muslim world, the first of which opened for business in the ninth century AC. The Muslim public and doctors could buy medications collected from all over the Muslim world. Whereas in the West nowadays it is customary to coat pills with sugar, the Muslims used rose water and perfumes. Pharmacologists were examined and licensed, and their shops were routinely inspected.[36]

As seen in the above discussion of eminent physicians, there was hardly any distinction between medical practice and pharmaceuticals, for the study of medications was an essential part of the study of medicine. Many physicians wrote about medications in some detail, as part of medical texts to be studied by other physicians. As a result, chemistry and botany were largely considered more useful in the preparation of medications than as separate disciplines. Many eminent physicians created new remedies.

Al-Kindi, discussed earlier in this chapter, also studied pharmacology extensively as part of his medical training and practice. The person who treated pharmaceuticals as worthy of a separate field of study was Abu Mansur Muwaffak, an Iranian court physician to the Prince of Herat in the fourth/tenth century. His work on *The True Properties of Remedies* brought together information on medications from Greek, Indian, Syriac, and Muslim sources. The systematic study was classified under four headings according to the action of the medicines, totaling 585 (466 derived from plants, 75 from minerals, and 44 from animals). Muwaffak included an introduction to general pharmacological theory. His work includes the making and surgical use of what was later known as plaster of Paris. Muwaffak's writing was also the earliest scientific treatise in modern Persian.[37] The Palestinian physician, al-Tamimi, who was a contemporary of Muwaffak, experimented with medications and wrote several works on pharmaceuticals. Among his treatments he included a discussion of the effects of food on human health. Another contemporary, Ibn al-Jazzar (c. 898–980 AC) in Qayrawan, Tunisia became famous for his book, *Traveler's Provision*, which proved to be of immense help to travelers and thus became a best seller. It described all kinds of ailments affecting travelers and offered remedies. Especially valuable was the extensive discussion on contagious diseases, including the causes of a plague in Egypt. One outstanding feature of the book concerned maladies due to changes in environment and climate. For example, pilgrims who went to Makkah to perform the Hajj suffered from a discomfort that made their lives miserable if they came from arable lands. The very dry climate in Makkah caused the swelling of the mucous membrane of the nasal cavities, which is known today as rhinitis.

The outstanding contemporary pharmacologist was Masawaih al-Mardini, who practiced in Baghdad and later, until his death, served as court physician to the Fatimid Caliph al-Hakim in Egypt. He devoted his professional years to the study of Islamic medications. Early on, he wrote a work on purgatives and emetics, then another on remedies for each disease known at the time. His major work was a complete pharmacopoeia in 12 parts, which was very well received in the world of medicine and also remained for centuries the standard textbook for pharmacology in the West.[38]

Of special interest also is Symeon Seth (eleventh century AC), a Jewish doctor who was living in Byzantium during this time and who exemplified the progress Muslims had made in medicine and pharmacology. Seth was one of several who reversed the Muslim intellectual tradition of translation from Greek into Arabic. Seth translated Arabic into Greek, concentrating on remedies from the Muslim world. His first major work was a dictionary focusing mostly on the medical properties of certain foods (most of the material came from the Muslim world and some from India). In this work, he introduced Arabic words into the Greek language. These were words that were also adopted in the West in translations into Latin, for example, camphor, musk, ambergris, julep, and syrup. Sarton points out, "Most, if not all of these drugs and spices are here mentioned in Greek for the first time."[39] Seth also wrote a botanical dictionary. It seems most likely that was when botany began to emerge as a distinct science to be studied separately from medicine. Ascribed to al-Bakri of Cordoba is a text on the plants and trees of Muslim Spain.

Medical and pharmaceutical knowledge spread throughout the Muslim world owing to scholars traveling to the exceptional medical schools to learn from the masters. There were also highly skilled physicians who were born in one region, studied medicine, and practiced elsewhere, establishing homes close to or far from their birthplaces. To extend their knowledge to their colleagues in their new homes, some also wrote books to assist them in their practice. Masawah al-Mardini, for example, was born in Upper Mesopotamia, practiced in Baghdad, and was later court physician to al-Hakam, the Fatimid Caliph in Egypt. He wrote works on purgatives and emetics. However, his major accomplishment was a compendium on pharmacology, compiled from what was known to Muslims at the time. It gained a wide audience in the Muslim world and was for centuries the standard textbook of pharmacy in the West.[40]

Another physician from the same region who also settled in Egypt was Ammar ibn Ali al-Mawsili. His contributions came from his own findings. He was, according to Sarton, "the most original of Muslim oculists." The most valuable part of the work he wrote on the eye and its diseases and remedies was that dealing with surgery, including "six operations for cataract, notably an operation for soft cataract by suction." Ammar's contribution was overshadowed by a contemporary who became more famous, Ali ibn Isa, already discussed above.[41]

An oculist who did not write in Arabic but in Persian was Ibn Mansur al-Jamani. His success is reflected in the name by which he was

popularly known – Zarrin Dast – which means "the Golden Hand."
His outstanding contribution to medicine was a work on ophthalmology entitled *Nūr al-ʿUyūn* (The Light of the Eyes). Another Iranian who achieved prominence from his work on pharmacology was
Abu Mansur. He wrote a book in Persian, which was published in
359/970. It described 585 medications, 466 of which consisted of or
were derived from vegetable sources, 75 mineral, and 44 animal.

Patient Care

The Muslims were noted for their hospitals. Juan Vernet describes
the hospital as an "eastern institution." Although the Muslims did
not invent the idea of a center for medical treatment, they were the
first to establish the kind of efficient hospital that the world knows
today.[42] Meyerhof notes that the West learnt about the hospital from
the Muslims during the Crusades.[43] Sixty-five years after the death
of Prophet Muhammad in 632 AC, the first major Muslim hospital
was built in Damascus in the reign of the Umayyad Caliph al-Walid.
During the Abbasid era, major hospitals were established in Baghdad, Cairo, and other parts of Egypt. Adud al-Dawlah founded one
of the earliest hospitals in Baghdad. Many smaller ones served local
neighborhoods, some of them infirmaries and/or dispensaries. An
unnamed Jewish traveler visiting Baghdad around 555/1160 discovered that this city alone had sixty of these medical establishments.
In most of them, treatment and medications were provided free of
charge.

Much thought was given to the planning of the biggest hospitals,
which were eventually to be found in every large Muslim city. They
consisted of more than just buildings to house medical facilities, as is
evident in Cairo's al-Mansur hospital. It comprised four courtyards
with fountains, separate wards allocated to "important diseases" and
to women and convalescents, outpatient clinics, "diet kitchens," and
an orphanage. It also had a well-stocked library, lecture rooms, and
a mosque. Both male and female nurses were employed. The hospital authorities took into account that many patients were unable
to return to work immediately after leaving the hospital, so they

provided financial support during their convalescence.[44] In the large hospitals, there were separate wards for the mentally ill, and most notable was (and still is) the humane and kind treatment of the insane.[45] As mentioned above, almost all the large hospitals were also schools of medicine. The most famous of them was appropriately named the Hall of Wisdom. This description makes more sense in Arabic, Farsi, and Urdu, since the word for physician, *ḥakīm*, is derived from the root word for wisdom, *ḥakama*.

This discussion of the Muslim contribution to medicine, as in other fields, is evidence that the flowering of Muslim mediscience was the result of the creative synthesizing of Islamic knowledge with that of other and earlier civilizations, especially ancient Greece. This chapter has also demonstrated the far-reaching and effective impact of Islamic medicine. Most Muslim physicians were famous in other fields of science, clearly indicating that the Islamic paradigm of knowledge of the medieval period was thorough and comprehensive in its focus.

II

ARABIC LITERATURE

THERE HAVE BEEN two more significant and most welcome constants throughout Islamic civilization. One is literature and the other, to be discussed in Chapter 13, is art. Although both disciplines existed in the Muslim world long before the advent of Islam, there is no doubt that Muslim creativity developed them to heights that place Islamic literature and the arts firmly at the top of humankind's achievements in these fields.

Since the Muslim community is not confined within geographical borders, Islamic literature and the arts include those created by Muslims in non-Muslim countries. Nevertheless, there are characteristics in Muslim literature relevant to this chapter and the next that ought to be made clear at the outset. In literature, the basis is language and, more important, how it is used. Each culture has distinctive forms, metaphors, symbols, and motifs and this is especially true of Islamic culture. Let me give a parallel, personal example. It was only when I taught Western literature, mainly British and American, that I realized that it strongly reflected a Judeo-Christian-Graeco-Roman heritage. Even minor details in, for example, a novel showed the residue of a Christian or Judaic bias in a work by an author who insisted that he or she was an atheist.

Muslim literature reflects the ethos of the Muslim world and, hence, has distinctive features. One is, of course, the knowledge writers acquire of the Qur'an and Islam from childhood onwards. Until the end of the twentieth century, that knowledge was thorough. The other feature is the principle that the community is more important than the individual, except in modern literature influenced by the West, where the focus is solely upon the individual without regard to society.

Pre-Islamic Arabic literature is highly relevant to this discussion, since it inspired the Muslim Arabs to continue their rich literary tradition, especially in the skilful use of language. That literature consisted primarily of poetry, oratory, and the tale (usually tribal history that became legend) and was rooted in tribal culture and restricted to certain themes. Nearly all the themes had a common focus: the exploits of an exceptional (usually male) figure, who excelled in conquering another male or an enemy tribe or a woman or all three. Another common theme, essential to many of the exploits, was vengeance.

In many tales or poems, a historical person, a major character, or the writer's alter ego plans a clever stratagem to gain an end. This led to a literary tradition at the center of many of the *Arabian Nights* or Mullah Nasruddin stories. The title of a collection of tales following this tradition (translated into English by René R. Khawam) has best described it: *The Subtle Ruse: The Book of Arabic Wisdom and Guile*. This collection is about Caliphs, kings, sultans, governors, judges, attorneys, witnesses, and devout men resorting to a ruse, mostly to achieve some honorable goal.

At times, a historical incident rendered into legend shows such "cleverness" at work. Reynold Nicholson, in his *Literary History of the Arabs*, narrates a story that is a good example. The incident was a migration from Marib in southern Arabia. To provide a reason for the migration, a much later, also historical, incident is attached to the first: the destruction of a dam so marvelous that its reputation continued among the Arabs well into Islamic times.

The wife of the king of the Marib, the story goes, dreams that the dam will be destroyed. The king is at first skeptical until an event in the dream tallies with what is happening on the dam. He wants to move from the area, so to prevent the tribe from becoming suspicious, he arranges a quarrel with his son. In public, the two come to blows and the king declares he will not live in a place where he has suffered the indignity of a son hitting his father. He sells his land and possessions, then tells his people the real reason for his departure. He sets "out from Marib at the head of a great multitude." Soon afterward, the dam bursts and floods the country.[1]

Other legends tell of Bilqis, the Queen of Sheba; Asad, the hero of a battle against Persia avenging the murder of a son; the adventures of Asad Kamil and the three witches; Numan renouncing a kingdom to serve God; and Adi, the poet, whose adoration of the woman he loves changes her attitude toward him from intense dislike to love. Historical facts in legends such as these are embellished with soothsayers and cunning means of wreaking vengeance.

Jadhima occupies a special place in both fables and proverbs. This hero is so proud that he proclaims his only close companions are two stars in the sky. During one of his conquests, he kills the husband of Zabba, a princess of Mesopotamia. Zabba is now the queen and as a courageous and resolute woman, she plans a ruse to avenge her husband's death. She succeeds in entrapping Jadhima and bleeds him to death, making sure his blood is collected in a golden bowl. She tells him she is doing so because a soothsayer had predicted that if a single drop were spilt, the murder would be avenged. Two men plan the vengeance, Jadhima's nephew and son, who, by means of a stratagem, succeed in overcoming the queen's forces and trap her in a tunnel she has built as a means of escape. However, the vengeance is not entirely theirs. She sucks poison secreted in her seal ring and, dying, boasts that her death has come by her own hand.

These stories were published around two centuries after the advent of Islam, during the Abbasid era. The most outstanding of these anthologies is *Kitāb al-Aghānī* [Book of Songs], collected by Abu al-Farraj of Isfahan and consisting of twenty volumes. Ibn Khaldun, the great historian, notes, "It comprises all that [Arabs] had achieved in the past of excellence in every kind of poetry, history, music, et cetera."[2]

Poetry

The protagonists in these pre-Islamic stories and legends were not only kings but also tribal heroes. The difference was in the telling:

the bedouin stories were told in verse and, thus, singing poetry in praise of desert heroes became a tradition. When a bedouin mentioned a historical exploit in Islamic times, he was asked to cite verses as evidence and, as a result, poems were invented to support the exploit. An authentic body of legends in poetic form was collected during Islamic times in Baghdad, Aleppo, and other cities and labeled *Ayyām al-ʿArab* (The [Battle] Days of the Arabs).

The content of later poems changed. Gone was the belief that the poet was in contact with the supernatural, that is, *jinn* or devils, who endowed him with magical powers. Poetry had now become an art. There were fewer embellishments and, except in a very few instances, less reliance on the supernatural. Vengeance still prevailed in some of the stories. However, there was more intertribal warfare, in which physical prowess and cunning played increasingly important roles. Sexual conquests were also emphasized thematically.

The Pre-Islamic Age, which Tuetey described as "the Golden Age of Arabian Poetry," lasted a hundred years, beginning about 500 AC.[3] The poets were living heroes in Arab culture, who sang about past heroes in Arab legend and history. Nicholson quotes Ibn Rashik in describing families wishing one another "the joy…of the coming to light of a poet" and entire tribes celebrating the appearance of one, "for a poet was… a means of perpetuating their glorious deeds."[4] The "Great Four" poets were Imru al-Qays, Asha, Nabigar, and Zuhair.[5]

There was further glory for the poet if he excelled and his poem won a prize at the poetry contests held at the annual fairs at Ukaz, close to Makkah. There were usually seven winners and their poems were embroidered in gold and hung on the Kaʿbah. The most sacred place was chosen for such an honor, reflecting the high regard the Arabs had for their poetry. The fame of both the poets and their *qaṣāʾid* (odes) spread when professional reciters delivered them all over Arabia.

The most famous of these poems that have come down to us are known as *Muʿallaqāt* (*The Suspended Ones*), also known as *The Seven Odes*. Their authors include Imru al-Qays, Antarah, and Labid. Sells divides the odes into three distinctive movements: the *nasib* or the remembrance of the beloved, the journey, and the boast.[6] The

Muʿallaqāt inspired Tennyson to write the opening lines of one of his best-known poems, "Locksley Hall."[7]

In English translation, the odes read well, for the language is lucid and the images are apt. Nevertheless, to appreciate the richness of the poem, one has to know Arabic because, in Charles Tuetey's description, "It is rich in words carrying highly specific meanings that in English would require a whole phrase rather than a single word."[8] To appreciate the Arabic futher, one should listen to a qualified Arab reciter. Even today, there are many Arabs who have memorized the entire *Muʿallaqāt* and who need no inducement to recite it for anyone who wants to hear it.

Despite the popularity of the *Muʿallaqāt*, Tuetey considers it a poor choice as an introduction to pre-Islamic poetry, declaring that there are other poems "better preserved and superior," a selection of which is given in his *Classical Arabic Poetry*. Although their language and imagery are just as rich, the expressions are more economical, relying heavily at times on allusion, and the themes are different. In twenty lines, for example, *Mutalammis of Dubai'a* depicts two men bent on vengeance, past wars against the Himyar kings, the setting around a castle during harvest time, and the men calling out, "If you come as friends, we shall come the same; if not, you shall find us the harder to meet."[9]

According to Ashtiany, the "medieval [Arab] urban men of letters… regarded bedouin poetry as their classical heritage." Ashtiany singles out Jarir and Farazdaq (both of the Umayyad era) as poets who "cast [their poetry] in the archaic mold or with archaic features."[10] However, by that time there were changes in Arabic literature, largely influenced by Islam. The most important factor was the language of the Qur'an, for there had never been nor has there been anything like it. Every Arab who listened to a skilled recitation of the Qur'an was struck by the beauty of its language.

Nevertheless, the Qur'an did not, as some believe, prevent poets from pursuing their skill, even during the life of the Prophet. Poets who opposed him attacked him in their poetry. The Prophet asked Muslim poets to respond and they did so, particularly Hasan, who was most skilled in the art of biting satire.[11] The first four Caliphs, especially Umar and Ali, according to Jayyusi, showed greater interest than the Prophet in poetry, with a particular preference for works that were rooted in "noble values" and Islamic morality.[12]

The Umayyad era was one of transition, leading to greater creativity among the poets and more fluid and lucid language. Jayyusi describes it as "a new artistic freedom," in which poetry "reflected the movement of a spirit set free from an established way of life" in an age "not yet spontaneously and completely Muslim." A new kind of poetry called the *ghazal* was now being written. It was a different kind of love poem, which was to become one of the most widely used forms in the Muslim world from that time.[13]

Earlier during this period, rhapsodic poetry took a different form called the eulogy, which was mainly to be recited though it was also recorded. It became more popular among the increasing number of both rulers and poets. The poets turned to eulogizing to earn a living, one of whom to achieve fame was a Christian called al-Akhtal, a favorite of the early Umayyad Caliphs.

The love poetry of pre-Islamic times was written again after the coming of Islam and, in addition, became part of the music and song, which under the Umayyads reached the sacred cities of Makkah and Madinah. Two women, Jamila and Azza, are credited with reviving Arabic music and adapting Arabic poetry to be sung. Jamila, in particular, became a very famous singer. When she returned to Madinah from a pilgrimage to Makkah, the people of Madinah lined the streets to welcome her home.[14]

At about the same period, poets resorted to ambiguity, so that a statement could on one level be interpreted literally and, on another level, be considered erotic. Tuetey gives an example from a poem written by Umar ibn Abi Rabia: "From Zainab nothing unfitting I gained but a scarlet robe that the two of us shared."[15] When pressed for an explanation of this line, Umar explained that it had started raining when he was with Zainab and he asked his servant "to cover us with a robe of mine." Umar ibn Abi Rabia's poetry was set to music. Umar's poetry, Nicholson states, was condemned by devout Muslims as "the greatest crime ever committed against God."[16]

Later, love and revelry poetry in the Umayyad courts dispensed with ambiguity. Outside the courts, too, poets indulged in ribald poetry as well as invective and biting satire, the latter directed against anyone who dared say anything negative about the poet. Farazdaq and Jarir stand out as examples, whose enmity toward each other added to the bitterness of their poems. Both came from the Tamim tribe.

Farazdaq was the more cunning, more persuasive, and much more scandalous in his behavior. He was uncouth and this shows in his poetry, which has been described as "rugged."[17] Farazdaq has received high praise from modern literary critics. Jayyusi considers him "one of the foremost poets of the Umayyad period."[18] Tuetey gives the impression that his poetry was part of the era's "satire developed to a fine art." Farazdaq's poems were certainly popular, most likely owing to his scandalous way of life and the vituperation he directed against his enemies. His poem about the governor of Iraq, for example, tells him that the clink of cash might change overnight to the clank of chains.[19] Farazdaq warns the ruler of Hijaz that he "may as well seek lions to beat with a stick," rather than refuse to surrender Farazdaq's wife who had sought refuge with the ruler. The marriage itself was a scandal. Farazdaq had, by a ruse, prevented his cousin Nawar from marrying another and insisted she marry him. They quarreled incessantly and she fled to Makkah. Eventually, he divorced her although he regretted it soon afterwards. Before, during, and after the marriage, he constantly wrote about Nawar.

The polar opposite of Farazdaq was Jarir, a gentle love poet given to piety and contemplation. Although his love poetry lacks passion, his satires are as good as the best written at the time. His skill is demonstrated in an incident in which criticism was directed at Rai al-Ibil, who wrote that Farazdaq was superior to Jarir. When Jarir confronted Rai, Rai's son spoke, calling Jarir "this dog of the Banu Kulayb." Jarir wrote a satire in response and recited it to both Rai and Farazdaq. The moment Jarir recited the lines demeaning Rai's tribe, Rai rushed to his companions and exclaimed that they could no longer stay in Basra since Jarir had disgraced them. They left the city and rejoined their tribe, who in turn "bitterly reproached" Rai for the "ignominy" he had brought upon them.[20]

Jarir also experimented in a meter that lent itself, according to Jayyusi, to diction nearer to the spoken language of the Umayyad era. Jarir wrote most of his poems in this "new language," though, unfortunately, the verbal distinction is lost in translation. Jayyusi states that Jarir contributed to Ummayad poetry in developing "these [language] elements into harmony with current speech," in writing for "popular audiences," and in introducing wit and humor into his satires.[21]

Notwithstanding the popularity of Farazdaq and Jarir, Jayyusi singles out Dhu al-Rummah as "artistically the most important poet of his age and undoubtedly one of the greatest poets of the Arabic language."[22] Nicholson considers him "the last important representative of the pure Bedouin school."[23] Because he wrote in the manner of the odes of olden times, with very few eulogies or poems of self-glorification or satire, he was not highly regarded by his contemporaries or the critics who came after them. He was a master of description, however, and a genius in the use of language.

Dhu al-Rummah was born in the desert and was well read in both the Qur'an and the pre-Islamic poets. He went to Kufa and Basra, where he met his contemporaries, although he discovered that he did not fit into an urban milieu. His one outstanding asset, Jayyusi states, is "a richness of language which few poets could combine, as he did, with fine poetic creativity."[24] His imagery is all-inclusive, dominated by the sense of touch, and conveys with poignancy the experience of the desert. His poetry differs from that of pre-Islamic times in its depiction of realism: mirages, fountains without water, the wilderness, the heat of the sun, and the toil of desert life, with the emphasis on fatigue.

Prose

There was development in the writing of prose, although oratory was still the primary means of expression in regions where literacy was just starting to spread. The beginnings of a literary, written prose consisted of, as Ashtiany aptly describes it, didactic epistles. Ashtiany makes a couple of fine distinctions in the study of the prose of the Umayyad era. Noting that Arabic was the language of "a complex cosmopolitan culture" beyond the borders of Arabia, she says that Arabic should be understood as a linguistic, not an ethnic, label, while literature fits into a broader category. These distinctions are essential because much of the literature of the Umayyad era was largely religious.[25]

Old legends were written down, although most early recorded works were historical. The most popular narratives were the *maghāzī*, the stories of the early wars of Islam in which the Prophet participated and which took place mainly in and around Madinah. These narratives were embellished, in some versions considerably. The most famous of the *maghāzī* was a compilation by al-Waqidi.

The outstanding prose work of the time was a biography-history of Prophet Muhammad by Ibn Ishaq, written toward the end of the first century AH. Although the original no longer exists, there remains a recension by Ibn Hisham. The biography is based on interviews with people who knew of the Prophet from information handed down by relatives or Companions. Ibn Ishaq listed the sources of information and noted he was reporting what others said. His method of a chain of authorities leading back to the time of the Prophet was also used for the compilation of the Hadith, also known as the Sunnah, "the way of the Prophet," which is, after the Qur'an, the most important religious guidance for Muslims. The authentication of the Hadith was the lifetime work of the two most widely used compilers, al-Bukhari and Muslim. They were meticulous and painstaking in sifting the valid reports from the rest, based on the integrity of the people who transmitted them.

More prose was written during the Abbasid era. This was not because the Abbasid era was longer – approximately five hundred years compared with less than a hundred for the Umayyad era – but because richer prose developed under a different, more sophisticated and cosmopolitan culture engendered by a new Caliphate. Equally important, this prose challenged the dominant status poetry had achieved both before Islam and in its first century and a half. There was also a new kind of literature known as the *adab* or "refined" prose, which Pellat divides into three types, all of them didactic: one aimed at inculcating "ethical precepts," another provided a general education, and the third was a guide for members of the various professions.[26]

Usually, the naming of literary periods after the rulers of the time is a convenience rather than a demarcation between the kinds of literature written at a particular time. Nevertheless, as with some other literatures (that of the Elizabethan era in England, for example), a distinction should be made between the Arabic-Islamic literature of the Umayyad era and that of the Abbasid era. The rule of the Abbasids made an enormous difference to literature, as it did to philosophy, the sciences, other branches of learning, and the arts.

This description does not apply to the entire Abbasid era. Nicholson divides the "Abbasid House" into two stages. The first created the atmosphere of learning, totaling around a hundred years, from the second Abbasid Caliph al-Mansur to al-Wathiq. This was also the time of the two kinds of sciences: those connected with the Qur'an and Islamic culture (including literature), and those derived from the "outside" (philosophy, the natural and physical sciences, and medicine). In view of all this intellectual activity, one can see why prose dominated. The second stage of the Abbasid era, from the time of al-Mutawakkil, was a period of decline.[27]

Literary prose dominated owing to increasing sophistication, and was enhanced by more learning and wider contact with the richness of other cultures, especially that of Persia. Nevertheless, it did not replace pre-Islamic literature. On the contrary, poetry was held in greater esteem, diligently studied by poets because of its "pure" and "classical" traits. Some poets imitated the old odes by, for example, beginning their poems with a description of a deserted camp, as did the traditional poets in earlier times.[28]

More stories were written at the beginning of the Abbasid era. They consisted of epics depicting the heroes of the Muslim conquests and their feats, as well as histories, biographical dictionaries, chronicles, and enchantments. Some of the stories were translations from the Pahlavi (literary Persian) texts, including *Kalīlah wa Dimnah* (originally the Sanskrit *Panchatantra* – Five Occasions of Good Sense), *The Khudaynamah* (Book of Kings), and the *Kitāb al-Tāj* (Book of the Crown).

Of these, the most popular was *Kalīlah wa Dimnah*. Only the Arabic translation exists and from it there have been translations into a number of languages, including English, and it is still in demand today. *Kalīlah wa Dimnah* was composed in Sanskrit between 300 and 500 AC and is said to be the work of a Brahmin for a king who wanted to impart wisdom to his naïve and lazy sons. Therefore, to call it a book of fables, as it is so often described, is to minimize its import. The tales are complex and lengthy and provide material for philosophical analysis.[29]

The principal protagonists are two jackals called Kalīlah and Dimnah. Around the two are narrated many interrelated tales about mammals and birds. Their behavior is human; they are wise and at times cunning; and they convey morals and deliver aphorisms, largely dealing with politics. According to Hornstein, "the medieval beast epic – and consequently most modern fables – derive ultimately from the Indian tradition."[30]

The translator of the Pahlavi texts was Ibn al-Muqaffa. Latham places him in "a central position" in "the annals of Arabic literature...for it is he who opens the door to the golden age of Arabic prose writing." These remarks become more significant when Ibn al-Muqaffa's background is taken into account. He was born an Iranian and was a Manichean before converting to Islam. He learned Arabic in Basra and became so proficient in the language that he ridiculed native speakers of Arabic who did not use their language well. He held secretarial positions in the administration of Iraq until he started translating Pahlavi texts into Arabic.[31]

Ibn al-Muqaffa proceeded to compose original works, where he revealed his most remarkable command of the Arabic language. This proficiency is especially evident in his preface to his most notable work, *Kitāb Adab al-Kabīr* (The Comprehensive Book of Rules of Conduct). The preface is very short, and states that the knowledge of his time depended heavily on the experience of the ancients. He believed the early writers to be physically and mentally superior to his contemporaries and that the later writers' undertakings consisted primarily of elaborating on the material they had inherited.[32]

The remainder of the *Adab* addresses princes, ministers, advisors, courtiers, and other administrators. Ibn al-Muqaffa's advice is very practical and is as applicable today as it was to the rulers in his audience. He advised princes not to succumb to flattery, to cultivate the companionship of "moral" persons, and seek advice from qualified people. He asks those in the service of the prince to respect him as one would respect a father. He discourses on the relations between friends and emphasizes the sacrifice of one friend for another. His counsel on maintaining good physical health is apt for today's world: to be moderate in eating, drinking, and sex.

Ibn al-Muqaffa wrote other prose works dealing with rule, authority, law, ignorance, and knowledge. Many of the writings are aphoristic and attest to his wisdom and meticulous attention to language. On the basis of language alone, none of his works could be considered minor. Ibn al-Muqaffa used every known device from the classical school, some of which were complex. The descriptions of many of these devices alone would fully occupy a grammarian in explaining them: for example, one device is known as an "alliterative quasi-anaphoristic repetition."[33]

Of all the literary works from this early literary period, the most popular and most famous work is, of course, *Alf Laylah wa Laylah* (*A Thousand and One Nights*), also known as *The Arabian Nights*. This splendid collection of stories exists in Syrian and Egyptian editions. The Syrian edition is considered authentic, recently and painstakingly shaped into a definitive version by Muhsin Mahdi, from which came the first, most readable modern English translation by Husain Haddawy. The Egyptian version contains too many deletions, modifications, additions, anecdotes, and worse, fabrications, almost all of which considerably disturb the unity and purpose of the earlier Syrian version.[34]

The original work was very important. Many of the stories were translated from the Persian *Hazar Afsana* (Thousand Stories). Almost all references to the *Arabian Nights* mention this source and leave it at that. However, there are also bedouin stories and Arab folk songs, as well as legendary tales from South Arabia presented to the first Umayyad Caliph, Muawiyah. There was an important difference in the old tales added to the *Arabian Nights* in that they became teaching stories for the Muslims. Therefore, although many of the stories were derivative, the final shape was, in Ashtiany's words, "thoroughly Islamicized."[35]

This process affected both the organization of the tales and their deeper meanings. Under Islam, they were no longer recorded simply for their entertainment value. There is great significance in the way the stories are told and how the entire work and many of the individual stories are framed. The primary reason for their telling was to save lives and, hence, an entire nation.

Subtleties escape readers of the stories in translation, although Muhsin Mahdi has clarified some of them. For example, Scheherazade, the name of the narrator of the tales, means "noble race." To assist her in her task, Scheherazade seeks the help of her sister Dinazad. Dinazad means "noble religion," signifying, according to Mahdi, the possession of "a secret wisdom."

In addition, Scheherazade also possesses a "secret knowledge," which is essential for pacifying the king, a knowledge she demonstrates in giving a different interpretation of the story told by her father to deter her from marrying a king who is determined to kill every woman he marries. Her ultimate goal is greater, however. To overcome aggression, personified in the king, Scheherazade uses not counterviolence, but wisdom, encapsulated in the palatable form of the enticing stories she tells.

Each of the stories carries deeper meanings, again clarified by Mahdi. The first story deals with a pious merchant who kills the invisible son of an invisible demon when he throws away date pits. It addresses the dilemma of how far a person is responsible for a murder he commits accidentally. The stories that follow concern ransoming lives, the dangers of lying, delusions, the necessity at times for immediate action, the uses and abuses of power, and using religion to gain political power. One of the early stories depicts the restoration of a kingdom where Muslims, Jews, and Christians live together in harmony.[36]

The richness of *Alf Laylah wa Laylah* is too vast and can only be hinted at here. Like all highly complex works of literature, these *Arabian Nights* delve into the intricacies of life with their attendant moral dilemmas. The stories are filled with the supernatural because of forces in the world beyond ordinary human perception that can be characterized only by metaphor or symbol. The common denominator in all the stories is wisdom. *Alf Laylah wa Laylah* has endured through the centuries. This book is officially banned in many Muslim countries because of its frank descriptions of human bodily functions and sexual intercourse. The English translations are in two versions, one for children and one for adults! This indicates that the Muslim societies were much more open to knowledge than the present ones.

Exceptional Writers and Poets

The Abbasid era was a time of increasing creativity in all areas of human endeavor, reaching heights farther than those accomplished before. Since literature (of which *Alf Laylah wa Laylah* is a specimen) cannot be encompassed in a chapter, the focus here is therefore on exceptional prose writers and poets.

Of these, al-Jahiz (776–c. 869 AC) was an unusual figure early in the Abbasid era. Although he had no formal schooling, he achieved the status of one of the most brilliant masters of Arabic prose.[37] He learned to read at a *madrasah* and after that led what appeared to be an idle life, working at times only to earn a little money, but mostly relying on friends to provide him with food and shelter. All the while, however, he learned from experience and observation, for his quest for knowledge was insatiable. Al-Jahiz was an avid listener at many kinds of discussions all over Basra, especially in and around the mosques. Pellat gives an excellent example of al-Jahiz at work, absorbing knowledge. He listened to philologists questioning the bedouin at the encampment on the outskirts of Basra and then listened with equal attention to the same philologists as they lectured on what they had learned from the bedouin. Among the lecturers, Pellat states, were scholars "who played a key role in the development of Arabic culture."[38]

In spite of this participation in the intellectual milieu, al-Jahiz still maintained relations with his own people, the lower classes, the laborers, artisans, and the "underworld." Hence, when he started to write, he drew on practically every aspect of the life of Basra. The titles of his works more than adequately describe their contents, such as *The Guidebook on the Conduct of Sovereigns*, *The Book of Eloquence and Exposition*, *Questions and Answers on the Subject of Knowledge*, *The Book of Animals*, and *The Book of Misers*. Al-Jahiz is said to have written 231 books, of which only 24 are extant. In one of his works, al-Jahiz lauds the black races as superior to the white, which is aimed, according to Pellat, not at "disparaging" the whites, but "to undermine Persian Shuʿubi pretensions to racial and cultural superiority to the Arabs."[39]

Many of his books must have been popular because he wrote about the people of his milieu, very many of whom were recognized by his readers. One of his stories concerns a judge of Basra, who maintains such a formidable and rigid dignity that he hesitates to use words unless absolutely necessary. From his lofty position, he communicates in sign language until one day, when the court is filled to capacity, a fly lands on his face and crawls all around. He loses his composure and the entire court bursts out laughing.[40]

Another incident must surely have served as the best example of miserliness. A person from Marv always stayed with a hospitable merchant in Basra and at the end of each visit was profuse in his gratitude. At the same time, he wished his host would visit Marv so that he could repay the merchant for all his "kindnesses" and "goodness." Sometime afterward, the merchant was on his way to Marv. It was a long and arduous journey and he looked forward to resting at the home of the person who had been his guest a number of times. When he finally faced his guest, the man gave no sign of recognition. The merchant took off his traveling clothes and, receiving no response, his turban and then his cap. Just then the guest stopped him, saying, "If you were to take off your skin I still wouldn't recognize you."[41]

Al-Jahiz exemplified the *adab* in both style and content. He is rightly considered one of the most outstanding writers of Arabic prose and is especially known for his lucid style. The content of his *adab* works, according to Pellat, fulfill the requirements of all three types of *adab*. The books are aimed, Pellat says, at "the study of manners and morals," for al-Jahiz analyzed the character of all classes of people, sparing none where criticism was necessary. He was consistent in advancing the positive qualities of life, which is why he is one of the prominent voices in the history of early Islamic thinking. Muslim scholars called him "the teacher of reason and polite learning."[42]

An unusual prose work that also continues to be famous is the philosophical allegory by Ibn Tufayl (d. 581/1185), *Ḥayy ibn Yaqẓān* (The Living Son of the Vigilant). The hero is so totally isolated on a deserted island that he does not even know that other human beings exist. The solitary existence has a special significance. It is a demonstration that, left on his own, the Living Son of the Vigilant was "able to develop to the highest level and reach the vision of the Divine… after he has passed through all the states of knowledge, until the universe lies clear before him."[43] If this work appears more philosophical than literary, then it should be remembered that Ibn Tufayl was recognized as a philosopher rather than as a writer.

A prose writer also widely known for his enormous library was al-Sahib ibn Abbad (326/938–385/995). He declared that his collection was so vast it would have required four hundred camels to transport it.

Ibn Abbad was of Iranian origin and became a master of Arabic prose. He came from a pious family and benefited from excellent teachers and eminent scholars. Some well-stocked libraries were at his disposal, although he continued to buy his own books until he amassed his famous collection. He gained his experience at court and on the battlefield with several successes in campaigns on foreign soil. As a vizier, he acquired a wide reputation.

Ibn Abbad's writing encompassed several areas. In addition to poetry, he wrote on theology, history, philology, and literary criticism, and conducted a voluminous correspondence, both official and personal, which ran to thirty volumes according to one authority, or fifteen according to another. Although, like his father, he was interested in traditional religion, he wrote instead on *kalām* (theology). In many of his works, his wit had a sharp, biting edge to it, and he was known to be malicious. In his poetry he, as did many writers of the time, resorted to verbal acrobatics.[44]

Ibn Abbad was noted most for the prose style that marked his "epistle," an exemplary use of language that Tha'alibi, supported by many literary critics, declares to be inimitable. Ibn Abbad was, in fact, regarded as an exemplary writer.[45] Ibn Abbad was also one of the fortunate writers who, having either affluence or political status, needed no patron, since his position as vizier enabled him to write the epistles as part of his job. The next eminent prose writer of the Abbasid period, Abu Hayyan al-Tawhidi (c. 930–1023 AC), was not so fortunate and, later in his life, he had to approach Ibn Abbad for patronage. Al-Tawhidi was largely neglected during his lifetime. Those of his works that have survived run to over 5,000 printed pages and consist of *adab*, polemics, and literary history, as well as calligraphy and Sufism.[46]

Although al-Tawhidi's writings are, in addition to their literary qualities, important to the intellectual history of the period, they are as relevant today as then. He was idealistic, yet, at the same time, realistic enough to realize that the ideals he upheld were not easily achieved. He ascribed idealistic purposes to literature, believing that "the ideal man of letters" could use his writings to resolve the conflicts of state and to help people. Marc Bergé calls him "a Muslim humanist." He practiced what he preached, he treated every person as an individual, whether beggar or vizier.[47]

Al-Tawhidi's writings clearly had a moralistic purpose. In his first book, he attributes his "pearls of wisdom" first to the Qur'an, second to the Sunnah of the Prophet, third to reason, and fourth to experience. His influence on al-Ghazali was considerable. Of particular interest is al-Tawhidi's ordering of the power of the state. The common tendency in those days was to relegate almost total power to the rulers, the ruling classes, and those who supported them, especially the military. Although al-Tawhidi recognized this, nevertheless, he added that rulers should consider the ordinary people as well. Al-Tawhidi gives a most telling example of Ibn Sadan, a vizier, complaining that the ordinary people knew the secrets and the affairs of the rulers, and discussed them in public.

Regarding the lower classes, al-Tawhidi gives reasons for their condition, reasons as valid today as they were then. Their lives are occupied, he stated, with "getting a living and wondering where the next meal is to come from." They were fortunate, al-Tawhidi said, if they got "a rag or two, to cover their nakedness, not to adorn themselves." He emphasized religion as the basis of society and state and, at the same time, regretted there were few pious people. He esteemed learning, although he criticized the contentious among the scholars. He rejected materialism. However, in his analysis of society, he completely ignores military leaders.

Bergé describes al-Tawhidi's last moments. The people around his deathbed insisted he call upon God because of the "terror towards which we are all hastening." He said to them, "You behave as though I were about to go before a soldier or a constable; but I am going to meet a merciful master." Those were his last words.[48]

The *Maqāmāt*

Increasing interest in prose style led to a new form of composition known as the *maqāmāt*.[49] Beeston criticizes modern writers for defining *maqāmāt* as "an assembly." He prefers "standings," because the person who narrated the stories spoke in the literary style known as *sajᶜ*, which was delivered standing.[50] The *maqāmāt* was a kind of writing unlike any other, and its dramatic style was in itself new. The hero was "a witty, unscrupulous vagabond journeying from place to place and supporting himself" with gifts he received for "his impromptu displays of rhetoric, poetry, and learning." These "displays" gave the writer an opportunity to demonstrate his skill in puns, innuendos, ambiguity, *doubles entendres*, and other verbal play. For example, a man approaches the narrator of the *maqāmāt* and says that he has a young man "of yellow paternity" and asks that the narrator provide him with "a yellow bride." The narrator does so. Beeston identifies "the yellow pair" as gold coins. The role of the narrator is to tie together all the stories that happen in different places. The narrator runs into the hero in these places and "reports" what he sees and hears.[51]

Ahmad ibn al-Husayn al-Hamadhani (358–398 /968–1008) invented the *maqāmāt*. Among his innovations were the use of *saj* ͨ, previously the medium of sermons, as a method of narrating stories; the introduction of a fictitious narrator instead of some famous person; and the tacit understanding that he was writing prose fiction. The master of the *maqāmāt* who recognized al-Hamadhani as its originator was Abu Muhammad al-Qasim (446–516/1054–1122), who soon became known as al-Hariri (from *harir*, "silk") because he was engaged in the silk trade. His book is known simply as *Maqāmāt*, as though there was no other similar book ever written. This in itself is a high and well-deserved tribute to al-Hamadhani.

The *Maqāmāt* has been considered since its inception to be next to the Qur'an as a treasure of the Arabic language. Al-Hariri's book is an exemplary demonstration of the basis of the *maqāmāt* in which, as Nicholson notes, "the story is nothing, the style everything." Yet Nicholson goes on to say that the "knaveries" of the major character, Abu Zayd, are pardoned because of his "wit and wisdom." Though these are conveyed in practically every turn of the Arabic language, they are delightfully enhanced by the stories of roguery, artifice, guile, deceit, and other means Abu Zayd uses to gain a living. In short, al-Hariri's *Maqāmāt* defies description. It has been read as entertainment and its text has been included in school curricula.[52]

In a passage later added to the original *Maqāmāt*, al-Hariri gives a list of what is contained in its writing: "language, serious and light…a dignity of style…jewels of eloquence…verses from the Qur'an… choice metaphors…Arab proverbs…grammatical riddles…double meaning of words…discourses and orations…and entertaining jests." Al-Hariri also insisted that his work had "a moral purpose."[53]

Al-Hariri's *Maqāmāt* has delighted readers of all kinds, in the original as well as in translation (the most recent retold in English by Amina Shah). Praise for the work from literary critics has been consistently high. The highest tribute was surely that expressed in verse from the pen of Zamakshari, one of the most prominent interpreters of the Qur'an. The last two lines of the tribute read as follows: "Al-Hariri's *Maqāmāt* is worthy/For each line to be written in gold."[54]

The Abbasid era was a time of abundant prose. In addition to religious and Sufic works, which formed the bulk, there were books on history, geography, travel, philosophy, and biography. The religious works included the most important after the Qur'an – collections of hadiths, the canons of the four schools of law, and the works of Imam al-Ghazali. The most outstanding writers of history were al-Tabari (224–310/839–923) and al-Masudi (d. 345/956). Al-Tabari wrote both religious and historical works. His commentary on the Qur'an is vast and his universal history consists of several volumes.

New Poetry

Also during the Abbasid era there appeared an abundance of poetry best described as new in both content and style. Poets wrote on a much wider range of subjects, their horizons extending not only geographically but also philosophically. The Muslim world had reached the farthest known extents of the hemispheres, as far as China in one direction and Western Europe in the other. Philosophically, there was, above all, the Iranian influence providing a much-needed additional perspective of "another world" and bringing to Arabic poetry, according to Nicholson, "elegance of diction, depth and tenderness of feeling, and a rich store of ideas."[55] Translations from Persian, Greek, and Sanskrit also contributed their influence, and there was the hedonistic nature of the Abbasid court, which knew no limits.

In style, there were new kinds of poems and techniques. The pleasures of the court resulted in the poetry known as *khamriyyah* (from *khamr*, wine) and *tardiyyāt* (hunting). Feeling was given greater expression in the *ghazal* (lyrical poetry, largely devoted to love themes). Two other kinds were directed to the more serious-minded – *zuhd* (a kind of devotional verse) and *badīʿ* (an ornate poetry of mannerism, often filled with conceits).

The *qaṣīdah* (ode) underwent a transformation, too. Badawi writes in distinguishing the old style from the new as "Primary and

Secondary *Qaṣīdah*." His discussion of the differences is worth noting. The primary *qaṣīdah*, he states, had a function in addition to the literary: it encompassed the values of the tribe and was therefore a "ritual," with the poet invariably identifying with the tribe. Its secondary function, on the other hand, was literary, based on "literary experience" with hardly any "self-praise," the poet often singing "the praises of his patron."[56]

Here, too, it is necessary to focus on the following poets who made contributions to their art or whose works achieved high merit: Muti ibn Iyas, Abu Nawas, Abu al-Atahiya, Abu Tammam, al-Mutanabbi, and Abu al-Ala al-Maʿari.

Muti ibn Iyas (d. 787 AC) belongs here for a historical rather than an Islamic reason. That he was a bridge between the Umayyad and the Abbasid eras is not in itself praiseworthy. His accomplishment was that he is recognized as the first of the wine poets of the new school of poetry and that he, together with a companion, brought his wine poetry to Baghdad. He had the reputation of being a profligate in the hedonistic Abbasid court. His poetry, extolling wine and love, has nevertheless been praised for its elegance.

His successor in imbibing, debauchery, and drollery, Abu Nawas (d. 813 AC), achieved far greater fame than any other poet. Abu Nawas is characterized in the *Arabian Nights* as a companion to the Caliph Harun al-Rashid. Although this most hedonistic poet of the Abbasid era had been given a sound religious education, yet he believed, as Nicholson expresses it, "that pleasure was the supreme business of his life."[57] Abu Nawas wrote all kinds of poetry, including hunting poems, *qaṣīdah*s, and love poetry. However, his wine poetry made him widely known and imitated. His drinking songs provide a more than adequate answer to the question one might ask about him: how can anyone write so many poems about a single subject? He wrote about the wine itself, the person who served the wine, drinking companions, singers, and inn keepers. He told stories about drinking. In one of these stories, he and his companions see a comely female wine seller one night. Then, realizing they do not have enough money to pay for the wine, he offers "one of us in pawn." She chooses him and adds that she will keep him a prisoner forever.

Abu Nawas outshone every other poet at the court of Harun al-Rashid and he was the poet of Harun's successor al-Amin. His writing was versatile, ranging in style from satire to song to elegy to ascetic poetry. His innovative alterations to the traditional *qaṣīdah* form were considered, in Schoeler's description, "daring."[58] In his love poetry, there was such a heavy reliance on metaphor that lines upon lines were entirely figurative descriptions.

Abu Nawas is said to have repented toward the end of his life, although some even today question his sincerity. Nicholson believes it to be genuine owing to aging, and quotes a line from Abu Nawas's poetry: "the Devil was sick, the Devil a monk would be." Abu Nawas turned to the writing of *zuhdiyyāt* (ascetic poetry, from *zahada*, "to abstain from gratification"). He spoke against vanity, especially those who considered themselves royal. "Every living man is a mortal," he insists, and "the son of a mortal."[59]

Poet Abu al-Atahiya (748–828 AC) was the opposite of Abu Nawas for most of his life. Early on in his writing career he wrote love and drinking songs, but he soon abandoned the hedonism of the court and lived as an ascetic. Although he was accused of being a free-thinker, he was closer to Islam than many of his contemporary poets. Nicholson describes Abu al-Atahiya's poetry as tending toward the philosophical, for it is filled with melancholy and pessimism. "The world is like a viper," Abu al-Atahiya said, "soft to touch but spitting venom." He believed that the world was transitory and vain and that wealth and pleasure were of no use. His most remarkable skill was, according to Nicholson, the use of plain and ordinary language in his poetry. This tendency matched his egalitarian nature. Men may vaunt "their noble blood," he believed, but no lineage can match "righteous deeds."[60]

His contemporaries did not regard him highly, although this mattered little to him. He saw in the middle and lower classes "religious feelings and beliefs...which led them to take a more earnest and elevated view of life." Abu al-Atahiya felt the need to exhort others, especially in his "Proverb Poem," rendered in rhyming couplets. Schroeder recognizes him as a forerunner of the didactic poem in Arabic.[61]

Another poet who was not lauded by all the critics was Abu Tammam (804–845 AC). Many critics rejected his poetry, most likely because he insisted on following the classic tradition in an age dominated by new poetry. Abu Tammam compiled an anthology, the *Ḥamāsah* [Fortitude], which achieved the status of being one of three principal collections of early Arabic poetry. He composed this anthology during an unplanned, prolonged stay when he was snowbound. He found in his host's library a fine collection of Arabic poetry, a substantial portion of which was of the pre-Islamic desert genre. He was so judicious in his choices that a critic remarked that he was "a better poet in his *Ḥamāsah* than in his poetry."[62] Abu Tammam's objective in putting together the *Ḥamāsah* was to demonstrate "the virtues most highly prized by the Arabs." [63]

Nevertheless, other critics, who appreciated metaphoric language, praised Abu Tammam's poetry. "To give his poetry vigor," Tuetey says, "[a court poet, which Abu Tammam was] will resort to ingenuity in the figurative."[64] Badawi described Abu Tammam's style as "a predominantly archaic, formal, and high-sounding mode of expression." Abu Tammam had a fondness for speaking entirely in metaphor. In one of his poems, he asks the reader to accept "this [pearl] necklace...of art and nature...fashioned by one who is skilled in thought."[65] Here, the necklace symbolizes his poetry. In another poem, beginning with the intriguing statement, "Sword tells more truth than books,"[66] there emerges, despite an overly heavy reliance on metaphoric language, a remarkably vivid picture of the conquest of a city. Abu Tammam's influence was considerable on *badīᶜ* and *rūmiyyāt*, for example, and the use of language. With regard to the latter, Tuetey says, "In effect, Abu Tammam created a manual of style that no poet after him could afford to ignore."[67]

In every era, an author is singled out for the highest praise and is labeled "the greatest." At times, more than one writer receives this designation, for a survey of an era can produce many poets who are described as "the greatest." However, highest praise does belong to two poets of the Abbasid era: al-Mutanabbi and al-Maʿarri. Abu al-Tayyib Ahmad ibn al-Husayn (d. 965 AC), better known as al-Mutanabbi, lived among the bedouin and thus acquired a greater knowledge of the pure Arabic language. He went out in search of patrons until he reached the court of Sayf al-Dawlah in Aleppo. The ruler and the writer had much in common, since both were men of the desert, and had intellectual as well as military interests. In Sayf al-Dawlah, al-Mutanabbi found a hero close to Arab ideals: someone who was at home in the library and in control on the battlefield, for the prince fought side by side with his men. Al-Mutanabbi's admiration of the prince was not just that of an observer, for he also fought in the prince's battles.

The relationship between poet and prince was more than that of patronage, since al-Mutanabbi was genuinely fond of Sayf al-Dawlah. His poetry was of a higher standard while at the royal court than after his departure. However, he was forced to leave, since he had too many rivals and enemies who finally succeeded in turning the prince against him. Al-Mutanabbi again moved from place to place. Later, Sayf al-Dawlah invited him back to his court, but the poet did not return. He and his son were killed while on a journey to Baghdad.

Al-Mutanabbi was a proud person, fully aware of his gifts and his achievements, and boastful about them, although he was known to grovel for coins thrown at him. He was the son of a water-carrier but took pride in proclaiming in one of his poems, "My glory is my own and does not come from my ancestors." He admonished others to "seek glory even if it be in hell, and shed servility even if it be in heaven." In the poems where he lauded himself, he also demonstrated contempt for people.[68] Yet al-Mutanabbi deserved the overwhelming amount of praise he received. Many of his admirers considered him to be divinely inspired, like a prophet, a claim made by the poet himself. Since they were unable to label him as such, they called him *almutanabbī* ("the would-be prophet").

Al-Maʿarri, the other great poet, admitted that he tried to improve on al-Mutanabbi's poems but failed. Al-Thaʿalibi, a critic of the next century, wrote that al-Mutannabi's poetry appealed to both the scholar and the person who read poetry for pleasure. Although al-Thaʿalibi pointed out weaknesses in al-Mutanabbi's poetry, he discussed at length the original features of the poet's style. Nicholson sums up these qualities: "elegant expression, subtle combination of words, fanciful imagery, witty conceits, and a striking use of rhetorical figures." Reiske, Nicholson adds, compares al-Mutanabbi, "a master of...proverbial philosophy," to Euripides because of his moralizing.[69]

According to Tuetey, al-Mutanabbi had "a high sense of honor," which was clearly evident in his poems, especially those addressed to Sayf al-Dawlah. One of these poems, Tuetey states, demonstrates "a standard of conduct that was later to become known in the West as 'chivalry.'" Perhaps it was because al-Mutanabbi expressed so vividly the Arab ideals that many recognized him as "the greatest poet of all."[70]

The other great poet, Abu al-Ala al-Maʿarri (973–1057 AC), shared al-Mutanabbi's contempt for people, though for a very different reason -- because, in Abd al-Rahman's description, the people "were content to hug their chains in sleepy irresponsibility."[71] Statements like this have led critics to doubt al-Maʿarri's faith. That he was bitter, of that there is no doubt. He was blinded at the age of four as a result of small pox and raged against his fate. A line in one of his poems implies that he blamed his father. In another poem, he wishes he had not been born. In his most bitter lines, he declared all men to be evil and, as Nicholson notes, "universal annihilation as the best hope for humanity."[72]

Like most poets of his time, al-Maʿarri went to Baghdad in an effort to make a better living as a court poet. It was an arduous journey for a man of his condition and he wondered whether it would be worth it. Nevertheless, his fame had preceded him. His poems were recited at al-Mansur Mosque and at an academy of poets, and the learned welcomed him. For a person eager to broaden his mind, it was an appropriate time to be in Baghdad. There were religionists and philosophers from many parts of the world there, including Buddhists, Zoroastrians, Jews, and Christians. Though he lived in

Baghdad for just a year and a half, this experience of the world made an enormous difference to his life.

Al-Maʿarri's stay was cut short when he received word that his mother was on her deathbed. However, she died before he arrived home and this added to his bitterness. In his view, no one else equaled her in gentleness and a caring nature. Al-Maʿarri secluded himself, lived as an ascetic, became a vegetarian, and led a life of contemplation and writing poetry. Nevertheless, he was not entirely a recluse, since students came to him regularly, as did visitors from all over the world. The eminent Iranian poet Nasir Khosrow remarked that when he visited, there were over two hundred people there from all over the world to hear al-Maʿarri lecture on poetry.

Al-Maʿarri's major poem, *al-Luzūmiyyāt* (The Unecessary Necessity – the full title of which also refers to the rhyme-scheme), made a great impact, both negative and positive. The primary criticism was that the poem was filled with doubt and despair, and hence, too negative. To the critics the poem also gave the impression that life was meaningless. Nevertheless, seen from another viewpoint, the poem is rich and incisive. It is full of insights of, in Tuetey's words, "a mind passionately in search of truth."[73] Abd al-Rahman sums up al-Maʿarri's works by describing his major poem as follows: "[It embraces] all aspects of his personality, as a very human writer, as a thinker and as a scholar deeply imbued with a feeling for the Arabic language."[74]

Many have also questioned al-Maʿarri's faith in Islam. He knew his religion well, for he had learned the Qur'an from the leading scholars of his town and the Hadith from his father and other leading authorities. He "proved so proficient at the Islamic sciences"[75] that he was sent to Aleppo for further studies there. He never deviated from a strong belief in God, and his self-denial and piety were never in question. What al-Maʿarri did, however, was to criticize the Muslims, which aggravated them, in the same way as justified criticism annoys the Muslims of today. Al-Maʿarri expressed his criticism bluntly in one of his poems. "Praise God and pray," he told the Muslims, "walk not seven but seventy times around the Kaʿbah, but remain impious." He said, "religion [is] bent and abused to serve political ends," and that Islam, as well as other religions, had simply become a social convention. He singled out injustice as "the worst of crimes." If hate had not become "man's natural element," he stated in one of his poems, mosques and churches would have existed side by side.[76]

His poems translated into English read as fresh as most poetry written today:

> I visit the loved ones, sunken in sleep,
> past curtains drawn by the months and the years.

> the harassments of life
> with radiant smile
> outfacing the shadows that at length must win.

And these lines sound as though he were addressing us directly:

> Truth stands pale where the shadows fall
> while falsehood walks the public squares.

> Society's rule is expedience first,
> pride in the trivial, unction in praise.

Although al-Maʿarri might have been bitter at times, yet, he never surrendered to despair. According to Tuetey, he "acted on the high ideal of fairness and tolerance that his poetry so decidedly upholds."[77] He pursued the life of a poet whose goal was the edification of humankind toward improving the lot of all creatures. He was by means of much of his poetry the finest of teachers. "The gist of his moral teaching," von Kremer says, "is to inculcate as the highest and holiest duty a conscientious fulfillment of one's obligations with equal warmth and affection towards all living things."[78]

Women Poets

Although a great many women composed poetry during both the pre-Islam age and the Islamic Empire, nearly all their poems were either of the moment or never recorded. However, some of the poems have survived as a result of anecdotal interest. Maysuna, mentioned in Chapter 8, is noted more for the effectiveness of one of her poems than for her poetry in general. As a queen in the palace of the first Umayyad Caliph, she wrote of her longing to return to the desert and Caliph Muawiyah granted her wish.

Nevertheless, there were women poets whose poetry earned them merit and wide recognition and who are still renowned today. Khansa of Sulaim bridged the pre-Islamic and Islamic eras and also gained the reputation of being the "greatest among the woman-poets of Arabia." Her most famous poem, often recited, is an elegy to her young brother killed in battle. The language is restrained yet moving. Khansa focuses on her brother's generosity – "a heart so quick to command in need" – and honorable death. When she recited her elegy at the annual fair near Makkah, Nabiga (an outstanding poet of the time) gave it the highest compliment. With the advent of Islam, she became a Muslim.[79]

The Umayyad era produced two major women poets: Humaida and Layla al-Akhyaliya. Humaida was the daughter of Ibn Bashir, a governor of Kufa under the first Umayyad Caliph, Muawiyah. She is noted for a poem of biting wit describing her marriage as that of a thoroughbred mare to a mule.[80] Layla al-Akhyaliya achieved greater fame. Her poems and details of her life were published in anthologies, and she was a familiar person at Caliph Abd al-Malik's court. Her most famous poem is an elegy to Tauba, the man she loved, who was killed in battle. Although her father had forced her to marry a disreputable man, she remained in love with Tauba for the rest of her life.[81]

During the Abbasid era, there were more female court poets. It became prestigious for both the Caliph and a woman poet to try to outdo each other in extemporaneously composing a poem. The Caliph usually produced the first line of a couplet and challenged the woman poet to complete it. The subject of the poem, choice of words, the knowledge of the world, the past, literary tradition and form, the witty retort, the rhyme scheme, and the figurative language – all of these were the weapons to be used in the battle. However, it was a battle where there were no winners, where both the contestants were lauded. This pursuit was in keeping with the sophistication and culture of the Abbasid world.

Some of the poems thus composed were recorded as part of history. Both at court and in the world beyond, there were a very few women poets whose exceptional creativity put them in the world of literature and whose poems have survived to this day. The major women poets were Layla, Mahbuba, Fadl, and Wallada, all of whom were identified simply by their first names. Layla was unusual in two respects, for she was prominent in two fields, the military and the literary. Her brother, Walid ibn Tarif, led a force of Kharijites against the skilled commander Yazid's imperial army and was killed in the battle. Layla took her brother's place and led his men in two battles against the enemy until her clan compelled her to relinquish her command. She wrote a eulogy for her brother Walid, though not the usual kind. It was, as Tuetey notes, "in the true bedouin tradition; it illustrates the reverse of imperial glory."[82] In the poem, she urges her people to "rise... against calamity's tide" and foresees death for the "great" enemies.[83]

Both Fadl and Mahbuba were at the court of Caliph Mutawakkil. Fadl was a free spirit in Baghdad, as was evident in her love poetry. Widely known was her love for a Farsi poet, Sa'id ibn Hamid. In fact, they wrote poems to each other. One of Fadl's outstanding poems expressed her longing to see Sa'id when he was on his deathbed. Mahbuba had an added gift of composing songs, which she sang at court and in Baghdad. Najib Ullah describes her tragic life. She loved the Caliph, and when he died, she was so grief-stricken that she abandoned her life of pleasure and mourned him until her own death. This angered the new Caliph and he gave her to a Turkish officer, who freed her on the understanding that she would leave the city. However, she secretly returned to Baghdad and died there "in complete obscurity."[84]

Love of Literature

The Abbasid era was also the time of the greatest number of Sufi poets who wrote in Arabic. They were eminent in both the high quality of their writing and the volume of their output, and they are still considered masters of Sufic poetry as well as Sufism. Among them the following are particularly important: Rabia, Hallaj, Ibn Burd, al-Raqashi, al-Junayd, Ibn Ata', al-Shibli, Abd al-Qadir Jilani, al-Nuri, Dhu al-Nun, al-Nuri, al-Basri, al-Shibli, Imam al-Ghazali, Ibn al-Arabi, Ibn al-Farid, Fakhr al-Din al-Razi, Abu Nuwas, al-Thaꞌalibi, Ibn al-Mutazz, and al-Shushtari.

Since the Caliphs and other men of culture in the capital cities were patrons of writers, most of the literary activities centered on those cities. Baghdad was, during the early years of the Abbasid Caliphate, what London was later to become – the center of literature. (Until the twentieth century, ninety percent of all English literature was written within a sixty-mile radius of London.)

However, soon there emerged other regions of a spreading Islamic civilization. These rapidly became, if not challengers, at least equal to Baghdad in many respects. The influence of Arab culture, language, and literature spread both East and West, resulting in "regional literature" in Arabic. The most notable blossoming took place in al-Andalus in Muslim Spain.

In al-Andalus, the love of literature was strong and its ruler, al-Mutamid, was a striking example. According to Hitti, he "possessed a sensitive and poetic soul." He was a poet himself and chose another poet, Ibn Ammar, as his vizier, so that he could challenge him. Al-Mutamid would compose the first line of a couplet and turn to his vizier to complete it. On one occasion, Ibn Ammar was not quick enough. One evening, when the two were walking beside the River Guadalquivir, al-Mutamid noticed how the wind wrinkled the surface of the water and immediately composed a line, describing the wind as "weaving the waves into mail." He then challenged Ibn Salah al-Din to complete the couplet. While the vizier pondered, a young woman washing clothes close by quickly provided the next line, stating that were the river "but frozen, no knight would it fail." Al-

Mutamid was so impressed with the young woman, Itimad, that he married her, made her his queen, and incorporated her name into his own.[85]

During this period, a skilled love poet called Ibn Zaydun was, in Chejne's words, the best writer in the traditional classic style in al-Andalus.[86] Most of his poems describe his love for Walladah, the daughter of a Caliph and herself a skilled poet. Walladah was a beautiful woman and a free spirit who, after her father's death, opened her home to poets and scholars.[87] Though Ibn Zaydun wrote Walladah a love poem described by many as the most beautiful love poem of the Muslims of Spain, and one of the most famous in general Arabic literature, the two never married.

Another writer, one who gained lasting fame, was Ibn Hazm. According to Hitti, he was "the most original thinker of Spanish Islam," whose criticism targeted kings, poets, and religious authorities. He described rulers as "the enemies of God" and soldiers as "bandits." He went so far as to declare that those people would "worship the cross" if they found it profitable. Ibn Hazm was one of the most prolific writers of Islam, and he is said to have written four hundred volumes on religion, history, tradition, literature, and other subjects. His genealogy of the Arabs is one of the most detailed of its kind. He was a poet, too. His most renowned literary work is *The Dove's Ring*, which Chejne describes as "an essay on love, its nature, and its manifestation in joy and suffering."[88]

Another literary flowering, in the Iranian region, was so magnificent that it deserves a chapter of its own and is therefore the subject of Chapter 12.

12

PERSIAN LITERATURE

IRAN IS THE greatest contributor to the civilization and culture of Islam outside the Arab world. Numerous scholars are included in the histories of Arab civilization because they wrote in Arabic, though they were of Iranian origin. Among them were Ibn Sina, al-Farabi, al-Razi, and al-Biruni. After the revival of the Persian language, a Persian literature emerged that soon achieved a dignity and eminence of its own.

The golden age of Persian literature is, indeed, one of the most remarkable periods in the history of both Iranian and Islamic culture. The works of illustrious poets such as Rumi, Saʿdi, and Hafiz have been translated into numerous languages, including many European, and even reached and were appreciated in North America. Among avid readers of these Persian poets were Goethe, Tennyson, Gibbon, Emerson, and Thoreau.

There was an enormous difference between the literary heritage of the Arabs and that of the Iranians. Although both Arabic and Farsi are rich languages, Arabic was largely oral at the beginning of Islam, whereas Farsi already had an extensive recorded literature, including the epic, a genre that became part of Islamic literature.

The Persian language can be divided into three distinct forms, each corresponding with a historical period. Old Persian lasted until around 300 BC, Middle Persian until the coming of Islam, and Modern Persian followed. Old Persian was already changing even before the Macedonian invasion.[1] Nevertheless, some of the literature of that early period did survive, including the *Avesta*, the sacred book of the Zoroastrians, and inscriptions narrating events in the lives of the kings.

The conquests of Alexander accelerated the change taking place in the Persian language from Old to Middle Persian, also known as Pahlavi, which was a collection of various dialects. Here again, the literary legacy consists of inscriptions, Zoroastrian writings (mostly the commentaries known as *Zand-Avesta*) and, in addition, poetry. These dialects have continued in use since then.[2] In fact, the Iranians, according to Levy, "clung to their accustomed ways of life [throughout Arab rule]. This may explain how they managed to retain the language they spoke basically unchanged."[3]

Nevertheless, the coming of Islam did change the Persian language. The Arabic script replaced the Pahlavi alphabet, with additional consonants for the sounds not found in Arabic. The old script disappeared in Iran but survived in Gujarat, India, where many Parsis (Zoroastrians) from Persia settled and thus preserved the early Persian literature. Arabic also further enriched the already rich Persian vocabulary. According to Aryanpur, "The single most importance influence on the Islamic literature of Iran was (and I should add, still is) the Qur'an."[4]

The Muslim presence, the Abbasids in particular, both borrowed from and contributed to the culture of Iran. The Caliphs began by learning about administration, the treasury, and palaces from the Iranians. Then they acquired knowledge of medicine, philosophy, and the sciences – already discussed in Chapters 8, 9, and 10. A very valuable Iranian contribution, during these early centuries, was the translation into Arabic of works from other languages. In return, the Arabs gave the Iranians part of their vocabulary, the religion of Islam, and their forms of poetry.

The *qaṣīdah* of the Arabs proved to be the dominant early form among the Iranians in its use as a panegyric. When the influence of Baghdad waned, the *qaṣīdah* became common among Iranian poets now writing in Persian. With regard to another Arab poetic form, the *ghazal*, Levy says that the Iranians did not "merely...borrow," they "fashioned...a separate lyric form." The format of the *ghazal* was still maintained.

A third poetic form created by the Iranians was the *rubāʿiyyah* or a quatrain, made famous by the English translations of works by Umar Khayyam. Despite the limitation to four lines, the *rubāʿiyyah* proved to be a vehicle for some of the most profound Persian poetry, and nearly every Persian poet at some time or another wrote in this form. Literary historians point to either of two poets as the first to introduce the form into popular use: Abu Shukur of Balkh or the Sufi Abu Saʿid. Abu Saʿid used the quatrain to express mystical thoughts. Since these were not easy to convey, he relied much more heavily on metaphors, a custom followed by virtually all of the subsequent Sufi poets.

Another Iranian form was the far more extensive *mathnavi*, consisting of a series of two lines connected by a rhyme, which Levy describes as a "doublet." Other than the metrics and rhyming required in the "doublet," there were no other restrictions on the *mathnavi*. Some works in this form extend into thousands of lines. The *mathnavi*, Levy states, is "regarded by Persians as embodying some of the masterpieces of their literature." The most famous of them is by Rumi, known simply as the *Mathnavi*.[5]

The earliest Iranian writings after the coming of Islam were entirely in prose and in Arabic. These were government documents dealing with the land and taxation, and they became of historical interest in later years. The compilers proceeded to write about related topics, mainly about the people. Some of this material eventually acquired a literary merit of its own and as part of other prose writings and poetry, including the epic. The Persian literary prose style was established early during the translations from the Arabic. One writer, Balami, who was a vizier, did not simply translate, but also adapted and skillfully rendered in Persian a work known as Balami's *Annals*.

Nevertheless, Farsi (Persian) proved to be of greater value as the language of poetry and therefore dominated the golden age of Persian literature, with one poet succeeding another during the five hundred years. The high esteem of these poets is demonstrated in their continuing popularity in Iran. In addition to the educated and urban dwellers, villagers recite lines from the poems of, for example, Hafiz and Jami.

The first to gain prominence as a Persian poet was Rudaki, who was blind. He achieved fame as the translator of the collection of fables from India known as *Kalilah wa Dimnah*. His poetry was excellent, enhanced considerably when, as a skilled singer and musician, he sang his compositions and accompanied his singing on the lute. He demonstrated these exceptional qualities during an incident concerning Amir Nasr, a ruler and Rudaki's patron. Amir Nasr had established a routine, traveling all over his realm in the spring and summer, and then returning to his capital, Bukhara. During one of these journeys, he became enamored with the city of Herat and lingered there as though he had no intention of returning to Bukhara. However, his retinue longed for home, so the captains of the army and the courtiers approached Rudaki. He composed a *qasidah* and the next morning sang it to Amir Nasr, lauding the charms of Bukhara. Amir Nasr was so overwhelmed that he rushed to his horse and headed for his capital city. His courtiers had to catch up with him to persuade him to put on his riding boots.

Later readers are surprised to see such a simple poem accomplishing what it did. Therein lies the genius, its simplicity and the skill with which Rudaki rendered it in song and music. All these skills enabled him to acquire a vast amount of wealth, so much that, according to Aryanpur, he needed four hundred camels to convey his possessions from Herat to Bukhara. Nevertheless, he is said to have spent his later years in poverty.[6]

Rudaki (858–c. 941 AC) was a prolific writer, though the output of 1,300,000 verses attributed to him has been exaggerated.[7] His verses totaled over one hundred thousand distichs.[8] However much Rudaki wrote, little has survived, although it is sufficient to attest to Rudaki's fame as the first major poet of Muslim Iran. Aryanpur sums up the major theme running through Rudaki's poetry: "...man's best strategy in an indifferent universe and in the face of an inevitable death is indifference toward material things." Nevertheless, Aryanpur states, Rudaki is also "deeply devoted" to the "pursuit of happiness." Among the lines Aryanpur quotes, are the following:

> Live happy, happy with the sable eyed
> For the world is naught but wind and dreams.
> Four things there be that ransom mortals from blame:
> Sound body, fair temper, wisdom, and good name.

Rudaki is little known outside Iran.

The other major Persian poets are world renowned. The next eminent poet, Firdausi (935–1020 AC), is famous for his epic, the *Shahnama* (The Book of Kings). It was not the first of its genre, for earlier poets had written similar chronicles. Of these, Abu al-Mu'ayid Balkhi's contribution, published toward the end of the third century AH, "was the most voluminous and authoritative book of its kind."[9] Another, by Abu Mansur, achieved wide popularity, which in turn led to Daqiqi's efforts to compose one. Daqiqi died after writing over a thousand couplets. They were of such exceptional quality that Firdausi quoted them extensively in his own work.

Firdausi devoted thirty years to the *Shahnama* and on that work alone rests his fame. He proved to be a poet worthy of his subject, or, more accurately, subjects, since it covers the lives of Persian rulers and heroes spanning four thousand years from 3600 BC to 651 AC. It is, in essence, the history of Iran before the coming of Islam and can be divided into two parts. The first part consists of the myths and legends of ancient Persia and the second part focuses on its history from the Alexandrian conquest of Dara to the Arab victories over the Sassanians.

The entire work totals around 60,000 couplets and is considered the most outstanding of Persian epics. The first presentable copy comprised seven volumes. Subsequent editions were published as illuminated manuscripts, illustrated with some of the finest Persian miniature paintings.

Firdausi made every attempt to avoid Arabic words and his work is therefore among the first Persian writings, if not the first, consisting almost entirely of Farsi vocabulary. His style, together with that of Rudaki, came to be known as the *Khorassani*, characterized by the use of the "simple, pure...diction" of the Dari dialect.[10]

Although the *Shahnama* has been described as non-Islamic, there is no doubt that, as Aryanpur states, monotheism "pervades" the entire work and that it is "shared" by the heroes. In one of its major themes, too, the epic reflects the Islamic principle that it is the individual's responsibility to avoid evil.[11]

The most tragic and moving episode of the *Shahnama* is the contest between Sohrab, the son, and Rustam, his father; the son leading his mother's people, the Tur, and the father fighting for the Persians. Neither is aware of the relationship, though Sohrab notices a physical similarity between himself and his foe, for he remembers his mother giving him details of Rustam's appearance. This evokes in him a love for Rustam. However, as he later explains to his father, he did not trust his eyes. Nevertheless, when he confronts Rustam, he suggests that the two meet amicably and come to terms. Rustam rejects this offer, suspecting it to be "guile." Father and son wrestle. Sohrab hurls Rustam to the ground and, as is customary, pulls out his dagger to kill Rustam. Rustam succeeds in avoiding death by telling Sohrab that the contest rules give the victory to the person who betters his foe two times out of three. This, Sohrab soon discovers, is a ruse, for Rustam had lied. The next wrestling match ends in victory for Rustam, who does not hesitate in fatally wounding Sohrab. It is then that Rustam identifies himself and Sohrab reveals that he is his son, offering as evidence a jewel that Rustam had given to his mother. "I sought [my father] in love," Sohrab said, "and die of my desire."

It would have been appropriate if the story of Firdausi's own life had been appended to the *Shahnama*, since it is as illuminating as most of the stories he told in his epic. Samarqandi, a later Persian writer, gives the details in his *Char Maqalah* (Four Discourses – on the lives of Persian poets). Firdausi, on completing the *Shahnama*, travels to Ghazna and, with the help of the Prime Minister, presents the seven-volume work to Sultan Mahmud, expecting his patronage in return. However, the Prime Minister has enemies and they influence the Sultan to grant Firdausi a meager amount. The poet is "bitterly disappointed" and gives the money away to a bath attendant and a sherbet seller.

Firdausi, realizing that the Sultan will take this gesture as an insult, flees and eventually settles in Tus. He then writes a scathing satire of a hundred couplets on Sultan Mahmud as a Preface to his epic and presents it to Shahriyar, the ruler of Tabaristan. Shahriyar informs Firdausi that Sultan Mahmud was influenced by others and is therefore not the kind of person depicted in the satire. He then buys the satire from Firdausi for a thousand dirhams a couplet, on the understanding that Firdausi will destroy it and that he will let the *Shahnama* "stand in [Sultan Mahmud's] name." Firdausi agrees and burns the rough draft of the satire.

Years later, the Prime Minister recites to Sultan Mahmud a verse from the *Shahnama* and the Sultan is so impressed that, when he learns that its author is Firdausi, he regrets the inappropriateness of the meager sum of money he has given him. He immediately takes steps to remedy the situation. This delights the Prime Minister, since he has for years made every effort to reinstate Firdausi's reputation.

Sultan Mahmud sends his own camels to carry a gift valued at sixty thousand dinars to Firdausi. As these camels enter through one gate of Tus, the corpse of Firdausi is being carried through another gate. Samarqandi concludes his narrative with what happens next. Sultan Mahmud offers the gift to Firdausi's daughter, but she rejects it. Sultan Mahmud then uses the money to repair a rest-house near Tus.[12] Incidentally, the name Firdausi means "a resident of Paradise."

Umar Khayyam is a good example of how readers can misunderstand a writer because they do not know the cultural background of the author and the text. Khayyam achieved fame in the English-speaking world with the FitzGerald edition of the *Rubāʿiyyah*. Some consider it more FitzGerald than Khayyam. The quatrains were very popular as expressions of, as FitzGerald himself noted, "drink and be merry."[13] Umar Khayyam's *Rubāʿiyyah* is far more complex than that.

One of the major problems in reading Khayyam is that in his homeland he was recognized as a skilled astronomer rather than as a poet. For Khayyam, poetry was more an amusement than a profession.[14] As a result, for a long time his poetry was not published in a single volume and there is still much dispute over how many quatrains he wrote. Early estimates range from 81, in Ali Dashti's estimate, to as high as "a corpus of at least 750."[15]

Another debate revolves around whether Khayyam was a Sufi and hence used the word "wine" in a purely figurative sense, "as a symbol of spiritual exultation." Aryanpur believes Khayyam was not a Sufi because he was "hostile...toward all organized religious bodies" and that in another work (*Noruz-Nameh*) Khayyam wrote, he recommended wine, saying, "Nothing is more beneficial to man's body than wine...."[16] Levy questions whether Umar Khayyam's passage on wine can be attributed to him.[17] The debate has been clouded by the overwhelming popularity of the FitzGerald "edition." Levy makes it clear that Fitzgerald "picked out those [quatrains] which suited his own thesis."[18] Idries Shah in his book, *The Sufis*, on the other hand, discusses and quotes Khayyam to demonstrate that in the original *Rubāʿiyyah* "Omar represents not himself but a school of Sufi philosophy."[19]

Aryanpur summarizes the *Rubāʿiyyah* as a progression of stages in Khayyam's life. It begins with a "rejection of material ends," moves to an erosion of his religious faith, resulting in a "contempt for religion" and a "rebellion against transience," to proclaiming "enjoy what you have," to "looking inward," and then repenting. And yet, Aryanpur states, Khayyam "never denies the existence of God." He, in fact, "renewed" his faith in a "benevolent God," asked forgiveness of Him, and also "guided" others to a similar path. Aryanpur recounts Khayyam's final hours, as described by the poet's son-in-law. Khayyam was studying a book on theology and when he "reached the chapter of the One and the Many," he stopped. He made his last will, prayed, and then did not eat or drink for the remainder of the day. After the last evening prayer, he headed for the mosque and declared, "O God, know that I tried to know Thee as best as I could. Therefore save me, for the knowledge of Thee is like a road toward Thee." He died soon afterward.[20]

Sufic Poetry

Sufic poetry ascended during those years and reached its pinnacle. The forerunners were distinguished Sufis of their time – Nasiri Khusrau, for example – and a few achieved higher reputations among the Sufis. Among these few was Sana‘i, who began writing as a court poet, proclaiming the court's hedonistic pleasures. It was only when he became a Sufi that he wrote much more, all of it so rich that it is still being studied, not only by Sufis but by others as well. He was the first to popularize the writing of *masnavis* and *ghazals* on mystical themes.[21] Sana‘i was a forerunner of the great masters yet to come.[22]

One of the first masters cited by Arberry was Farid al-Din Attar (1145/6–1221 AC), who "persevered in Sana‘i's footsteps all through his long life." Attar became a master of the Sufi allegory and is best known for his allegorical poem, *Manṭiq al-Ṭayr* (Conference of the Birds). A hoopoe represents the spiritual and calls his assembly of birds together to go forth in quest of a King known as the Simurgh, who dwells on Mount Qaf. It is a perilous journey, with the temptations of the material world distracting some of the birds from the quest. The allegory makes clear that "the Royal Road" is not for everyone, especially not for those who give in to "Sloth, Folly, or Deceit." Some of the birds make excuses for not continuing, some die, some are made to abandon the journey. At the end, the remaining thirty birds confront the Mountain filled with Light,[23] "And in the Center of the Glory there / Beheld the figure of Themselves." The significance of this particular goal was emphasized all along, from the title and the beginning of the poem to the end of the journey. The quest was for Simurgh, which in Farsi means thirty birds, the number that reaches the goal, which is the discovery of the Self. The poem is far richer than this summary indicates, for the book is filled with details about the stages, or Valleys in the text, that the Sufis experience on their way to fulfillment.

Attar wrote other allegories, three of them masterpieces of Sufic philosophy. *The Ilahi-nama* (Divine Book), which Attar himself described as a book of "revealed secrets," tells the story of a king whose six sons comply with his request to tell him of their fondest wishes. The wishes all turn out to be solely of the mundane world. The king then teaches them, with a series of anecdotes, the greater value of the spiritual and eternal world.

The second exceptional allegory, *Musibat-nama*, is about the world's grief, though not entirely, however. According to Schimmel, the book focuses on "the development of the human soul on its pilgrimage to God."[24] Its framework is particularly interesting. It is the Ascent of the Prophet through the seven heavens "to the near presence of God." In Attar's book, Arberry states, "the aspiring soul passes through 'forty stations' on its celestial ascent."[25]

The third masterful allegory, *Asrar-nama* (Book of Secrets) is, according to Aryanpur, "a book of poetry dealing with Sufi ideas," and is therefore beyond the scope of a brief summary. It has an additional significance, however, since it is the book that an older Attar gave to a young Rumi and proved considerably influential, which Rumi acknowledges in his own works.[26]

Attar attained the status of being one of the masters of the Sufis. Yet, true to Sufi custom, his outstanding quality was humility, which he demonstrated at the end of his life. Shah describes the incident in his book, *The Sufis*. Attar was well over a hundred years old when Jenghiz Khan invaded Iran. A Mongol took him captive and another offered a thousand pieces of silver for him. Attar made his captor refuse, promising him that there would be a better price. Another person "offered a quantity of straw." Attar said, "Sell me for the straw, for that is all I am worth." The captor was so enraged that he killed Attar.[27]

There is a continuity in Persian literature, as though each poet passed on his pen to a successor. This is true of Nizami as of other poets to come. There is a "continuation" of Sana'i in Nizami, in the telling of anecdotes to point to a moral, in his *Makhzan Asrar* (Treasury of Secrets) and the *Khamsa* (Quintet) or *Panj Ganj* (Five Treasures). However, Nizami is more than a worthy successor to Firdausi in the narrative poems he wrote, which Aryanpur describes as "epical romances."[28]

Iskandar-nama and *Khusrau u Shirin* are two of the stories that Nizami took directly from Firdausi's *Shah-nama*. *Iskandar-nama* tells of the life of Alexander and is divided into two parts: the first narrates his military exploits and the second dwells on the warrior's extraordinary mind, attributing some of it to Aristotle, who is also a character in the poem.

Khusrau u Shirin focuses, as the title makes clear, on two people in love. Khusrau, a Persian emperor, loves Shirin, an Armenian queen. However, Khusrau has a rival in Farhad, a stone-cutter. Shirin is attracted to Farhad and to test his worth, she gives him the task of carving a channel through a mountain. He is on the verge of completion when Khusrau sends him word that Shirin is dead. Immediately on hearing this, Farhad leaps from the mountain to his death. Khusrau courts Shirin and marries her. In the Western tradition, Levy implies, there would be "poetic justice." Nizami is realistic, however. Nevertheless, there was another kind of "justice." Iranians and, later, Indian Muslims felt that Farhad was more deserving of Shirin's heart, since he preferred death to living without her. When they refer to her, they link her name with that of the stone-cutter rather than that of the emperor, and so the story has always been known as *Shirin–Farhad*.[29]

Perhaps this linking was due to an earlier, traditional story of unrequited love, to which Nizami also devoted another narrative poem, *Layla u Majnūn*. By the time Nizami came to write this story, it was widely known in the Arab world, where it originated. Majnūn is not a name but a word meaning someone who has lost his mind. The word aptly describes the condition of the desert poet Qais, who is unable to marry Layla owing to family rivalry and who, nevertheless, is so obsessed with his love that he becomes a wanderer. Layla's father forces her to marry another man. When the husband dies, Layla and Majnūn meet but then drift apart, and Qais spends the remainder of his life wandering in the wilderness. Layla dies soon afterward. In Nizami's hands, the story achieves another dimension, when Zaid, a friend of both, dreams that their "immortal love" has a "mystical significance."

Nizami was a success during his lifetime. He dedicated his poems to various rulers and the rewards from his patrons included a village, five thousand gold coins, and five mules.[30]

Rumi: Islam's Greatest Writer

Most scholars all over the Muslim world agree that Rumi (1207–1273 AC) is Islam's greatest writer. However, he is more than a writer. Aryanpur calls him "the Supreme Mystic" and Schimmel associates him with "Love Triumphant." Shah places him among "the first rank of mystical masters" and says that even Samuel Johnson, though a stern critic, had this to say of Rumi: "He makes plain to the Pilgrim the secrets of the Way of Unity, and unveils the Mysteries of the Path of Eternal Truth."[31] Idries Shah also states that Rumi's writings were known in the distant parts of the world within a hundred years, since Chaucer referred to them in his works. Rumi's *Mathnavi-i Ma'navi* (Poem of Inner Meanings), Levy writes, "is the finest achievement of Persian mysticism."[32]

In one respect, Rumi stands out above others, for he is the Sufi of Celebration. In his life and in his works he celebrated love, the wonders of life and the world, of spring especially when the flowers bloom, the music of the reed pipe, sunshine, and the lifting of the heart, higher and higher. He was fascinated by the entire world, especially human beings and their behavior. He was highly perceptive, taking in a single glance what would otherwise require long and close observation. Rumi also contemplated the world, finding in all its manifestations greater significance than had hitherto been expressed. He is most widely known simply as Moulana, or, Our Master.

He lived at a time when an entire people and a great civilization were being destroyed by the Mongols. Nevertheless, he preserved a highly significant proportion of the essence of that civilization by a close study of the Qur'an, Islam, and his teachers – his father, Hallaj, Sana'i, and Attar among them – and by contemplation and the experience he gained as he traveled through the Muslim world. His family left their home in Balkh to escape the Mongols, a move that proved to be providential. During their sweep through the Muslim world, the Mongols were so destructive that of Balkh nothing was left. Rumi's family traveled to Nishapur, Baghdad, Makkah, and, after the pilgrimage, to Damascus. They finally settled in Konya, Turkey.

Rumi encountered Shamse-Tabriz, who had an enormous influence on his life. Shamse-Tabriz's behavior was extremely unconventional, and even outrageous in the opinion of the people of Konya. Nevertheless, he revealed to Rumi areas of the universe that had been previously beyond Rumi's imagination, and led him to far more profound levels of reaches beyond the mundane world. Shamse-Tabriz also inspired Rumi, as demonstrated in Rumi's lengthy poem written as a tribute to this most unusual teacher. According to Hodgson, in Rumi's devotion to Shamse-Tabriz, he "found a paradigm of his love of God: a participation, on a concrete level, in that free responsiveness to ultimate beauty in which he discovered the meaning of life."[33]

Of all Rumi's works, the richest and the most widely-read is his *Mathnavi,* the poetry of which is among the finest. His imagery is rich, yet clearly stated. There is a rhythm in the *Mathnavi* that matches the music of the reed in the water, a rhythm sustained all through this work, like a gentle stream flowing on and on. There are stories here and stories within stories, strong in their implications. When Rumi interrupts the narratives with a discourse, he goes beyond these implications and discusses the meanings of the stories on sublime levels. Hodgson divides this technique into three levels: "narrative, moral and metaphysical." Rumi is poet, storyteller, moralist, philosopher, and a leader of the mystical quest. To read his works is to know Islam, the Qur'an, and the world in its infinite variety, and also to learn of the range of human behavior.

Rumi's knowledge of people is clearly evident on the narrative level. The stories are entertaining and revealing, from the simple antics of schoolboys convincing their teacher he is not well so that they can have a holiday, to a vizier so devoted to his King that he sacrifices his life to solve for his master a problem otherwise insoluble, to a Caliph debating with Satan.[34] Hodgson singles out the last story as an outstanding example of the metaphysical level of the *Mathnavi.* Satan wakes the Caliph Muawiyah so that he will not miss the dawn prayer. Is Satan performing an act of piety? Muawiyah is immediately suspicious and insists on knowing the reason. A long dialog follows, dealing with questions regarding the role of sinful impulses;

the reason for the existence of sin; whether Satan is, as he declares, not as bad as he is made out to be; whether Satan is a servant of God; if everything is from God, how should a person react to sin; sin and choice; and whether Satan's complaint is valid, "that he has been made a scapegoat for people's own faults." There is far more to the dialog. Satan finally reveals why he has woken the Caliph. Had the Caliph missed the dawn prayer, his regret would have been so deep that it, rather than performing a ritual, would have revealed the great extent of his faith.

No summary can do the *Mathnavi* justice. The literary masterpiece has to be, Hodgson reminds us, directed toward a "complex individual," to be faced throughout that individual's complex life. It is also practical, "a summons to go beyond the routine." Its heroes have to "struggle" with "the inner soul on one side, and the whole cosmos on the other."[35]

The *Mathnavi* has a greater significance on the highest level, which deals with the Sufic experience. According to Shah, Rumi himself explained that his work had "meanings which...have no actual parallel in ordinary human experience."[36] The Sufis travel beyond the ordinary by developing "the basic elements which exist in every human being": love, enlightenment, and "self-work, whereby man becomes perfected." Rumi provides an excellent example of the latter: "Wool, through the presence of a man of knowledge, becomes a carpet." It is the "knowledge" that is of utmost importance. A "stone" to an ordinary man, Rumi said, "is a pearl to the Knower." The *Mathnavi* is of immense value to those venturing on the Path of mysticism, since it illustrates the stages in the Sufi's quest for fulfillment.

Nevertheless, the *Mathnavi* is also a treasure of wisdom for those not on the path, opening up avenues toward a better understanding of human beings and their universe. Understanding is the key word here and the best example comes from Rumi. Two beggars approach a house. One is given bread immediately and departs, while the other is made to wait for quite a while before he is given any. To understand the situation one has to look beneath the surface. The first beggar "was not greatly liked" and was therefore given stale bread. The other beggar "was made to wait" because fresh bread was being baked for him.

It is fitting to end this discussion of Rumi with a story from the first book of the *Mathnavi*, which is a particular favorite of mine. During the time of a most generous Caliph in Baghdad, in an isolated, arid area, a bedouin and his wife argue for days about whether he should journey to Baghdad to take advantage of the Caliph's generosity. The husband yields to his wife's pleas and agrees to go. The next problem is what gift he should take to the Caliph, since they have nothing. The wife suggests the rainwater they had been saving for a special occasion. Their well provides only brackish water and therefore the water they save from sparse rainfall is sweet by comparison.

The bedouin's next concern is to deliver the water safely. Back home, his wife prays that he succeeds in doing so. On reaching Baghdad, her husband is amazed. There are so many people here, most of them dressed in splendid clothes. Although at every turn there is something at which to wonder, at the entrance to the palace, however, there is the even more marvellous sight of petitioners emerging with rich gifts. The guards at the gate "smile" at his gift, yet accept it graciously. The Caliph is exceedingly generous. He fills the bedouin's empty pitcher with gold and adds other gifts. Then he gives orders that the bedouin, who had journeyed over "dry land," be conveyed back by boat along the Tigris.

The bedouin, seeing the vastness of the Tigris and its unceasing flow, bows his head in realization that, despite all this water at his disposal, the Caliph accepted his meager offering and rewarded him so bountifully. Rumi tells the story much more elaborately. The argument between husband and wife is the major portion of the tale, ranging from whether one ought to endure suffering due to poverty, or seek the bounty of the Most Generous, to what kind of a life one should live. Arberry summarizes Rumi's conclusion:

> Know, my son, that this whole world is a
> pitcher filled to the brim with wisdom and beauty.

The world is a single drop of the Tigris of God's
Beauty, which, on account of its fullness, cannot be
contained within any vessel.[37]

There is a great river on which to journey. There is also a need,
through Rumi, to pause every now and then and listen to the melodies
of the reed pipe.

Saʿdi

The other Persian writer as highly acclaimed as Rumi is Saʿdi (1183–
1284 or 1291 AC). Aryanpur states that Saʿdi is considered to be the best
of the Persian poets and one of the most widely read both in Iran and
abroad. Saʿdi is, like Rumi, both a teller of tales as well as a poet.[38]

Mention of Saʿdi here brings back a memory of the 1950s, when I
was in my mid-teens. It was my first encounter with Saʿdi. Cooped up
in a corner of an office, with numerous letters to write and far more
numerous documents to be typed in triplicate, working as many as
ten hours a day for a meager salary, I paused and read Saʿdi.

One of the tales he narrates has remained embedded in my memory over the years. It tells of a pious man who wanders along the
seashore and who is suffering great pain on one side of his body after
having been injured by a tiger. He keeps saying, "Thanks be to God
that I have fallen into ill-luck and not into sin."

Saʿdi himself knew the "seashores" of many a country. He was
born in Shiraz, lived and studied in Baghdad, and then as a Sufi
he journeyed to Syria, Turkey, Arabia, Egypt, and Libya, and,
according to the references in his writings, possibly to Turkestan
and India as well. These travels, too, were in quest of learning and
took up most of his years, after which he returned to Shiraz. There
he continued to live, some say, for the remaining thirty years of
his life, during which he wrote a prodigious number of books. His
fame traveled beyond the lands to which he had journeyed.

Of the numerous books he wrote, he is known especially for his,
in Levy's description, "didactic *mathnavis* of mystical-ethical lore" in
two books, the *Gulistan* (Rose Garden) and the *Bustan* (The Orchard).

Both are written in a lucid, inimitable style and consist of stories where Saʿdi, in narrating them, also explains their moral and ethic implications, and discusses them in the context of his experiences. Most of the stories are told in prose and the remainder in verse.[39]

At the beginning of the *Gulistan*, Saʿdi tells how he came to write it. He and a friend were in a garden and the friend was gathering flowers to take back to his home. Saʿdi said that the flowers would be no more in a few days and that he would offer the world flowers that would always remain fresh. And they continue to be so.

The story from the *Gulistan* most often quoted concerns a sea voyage of a ruler and his retinue. One of the servants had never boarded a boat and he was terrified of the sea. He could not stop trembling and nothing the ruler and the others did helped allay his fear. The king then turned to a "philosopher" on board, who recommended that the servant be thrown overboard and then rescued. From then on the servant was quiet. The philosopher explains, "A man does not appreciate the value of immunity from a misfortune until it has befallen him."[40]

Some of the stories Saʿdi narrates come from his experiences, some of them painful. One story tells of the time he grew "weary" of Damascus and wandered into "the Jerusalem desert," where he was enjoying "the companionship of the beasts" when he was captured by the Crusaders. He and Jewish prisoners were put to work at Tripoli, "digging clay." A leading citizen of Aleppo, who was passing by, saw him and with the payment of ten dinars effected his release. The citizen took Saʿdi to his home, "made" Saʿdi marry his daughter with a dowry of a hundred dinars. She turned out to be "a woman always scowling, disobedient, and growling," and who "made life wholly miserable" for Saʿdi. In a fit of abuse, she asked him whether he was the man her father bought from the Franks. He said, "Yes, I am that man whom he bought back from the Frankish chains for ten dinars, and delivered into your bondage for a hundred dinars."[41]

The *Bustan* was also written as a didactic work as indicated by its ten chapter headings, which include "Wisdom," "Compassion," "Love," and "Humility." This work is different in one major respect, for it begins with Saʿdi's reflections on memories of his early life and the regret that he wasted "bygone days...in foolish ways." Another regret is that he was orphaned as a child and thus deprived of his "father's care."

The *Bustan* has received very high praise. Arberry writes: "The interweaving of popular wisdom with appropriate anecdote is done with great skill."[42] Levy describes it as "facile and often beautiful verse."[43] In the eighteenth century, Arberry says, there was the hope in England that the *Bustan* would be rendered into "a suitably elegant version," but the *Bustan* "defies successful transplantation." Like much of Islamic poetry, it is difficult to translate. The *Bustan*, in particular, has proved one of the most challenging because, in Muhammad Ali Furughi's words, "this book has no like or parallel, either in Persian or in any other language, as regards elegance, eloquence, fluency, delicacy, charm, wisdom, and insight."[44]

Of the writers discussed here, Saʿdi was the most influential in the West. His writings, according to Shah, gave substance to the *Gesta Romanorium*, the source book of many Western legends and allegories. Saʿdi's influence can be found in German literature.[45] In addition, Saʿdi influenced the development of transcendentalism in nineteenth-century America. Emerson, in particular, was highly impressed with Saʿdi, and, in a preface to the first American publication, also stated that Saʿdi's stories and wisdom were already "familiar" to readers from Western writers who neglected to acknowledge their source. Saʿdi, Emerson added, "exhibits perpetual variety of situation and incident" and "depth of experience." Emerson praised the Persians for "their superior intelligence" and singled out Saʿdi as the poet who "inspires in the reader a good hope."[46]

This inspiration is especially evident in Saʿdi's other poems. He wrote a number of *qaṣāʾid*, some of them in Arabic, these odes being the last of their genre as a dominant literary form. Saʿdi wrote more *ghazal*s, which, according to Levy, have not received the attention they deserve. The focus of most of these lyrics is on love and friendship. "Indeed," Archer points out, "so sensitive was [Saʿdi] to friendship that he rated treachery or betrayal as one of the greatest threats to happiness."[47] Saʿdi was one of the two great masters of the *ghazal*.

Hafiz

The other great master was Hafiz (fourteenth century AC). Aryanpur singles him out as "the greatest *ghazal* writer of all time." A story attributes his first exposure to poetry at a clothier's, close to where he was apprenticed as a youth to a baker. The clothier wrote poems and sang them in his shop. So "pleasant" were the poems and the singing that people stopped to listen to him. Among the appreciative audience was Hafiz.[48]

Though orphaned early and apprenticed, Hafiz succeeded in gaining a sound education. As his name indicates, he had memorized the Qur'an and he also wrote interpretations of its sacred text. His poetic career began with the support of a number of rulers. Nevertheless, crises soon intervened and he had to resort to selling his other talent, which was beautiful handwriting. For long periods he was a professional copyist. Then there were the Mongol invasions. One of the subsequent rulers turned Hafiz's sons against him. Fortunately, the ruler was overthrown and his successor was a patron of the arts. However, Hafiz's ready reception at the court was short-lived.

Rival factions continued to wrench control of Shiraz until it was conquered by Timur. The new emperor differed from the previous Mongol conquerors in that he knew Persian and, furthermore, had read Hafiz's poetry. He therefore summoned Hafiz to his court and confronted him with lines he had written about a beautiful woman:

> If that Shirazi Turk would take my heart
> in her hand
> For the mole on her cheek I'd give Bukhara
> and Samarkand

How dare Hafiz offer to give away two great cities, of which Samarkand was the home of Timur, for the mole on the face of a Shirazi Turkish woman? Hafiz said, "It is because of such extravagances that I have fallen into such a bankrupt state." Timur's anger turned to pleasure at such a witty retort and he rewarded the poet.

Hafiz's fame spread as far as Turkestan and Mesopotamia. Rulers in Baghdad and India invited him to visit their courts. Hafiz's reputation was such that lesser poets used his name to sell their own poems or wrote poems that they passed off as the unpublished works of the master. His fame reached beyond Iran, beyond the Muslim world and into Europe. Here, his poems were first translated into Latin and then into English. Then there were succeeding translations of the same poems with nearly every generation because of the changes in the European languages. These translations attest to Hafiz's popularity in Europe and he became an important figure in the continent's literary history. Arberry, in his study of Persian literature, devotes more space to this history of Europe's interest in Hafiz than to the Western history of any other Persian writer. Meanwhile, newer translations of Hafiz have appeared in the West since Arberry.

In Iran, according to Aryanpur, his poetry was considered to be "divinely inspired."[49] It was enriched, too, from his enormous learning. The masters who were his teachers included Sana'i, Rumi, and Saʿdi. His works were filled with religious and historical allusions and he created his own compound words, which increased the difficulty of the translator's task.

Hafiz was especially adept at putting proverbial expressions into other contexts and either using them as allusions or giving them additional significance. Aryanpur gives as an example the use of the proverb, "To hide a drum under a rug" (meaning "the impossibility of concealing certain things"). Hafiz associates the drum with the army and its flag in the following lines: "My heart is overcast with cant and under-the-rug/drums/O happy time when I hoist the flag at the tavern." Aryanpur also points to Hafiz's "ingenious" use of conceits, giving the following excellent example: "Dear am I held among the Magians, for/The fire that never dies in my heart."

His popularity continues among the Iranians and as a result there are more books on Hafiz now being written in Iran than on any other poet. After all, Hafiz wrote a vast amount on the most appealing subject in Persian poetry: love, both human and divine. However, there is far more to Hafiz's poetry than this. Although some of his allusions might be forgotten, nevertheless, Levy states, "it is the music and charm of the verses that have remained."[50]

Among all the poets of Iran, he wrote poetry that makes the most skillful use of the widest varieties of poetic techniques and the handling of words. This was the conclusion of a lengthy in-depth discussion between two eminent twentieth-century authorities of Persian poetry: Qasim Ghani and Mirza Muhammad Qazvini. The two authorities have no hesitation in choosing Hafiz if asked to present only one poet to be honored above the rest. Qazvini quotes Jami as saying that Hafiz's poetry "is something near a miracle."[51]

Jami

Jami himself (1414–1492 AC) belongs to the canon of outstanding Persian poetry. He was recognized as a successor to Sa'di, Nizami, and Hafiz and was considered to be an equally skillful poet. However, Jami was more than a poet. He received his early schooling from his father, who was a learned man, and then he attended one of the best educational institutions of the time, the Nizamiya in Herat, the Timurid capital. He was an exceptional scholar as well as, in Aryanpur's description, "a man of unusually spiritual zeal."[52] This zeal led to his being elected the head of the Naqshabandi order of the Sufis. Babur, the first of the Mughal emperors, said that Jami was "too exalted for there to be any need for praising him."[53]

Jami's reputation was high at the court of Baiqara, the last of the Timurid rulers. The two exchanged letters and Baiqara praised Jami's genius in a book. In addition, Baiqara's vizier, who was also a poet, encouraged Jami and wrote a book on Jami's life and works. Jami's fame extended to a number of other Muslim rulers, including Babur (mentioned above) and Sultan Bayazid II of Turkey.

Jami sought to outdo his predecessors. When his *Kulliyāt* (Collected Poems) was published, it was an enormous tome consisting of poems written during his youth, his mature years, and his old age. Where Nizami wrote five epics, Jami wrote seven. Only when it came to Saʿdi, did Jami prefer a parallel work. Saʿdi's *Gulistan* had eight gardens, so Jami wrote the same number of chapters in a similar work. However, there was a difference between Saʿdi's gardens and those of Jami, for Jami's seventh garden is "a miniature anthology of Persian poets," with the author's "pointed criticisms" of them.[54] Jami also wrote a history of the lives of Sufis.

Jami's book of epics, the *Haft Aurang* (Seven Thrones), is a complex work containing some of his finest writing. The first, *Silsilat al-Dhahab* (The Golden Chain) deals with "ethical, religious and mystical matters."[55] The second, *Salaman u Absal* (Salman and Absal), is "an old romance imbued with mysticism," in which, Arberry says, Jami "took up a philosophical allegory that had not been treated by any previous poet."[56] The third, *Tuhfat al-Aḥrār* (The Gift of Free Men), addressed to his son as part of his education, is primarily a manual of ethics and also "a tribute to all the saints." In a similar vein is the fourth, *Subhat al-Abrār* (The Rosary of the Pious). It, too, is filled with theology, ethics, and mysticism, and illustrated with anecdotes.

The fifth, *Yusuf u Zulaikha* (Joseph and Potiphar's Wife Zuleikha) is a reworking of, in Arberry's words, "a romantic theme...which was a favorite with Persian authors." This story too, like Salman, is "imbued with mysticism." It is, Arberry says, "the most popular of all Jami's works, and deservedly so."[57] This work is enhanced with lucid and hence effective renditions of the poignant episodes, as is his sixth epic, *Layla u Majnūn*, also a retelling of a tragic love story that was already a legend in Arabic literature.

The seventh epic, *Khirad-nama-yi Iskandari* (Wisdom of Alexander) is unlike the others. As Arberry states, it "enabled Jami in the guise of the ancient legend of Alexander to write what is virtually a fourth didactic idyll."[58] Jami's work must be taken as a whole without regard to labels. Therefore, it is a fitting end to a period of remarkable creativity, the golden age of Persian literature. Jami was the last of that age. He died in 1492 AC. From what we know now, it was a year that proved to be of enormous significance in the history of Iran and India, as well as the Muslim world.

Impact on India

By the end of the fifteenth century AC, the Persian language and literature had spread to India and influenced the language and literature of the Muslims living there. This led to the creation of a new Indian language called Urdu. It was not a totally new language however, for it had its beginnings long before the Muslims arrived in India.

With the coming of the Aryans to India, a language developed that later came to be known as Indo-Aryan, consisting mainly of Sanskrit. This language spread across northern India and its regions of local dialects. As with any language, there was further development. into a form that was given a different name, that of *Khari Boli* (Upright Speech).

The earliest language the Muslims brought with them was Arabic, yet the newcomers were not of a sufficient number to maintain it. The next wave of Muslims was from Iran as well as from the North, the former Mongols, who now knew Persian. These Muslims were the ruling power and their language was that used at court and by writers. While Persian dominated as a written language among the Muslims in Delhi, those not connected with the court and the increasing number of new converts to Islam spoke Khari Bholi. Some of this language was included in written records and hence became the first of what was later to be known as Urdu. In fact, Urdu was gradually becoming a distinct language long before it was given its name.

The Mughals created their own civilization and, at the same time, a rich culture. Part of the culture was the continuation of the literary heritage they had brought with them, which in turn led to a new one. With the creation of the Mughal empire came affluence and the extension of patronage to poets from Iran. They came and stayed, and added to Persian literature, though with a difference. The poets refined their style, with a greater emphasis on subtlety, and it became known as the "Indian style" of Persian literature. The most outstanding practitioners of this style was the prolific Bedil.

Delhi was not the only Muslim capital in India, for there were small Muslim kingdoms in the Deccan. Although the rulers there were also patrons of poets from Iran, it was in their courts that the widely spoken Urdu became a literary language. The first major Urdu poet Vali began his career in Deccan and then moved to Delhi and was hence also the first to create an enthusiasm for literature in the "new" language. Political changes helped in its establishment. When Emperor Aurengzeb died, the immense power of the Mughal world died with him, and the empire was fragmented into small kingdoms. A British presence followed soon afterward. Urdu replaced Persian in the literary activities in Muslim courts, and the city of Lucknow, with its wealthy royal and aristocratic patrons, became the center of Urdu poetry.

By then, Urdu was already a common language among the Muslims, and it soon separated itself from the Khari Boli. Although it maintained the Hindi grammar, it adopted the Persian script and the vocabulary was largely Persian and Arabic with some words from Turkish. The Hindus then formed their own language, adopting the Devanagri script of Sanskrit and a large amount of the Sanskrit vocabulary. Among the early Urdu poets, the most outstanding include Sauda, Mir, and Mir Hasan. Sauda preferred the more complex form of the *qaṣīdah* and, since it had been avoided by many poets previously, he accepted it as a challenge to write largely in this form until he was recognized as its master. Most of his poems were focused on two areas. The first was a series exalting the nobility of Delhi. People preferred the second kind, a realistic treatment of his times in satire. Among the objects of his witty and sharply barbed lines were a glutton, a quack doctor, and an old man of ninety years who insisted on marrying a girl in her early teens.

The Persian language and its literature contributed unprecedented treasures to the Islamic tradition of literary arts. Imaginative themes and characters along with important literary styles marked this monumental period of Islamic civilization.

13

THE ARTS

TWO MOST BEAUTIFUL monuments in Spain exemplify the arts of Islam: the Great Mosque of Cordoba and Alhambra in Granada. The most impressive part of the Great Mosque of Cordoba, especially when one enters from the intense Andalusian sun, is the very strong feeling of having entered another world, one of coolness, tranquility, silence, a sense of spirituality, and apparently endless double arches as though extending to infinity. The whole impression is the result of the building's simplicity.

Outside, today, the Islamic architectural features are weather-worn, hence subdued. Inside, however, most of the building is nearly the same as when it was constructed. The interior consists of a multitude of slender pillars balanced by massive double arches. Despite these formidable structures, the atmosphere is one of light airiness, enhanced with a touch of red on the arches.

There is brightness here, too, and more color at the end of one corridor of pillars and arches. This is the location of the qiblah, the direction of prayer toward Makkah, and it is a richly decorated area. The cupola, filled with arabesques, is like the sun. The façade of the prayer niche dazzles, as though with gold. It has a horseshoe arch, with an arc of its own, of both sculptured and painted arabesques. The whole niche is framed, also with sculptured and painted arabesques and Islamic calligraphy in gold and blue. The mosque is so quiet and serene that one is tempted to linger there, sit down on the cool floor, lean against one of the pillars, and contemplate – perhaps about the civilization that created such magnificence.

Alhambra is magnificent, too, though far more complex. From the outside, it presents a formidable aspect, as if built to guard treasures. Inside, the treasures gradually reveal themselves and all their magnificence. If only one place is to be singled out as the epitome of beauty, this, in its tranquil surroundings, is it. Arabesques, geometric designs, and calligraphy adorn the walls, the floors, and the ceilings of room after room – all rendered in the browns, yellows, and reds of the earth, the different greens of plants, and the various blues of the sky.

Everywhere there are arches, all richly and delicately carved, some on slender pillars. Arches beyond arches disclose another elegant room, another region of splendor, or a vista of the surrounding countryside. The only sound and movement come from the fountains. There are pools, too, reflecting the magnificence of Alhambra in the calm of their waters. All the elements – earth, water, air, and the sun – are so exquisitely blended as to render the place a touch of Heaven on Earth.

The Qur'an emphasizes beauty in many places, especially in verse 7:32 – "Who is there to forbid the beauty which God has brought forth for his creatures..?" Later in the Qur'an, God adds that He has created "all the many colors...for you on earth" (16:13) and that He has caused the earth "to bring forth beautiful plants of all kinds" (50:7). Animals are beautiful, too (16:8). God also asks people to beautify themselves (7:31).

The Muslims took the beauty that God provided for them and, in turn, beautified the Qur'an and the mosques, that is, His Book and His houses of worship. They proceeded to beautify their other surroundings. Hodgson sums up the extent to which they succeeded. "[Islam's] visual arts," he says, "include surely the greatest ever known in which the element of sheer visual design could be given priority over all other considerations."[1]

Wherever one travels in the Muslim world today, one is surrounded by beauty great and small, from the rich designs of clothes and decorations of public buildings to the richer calligraphy, intricate geometric designs, arabesques, and especially the designs and calligraphy of the books, both sacred and secular, as described by El-Said and Parman.[2]

Book Illustrations

The extremely high regard Muslims had for books is evident in the way they beautified the texts and enriched them with illumination, using pigments such as pure gold and pure turquoise.

Islamic miniature painting is definitely among the most exquisite arts of the world. As a result, it has been recognized as the Islamic art. If miniature painting is put into a larger context – that of the illuminated manuscript page – a strong case can be made for the elevation of the illuminated work to a position of the highest eminence. It incorporates calligraphy, which was the earliest art of the Muslims, as well the most distinctive Islamic aesthetic form, being the arabesque that includes geometric design.

What is often overlooked is that centuries before they illustrated books, Muslim artists created exquisite pages, which were the earliest illuminated manuscripts of the Qur'an. Title pages especially, and at times the entire text of the Qur'an, were magnificently delineated. This is of such importance to the Muslim world that it will be discussed in further detail below.

It was much later that illumination reached another peak with the finest miniature paintings designated as Persian, Mughal, and Turkish. These were not the first illustrated pages, however. Previously, there were meticulous, realistic pictures overshadowed by the exceptional artistry of the later miniature paintings. The earliest extant illustrated pages were created to inform, rather than convey an aesthetic sense, since they were used in scientific treatises. The oldest pages that have survived were part of a book on astronomy, *The Book of Forms of the Fixed Stars*, by Abd al-Rahman al-Sufi. To help the memory "fix" the positions of the stars, human figures – for example, an archer on horseback – have red dots in appropriate places corresponding to the stars in the night sky.

From that time, scientific works were invariably illustrated. At first, there were texts translated from the Greek. However, the Muslim artists did not merely copy the pictures from the Greek books, for they created their own illustrations. Although there was some Greek and Byzantine influence, the Muslim creations were

different. They were no longer modeled – that is, rendered in light
and shadow to give the figures a three-dimensional effect – but
depicted on a two-dimensional level. Another change took place
owing to an increasing interest in expressing original scientific discoveries in artistic terms. More and more young talented Muslims
offered their services to patrons of learning and, as a result, illustrating books became a profession. This eventually led to painting
as an aesthetic form.

Paintings had been part of the Muslim milieu from long before
the inception of Islam. There was the painting of Mary, the mother
of Jesus, within the Kaʿbah, which the Prophet spared when he destroyed the idols on, within, and around that sacred building. The
painting no longer exists, probably destroyed during a fire.

In the early centuries of Muslim history, paintings adorned the
luxurious surroundings of the palaces of the Caliphs and the homes
of the affluent, for example, the frescoes on the walls at Samarra.
Because many of these works of art portrayed the human figure, care
was taken not to associate them with Islam, so as to prevent any sus-
picion of idolatry. Royalty and the aristocrats extended their thirst
for aesthetic luxury to books, and miniature paintings were created
to meet their demands. This in turn led to another change: the illustrations in the scientific works became stylized and the artists must
have been happy to demonstrate their creative abilities. The *Book of
Antidotes*, for example, had its text illustrated with medicinal plants
as well as depictions of the procedures required to cultivate them.
One page shows the activities on a farm: the cultivators working the
land, a servant bringing them food on a tray balanced on his head,
a donkey transporting a huge bag, a man with a sieve, and another
feeding two cows.

The first true Muslim miniature paintings were produced around
627/1230 to illustrate the *Maqāmāt* of al-Hariri and the Arabic translations of the *Kalīlah wa Dimnah* stories. However, this art form was
not restricted to illustrating imaginative literary works. In the same
century, paintings enhanced al-Mubashshir's book of "philosophical and moral anecdotes" and "a diptych at the beginning" of an

edition of the encyclopedia compiled by the Brethren of Purity. In later years, illustrations accompanied the text of history books. An example is Rashid al-Din's *Universal History*, which is profusely illustrated. However, a distinction must be emphasized here: these are paintings, not the meticulous miniatures of yet later times.

The illustrations in the *Maqāmāt* are remarkably vivid and give a semblance of what life must have been like in al-Hariri's days. They are not exactly realistic, though many of the details are true to life. Most of the faces are round and the only attempt to differentiate between them is in the way their expressions are rendered. This is evident in a painting of two people questioning villagers, in which two camels and their riders, the building, and the mosque in the background are realistically painted. Another painting, showing a prince being enthroned, consists of half-bodies surrounding the prince, who is identified by the goblet he is holding. Incidentally, the *Maqāmāt* had the distinction of becoming the unrivaled bestseller, firstly in the Arab countries and then in the rest of the Muslim world, a position it held until the invention of printing.[3]

Predecessors to Miniatures

Meticulous attention to small details in the other arts preceded the bejeweled miniature paintings. Examples were hammered and incised metalwork, some of which was also inlaid with silver or gold, details in the carpets, perhaps the most widespread and nowadays the most popular of the products of Islamic art, as well as details in ceramics and glassware.

These crafts existed long before Islam, and the Muslims continued the handiwork. More important to this discussion is what the Muslims did with the techniques they learned. A comparison with the arts of pre-Islamic times will demonstrate a major difference in that the Muslims refined the arts.

Carpets, for instance, had existed for over a thousand years before the coming of Islam. However, except for those made of plaited rushes, carpets were restricted to the palaces and homes of the aristocracy. They were decorated with designs, borders, and figures. With Islam came an increase in materials and production as well as in artistry, and carpets were now available to all. The interiors of mosques were soon completely covered with carpets, many of which originated in other parts of the Muslim world. At that time, both palaces and homes contained very few furnishings. Whether it was the residence of the Caliph or a merchant or a shepherd, the only furnishings consisted of carpets and cushions on which to recline.

Nomads especially benefited and carpets became an essential part of their portable household goods. Since they made their own, they now had improved fibers and a wider variety of dyes. The nomads created individual designs, many of which contained quite elaborate emblems, to identify each tribe. The central Asian tribes had similar emblems identifying them as belonging to the Turkmen race, but they were also different in detail, signifying a particular tribe as Tekke or Arsar or one of the eight others related to one another. Giovanni Curatola states that nomadic and semi-nomadic peoples and tribes had a huge impact on the development of Islamic artistic culture, in particular, the development of the carpet.[4]

Huge, profusely illustrated volumes have been written about carpets designated as Oriental, though mostly from the Muslim world. These texts discuss the different weaves, kinds of threads, patterns, and designs as well as their symbolic meanings. There were, for example, three different systems of looping the "knots:" Persian, Turkish, and Arab-Spanish. In addition there were twenty different types of borders. In studying dyes, authorities discovered a special quality in the dyes used almost throughout history, most of them of vegetable or animal origin. These were far superior to the synthetic dyes introduced around the middle of the eighteenth century. The earlier dyes were available in a wider variety of colors and the colors lasted. The synthetic dyes, on the other hand, were inclined to fade quickly. There were also differences in the designs of the carpets, depending on their origin: the Turkish-Caucasian were largely geometric, whereas the Persian were overwhelmingly floral.

The most intriguing and complex feature of the carpets is their symbolism. The significance of some of the symbols has disappeared

because there was no one to record their import when they were created by the designers. Others are difficult to determine, intricately
woven as they are into the overall pattern of the carpet. Nevertheless,
there are universal symbols that can still be identified. The tree, for
example, can be seen as the Tree of Life or the Tree of Paradise or, in
the case of the cypress, as a symbol of renewal and eternal life.[5] The
sun represents light, though in its symbolic context it is either the
light of religion that dispelled the darkness of idolatry or of knowledge that dispelled the darkness of ignorance.

Because carpets were easily portable, they were taken rapidly to
all parts of the Muslim world and thus their designs were carried
to local artists, who, in turn, either copied them or used them as
part of an art work that they created. Oleg Grabar gives a good
example in his book, *The Formation of Islamic Art*. Noting that artists
"[transferred] effects from one technique to [another]," he cites the
mosaics from Khirbat Minyah that borrow from carpet designs "by
the apparent indication of the weaving technique."[6]

The most widespread use of the carpet all over the Muslim world
was the prayer rug. It was one of three important things the Muslims
carried with them when they went traveling (the other two were the
Qur'an and water). The prayer rug identified their region of origin,
demonstrated to the host people the kind of work other Muslims
were doing, and made the designs widely known.

Perhaps the early prayer rugs were of a simple design, although
it was very likely that it consisted either solely or mostly of a rep-
lication of the *miḥrāb*, the niche in the mosque that indicates the
direction of Makkah. The design of the *miḥrāb* design was individual, since it was a semblance of the one in the mosque with which
the designer or the carpet weaver was familiar. This is clearly evident in the rugs woven in Anatolia. There were thirty-two distinct
miḥrāb designs, each identified with a different region. Some regions
had more than one. Konya, for example, had two different designs.
Prayer rugs with *miḥrāb* designs already existed as early as 743/1343–
44, for a miniature painting illustrating a story depicts a rug of this
type.[7]

Other features were added to the prayer rugs, the most common being the border, made up of geometric variations or garden decorations. The latter was a reminder of the gardens of Paradise, since regular prayer was one of the means of reaching them. Another addition was taken directly from the *miḥrāb* on which the artist modeled his design: the lamp hung from the top of the arch of the *miḥrāb*. Here again, the kinds of lamps depicted varied according to their geographical regions of origin. Some designers of the prayer rug had more space to work with below the lamp, so they added a floral decoration to fill it. Other designs were added above the arch, such as illustrations of the Kaʿbah in Makkah, often accompanied by pictures of the Prophet's mosque in Madinah.

At the beginning of the European Renaissance, carpets were among the most desired of products from the Muslim world. The heaviest trade was through the Italian ports of Genoa and Venice. Italy derived an additional benefit from the carpet trade, because when the country started manufacturing its own fabrics, the designers copied the designs of the carpets that had been imported.[8]

In many parts of Europe, the Muslim carpets were appreciated for their rich designs and were included in the paintings produced by some leading European artists. In the foreground of his painting, "Girl Asleep," Jan Vermeer has two carpets that occupy a third of the canvas. In "The French Ambassadors at the English Court," a painting by Hans Holbein the Younger, the ambassadors stand before a table covered with a carpet meticulous in every detail. A place of honor is given to a carpet that has as its most prominent feature "a pseudo-Kufic inscription," for it is placed at the feet of the Virgin Mary in Andrea Mantegna's painting, "Pala di San Zeno." Another honorable placement of a carpet is in Diego Velasquez's painting, "Joseph's Bloody Coat Brought to Jacob": to accept the coat, Jacob steps on a Muslim carpet.[9]

Ceramics and Glass

When defining ceramics, a distinction must be made between two kinds. One kind, better described generically as "pottery," is that which is indigenous to the lands that became Muslim. Pottery is among the most universal of crafts, if not the most universal, and of course it is the earliest. The artistry was demonstrated in the way the pottery, invariably utilitarian, was decorated. This is, incidentally, proof that a propensity for art must have been innate in the human being from the earliest times. The other kind of ceramics is finished with a glaze or luster.

The accepted notion of the glazed Islamic ceramics is that the process was derived from China. Manners, an authority on Chinese ceramics, makes it clear in his *Ceramics Source Book* that this was not so. The Muslims, he writes, "did not adopt the Chinese stoneware and porcelain technologies," but Chinese imports "encouraged them to refine their own materials." He adds: "the most interesting Islamic wares…were derived from their own rich and developing artistic tradition."[10] Muslim artists later contributed to the art of ceramics in China, when the Muslim process of metallic glazing was carried to that country. Both facts – that Muslims developed a process on their own and contributed to China – are supported by Caiger-Smith, who is a professional tin-glaze potter. A display in the Royal Ontario Museum contains this relevant information: "The use of cobalt blue in Islamic pottery played a role in the development of China Blue and White."[11]

The basic technology of glazing already existed before Islamic times: the use of alkaline and lead, and the frit technique enabling the potter to add the glaze. However, the major differences between those early methods and what the Muslims created are like the differences between a bicycle and an automobile. Manners also discusses two most important Islamic contributions to the art of ceramics, important not only for the Muslims, but also for the rest of the world. The first, according to Manners and Caiger-Smith, was the Muslims' "reinvention" of the tin glazing that had been lost. It was the tin glaze that, when introduced to Europe, became one of the dominant techniques of pottery in the West.

The other technique the Muslims created to add luster to ceramics was the use of the metallic glaze. In another book, Caiger-Smith points to areas around Baghdad where this technique was used. An unusual feature of this pottery was that it was multi-colored, whereas later, the lusters consisted of single colors. The metallic lusters became the most widely used in the Muslim world, including Muslim Spain, where they were developed into the Hispano-Moresque tradition.

Muslim luster techniques entered Europe primarily through Spain, though at first via Italy. Italy had been buying this glazed pottery from the Muslim world for three hundred years before it started producing its own. The ceramic plates that Italy bought in abundance from the Muslim world – Egypt and Spain, in particular – were used to decorate the walls of churches. The early Italian word for luster – *majolica* – was derived from the Spanish. From the Muslim world the luster techniques soon spread all across Europe and to other regions as well. "The pottery of Europe...," Manners says, "owes a great debt to Islam."[12]

In the use of glass and rock crystal, too, the Muslims excelled. However, it would be more accurate to say that for centuries, the Muslim world was most likely the only civilization during the Middle Ages to produce glass and rock crystal works of a high artistic quality.[13] The earliest "datable glass object" of the Muslim world was discovered during an excavation of the Fustat area in Egypt. It dates back to 155/772 and is distinctive in that it is decorated with luster painting. It is a bowl-shaped goblet with three borders: the top border consists of Arabic calligraphy, the second is filled with an abstract circular motif, and the third, occupying more than half the space, is floral.[14]

Among the earliest rock crystal objects is a goblet decorated with palmettes, which dates back to the Abbasid era and was produced in Iran. From about the same period and also from Iran, there is a blue glass bowl with similar palmette decorations.

Glass was easier to work with; hence, it was common throughout most of the Muslim world. In addition to its practical applications, it was used as decoration. The Dome of the Rock has mosaics consisting of clear cubes, while palaces were adorned with colored window glass. Size must have also become important in recognizing an art object as an outstanding treasure. A historical report mentions Umm

Hakim, wife of the Umayyad Caliph Hisham, as possessing a "cup of phenomenal size in green glass with a golden handle."[15]

The exquisite glass products were those especially decorated by using two techniques, the most exquisite of which are long-necked glass bottles and mosque lamps. The first of these techniques made use of gold and other attractive metals. The convenient method was to paint the object with a very thin layer of, for example, gold. A more complicated process was to gild the glass either before or after the object was fired. A serving piece, a glass bowl displayed in a museum, though fragmented, retains the golden luster it was given over eight centuries ago.

The other technique, used with or without gold, was enameling. The earliest use of this technique was in Egypt around 80 AH. The most outstanding was the Syrian school, which has never been equaled, especially in the production of enameled lamps for mosques. Some of these mosque lamps still exist and are displayed in museums, the Islamic Art Museum in Cairo having the largest collection. The enamel decoration has the added advantage of being in relief, giving the design an additional dimension. Almost all of the lamps have intricate floral designs interwoven with larger, more prominent Arabic calligraphy of sacred words. These mosque lamps, as well as the enameled glass bottles, are the most artistic glass products of the Middle Ages. No description would ever do them justice, since they have to be seen to be appreciated.

As mentioned in Chapter 6 on Trade, the glassmaking techniques of Syria were revealed to the artisans of Venice, which still profits from what it learned from the Muslim world.

Miniature Paintings

Ultimately, the success of an art work depends on how it affects the viewer, in other words, the pleasure one derives from it. The connoisseur, coming to Muslim art, takes the most delight in the Islamic miniature painting at its finest, as demonstrated in the Persian, Mughal, and Turkish miniatures. In sheer beauty, they match the excellence the Muslims achieved in the other arts.

The outstanding characteristic of the miniature painting is the detail meticulously and exquisitely rendered. I discovered this attention to detail when I made slides of small parts of Persian miniatures and projected them on a screen. One focused on a chess game and it was clearly evident the painter made every attempt to depict the chessmen accurately and did not try simply to convey a semblance. Details of a small part of another painting, enlarged to a width of five feet on the screen, retained much of the distinctness of the original. As anyone who has closely studied painting knows, the details are blurred when they are enlarged. However, this was hardly true of the Islamic miniatures.

It is because the beauty lies in their details that the Metropolitan Museum of Art in New York has made it convenient for visitors to have a closeup view of a group of miniatures. These are framed on a stand a little above waist level and there are chairs where the viewers can sit comfortably and examine the details closely. There was a similar display in an exhibition at a museum in Paris. There were other miniatures on the wall that could be viewed at close range. To appreciate them fully, some French men and women used magnifying glasses that they brought with them.

The miniature paintings are also enhanced because they feature the other Islamic arts, such as buildings (especially the domes and minarets of mosques), calligraphy (definitely among the best), gardens (with an enormous variety of flowers, plants, and trees), carpets (especially their designs), and clothes (in all their splendor). The miniatures of Iran give much more prominence, and hence significance, to architecture than do those of other regions. Most of these features are realistically portrayed, although there is a major difference in how this realism is presented. The miniature paintings in this particular respect are quite distinct from other paintings.

Papadopoulo refers to this distinction when he says that the miniatures are "theocentric rather than anthropocentric." The reference, he makes clear, is "the eye of God, rather than that of man." This enables the artist, he adds, to "show what takes place simultaneously inside and outside a building."[16]

There is therefore a disregard for perspective, since that viewpoint belongs to the observation by a human being. This is why carpets and gardens, for instance, are shown in full from the vantage point of a person looking down on the object. Other objects are not "sized" according to where they are placed. For example, a tree in front might be smaller than one far behind. It depends on what the artist wants to emphasize. In any case, perspective is limiting, because the subject of a painting is restricted to a single point of view. The Muslim artist, in ignoring perspective, is really stating that there are a number of viewpoints, that the earth is immense, and that a work of art should reflect that expanse.

More often the setting is given greater prominence. Take Behzad's "Yusuf Fleeing from Zuleikha" as an illustration of Saʿdi's *Bustan* (The Orchard), for example. Yusuf (Joseph) and Zuleikha (Potiphar's wife) occupy less than one-fifth of the miniature. The remainder depicts the splendor of a palace in richly decorated panels. Most of the designs of these panels are geometric, a few of them are filled with flower motifs, and five have calligraphic inscriptions. Gold is the dominant color, indicating that Yusuf is rejecting, not only temptation, but immense wealth as well. For his act of piety, he is soon imprisoned.

A vast amount of wealth went into the making of many miniatures. Muslim artists were not content with the use of the colors ordinarily available to them and, as a result, they proved to be, in Papadopoulo's words, "exceptional colorists." He singles out the color of Persian miniaturists for his highest praise. Later, when discussing the use of color by Muslim artists, Papadopoulo implies that they anticipated impressionistic techniques. To describe the way the Muslim artist saw the world, Papadopoulo quotes from Gaugin's advice to an artist: "How do you see this tree?" Gauguin asks. "Is it truly green? Then apply green, the most beautiful green on your palette. And this shadow pretty much blue? Don't be afraid to paint it as blue as possible." Referring to the Muslim miniature paintings, Papadopoulo added, "Here then we have pure colors, colored shadows, colors corresponding to the concept and logic of colors."[17]

To enrich their miniature paintings, Muslim artists created brilliant colors. They used abundant amounts of gold and a little less of silver. They powdered precious and semi-precious stones. They made every effort to achieve, in Papadopoulo's description, an "enamel-like sheen." After the miniature painting was complete, the artists went a step further and employed a technique that was the mark of their achievements: they burnished the gold and some of the colors. A selection of the finest examples was displayed at the Sackler Gallery of the Smithsonian Institution in Washington DC: the title of the exhibition aptly described it, "Gold and Lapis Lazuli."

Sound and Music

The Muslims believe that the arts that deserve to be labeled Islamic are "the sacred arts." This is why many Muslims reject labeling the miniature paintings Islamic art, because these works are associated with the luxurious lifestyle of royalty and the very affluent. Many Muslims also reject music as one of the Islamic arts. Some, because the Prophet spoke against it, disdain it altogether. Nevertheless, music has survived almost from the beginning of Islamic times and prevails in every Muslim region, including the Hijaz, where Islam originated.

Two reasons are advanced as to why Muslims have accepted and continue to accept music. One reason is given as a special designation – handasah al-ṣawt (the art of sound) – to distinguish it from other kinds of music. It is certainly a valid designation. The Prophet paid close attention to the quality of the recital of the Qur'an, that is, its "melody." The earliest "music" of the Muslims, going back to the first Caliphs, was vocal. The sound is so important that there were and still are recitals, mostly improvisations, which emphasize the voice alone; there are no words, and at times, no music, either.

There is an extensive body of literature on "the art of sound" in the Muslim world, written by eminent scholars, including the most prominent of Muslim theologians, al-Ghazali. These consist of discussions of theory, sound notations, systems, and instruments, and vocalizations for religious functions. Theory was considered part of the mathematical sciences and among those who wrote about it were philosophers and scientists, for example, al-Kindi, al-Farabi, and Ibn Sina, and the Brethren of Purity. There is a debate about whether the Western system of musical notation came from Muslim sources, since it is almost identical to that described by al-Farabi in his *Book of Music.*

The other reason is that music belongs to local cultures, and since the Muslims did not interfere with the customs of the people they encountered in their expansion, music was left alone. This, too, is a valid reason. The local sound of the music is clearly evident in the traditional kinds of songs and melodies and of instruments indigenous to different regions.

Scholars and others talk nowadays of the music of the Muslim world. The 1976 World of Islam Festival in London included both the music itself and discussions of the music, the musicians, and musical instruments. Jean Jenkins and Poul Rovsing Olsen, authors of the "official" book of the Festival, describe, in addition, "Islamic influences on the Music of the World," including China, India, Japan, and Mongolia. They add that European music owes to the Muslim world "an even larger debt."[18] According to James and Thorpe, Arabs introduced the lute to Europe from Muslim Spain.[19]

Arabic Calligraphy

The "sacred arts" had their beginnings soon after the extension of the first Muslim community.[20] It was also the beginning of Arabic calligraphy, one of the major Islamic arts. "Writing," Giovanni Curatola says, "on a par with architecture, is…the most exalted and important art form in the Muslim world, precisely because it is drawn from the Koran."[21]

The earliest written records of the language are those found on the tombs, as far back as the Nabatean Age. They were carved in stone and the inscriptions appear to have been set down haphazardly. The written language in those days was functional and was rarely used, owing to the lack of writing materials. That was why the earliest style of writing continued to be used for many centuries. Then came

Kufic, named after the city of Kufa, where it was developed. It consists largely of straight lines and angles, and it was the style in which the very early copies of the Qur'an were written, with the only variation being a slanting script.

During the first century AH, the Qur'an also had a script of its own, known as the Nashq script, which was developed in Makkah and Madinah. Curves were added to many characters, the words were quite distinct, the lines were straighter, and more attention was paid to the spacing of the letters and the words. It was beautifully written and thus initiated calligraphy as an art form. That the aim of the calligraphist was aesthetic is clearly evident in some of the copies of the Qur'an that have survived. A most beautiful Kufic Qur'an was produced in North Africa and was written in gold ink on blue vellum.

There was also, during the time of the Prophet, another style that was to become the most widely used. It was the cursive, flowing Naskhi, which had the advantage of being easy to read. A very early example is the letter the Prophet had sent, around the beginning of his ministry, to the ruler of al-Hasa in the Gulf.

In the western region, that is, in North Africa, there was a change in the Kufic script. It followed a pattern in which many of the characters were now cursive, some of the vertical letters were extended above the line and some of the curves extended below the line. As a result, distinctions were made between the Eastern and the Western Kufic.

With the increase in Islamic buildings, the Kufic was much more widely used as a decorative script, perhaps because of the ease with which it could be carved into or out of stone and, later, marble. The beauty of the calligraphy was then enhanced with the addition of flowers, leaves, and branches, thus creating a style that became known as foliated Kufic. With a slight change, that is, with the addition of knots to vertical letters, it was known as the knotted Kufic.

All of this led to the additional use of decorational Kufic on illuminated title pages or the chapter headings in books, especially the Qur'an, even though the rest of the book was in a cursive script. In the borders of carpets, the Kufic script was so intricately incorporated that it was hardly discernible and one had to isolate the calligraphic part to identify the letters. Later, the blending of Kufic elements into the design was done solely for aesthetic reasons.

The Naskhi script became the most widely used because of its fluidity, and it is the script in which most of the copies of the Qur'an are written. It was also the basis of a much wider variety of styles, among the most prominent of which are Thuluth, Muhaqqaq, and Rayhani. These, too, were the scripts of the Qur'an. A highly ornate – or even, affected – style, because of its long downward curves, was called *zulfi arus* or the "bride's lock of hair."

All of the styles were soon used in media other than pen, paper, and buildings; they now included ceramics, metal, fabric, glass, carpets, marble, silver, gold, and concrete. Most of them were inscriptions from the Qur'an, although there were also passages from poetry and, on tombs and other buildings, the names of rulers and other public figures.

In Islamic calligraphy, the focus has been almost entirely on Arabic. One reason is clearly evident in that it is the sacred language of the Qur'an and, therefore, holds the highest position in the languages of the Muslim world. The other reason is given by Titus Burckhardt in his book, *Art of Islam* "It was by the mediation of the Arabic language that the essential Arab genius was effectively communicated to Muslim civilization as a whole."[22]

In some of the non-Muslim countries in the West, where Islamic culture was held in high esteem, Arabic calligraphy was applied purely decoratively. "The characters," Papadopoulo states, "are generally only pseudo-Arabic." Without regard to words or their meanings, the calligraphy adorned, among other items, carpets, and borders of fabric. Arabic calligraphy was also used, according to Papadopoulo, "purely as decoration in Byzantine works, in early Italian paintings, and even on façades of medieval French churches, as at Le Puy."[23] "[E]ven now," James and Thorpe state, "there are silk covers in some churches that bear the Arabic holy text *Lā ilāhah illā Allāh* ('There is no god but God')."[24]

Then, with the adoption of the Arabic alphabet in Iran, another calligraphic style called the Taliq was developed there in the early ninth

century AC. Over a hundred years later, a prominent Tabrizi calligrapher, Mir Ali, combined the Naskhi and the Taliq to produce yet
another style that was as elegant as the latter was lighter. Since the
Muslim rulers of India spoke the Iranian language Farsi, they took
these styles with them to the sub-continent, where they eventually
became the scripts of the Indian Muslim language Urdu.

The first use of calligraphy as an aesthetic part of architecture was
in the Dome of the Rock. The next building to be so beautified was
the mosque of the Prophet in Madinah. The Madinan calligrapher
was Khalid Abu al-Sayyaj, who had gained prominence for his exquisite copies of the Qur'an and of poems and chronicles. On the south
wall of the Prophet's mosque, he inscribed in gold passages from the
Qur'an, beginning with the *ayah*, "By the sun and its splendor," to
the end of the text. From that time, Arabic calligraphy became an integral feature of the mosque, sometimes minimal, when the emphasis was placed on a singular, essential basis of Islam: only one word,
Allah, above the niche for the Imam, because God stands alone and
above everyone. This of course represents the basis of Islam, which
is *tawḥīd* (Unity).

Allah has also been the focus of the most various styles and decorations in Islamic calligraphy. In most of the artwork, it has been
expressed simply by the rendition of beautiful characters, and in other artwork, woven intricately into designs. It has also been the focus
of abstract art, a genre that Islam developed and that the rest of the
world did not fully recognize until over a thousand years later.

The Kufic script lent itself and in fact led to an abstract way of
expressing Unity. Perhaps the most sacred building of Islam, the
Kaʿbah, was an inspiration, since it is a simple cube. The word Allah,
mainly, and /or His attributes, as well as the names of prominent
Muslims, beginning with the Prophet, were made to fit into rectangular shapes. It was also a practical way of rendering calligraphy,
since many of the early mosques were built of brick. Although most
brick minarets were round, nevertheless, the abstract, rectangular
calligraphy proved convenient to apply and was wrapped around
the minaret.

Geometric Design

The genius of the Muslim artists, especially those of the early years of Islamic history, who were its originators, is also strongly reflected in the development of geometric design. This type of decoration is sometimes included in the art form known as the arabesque, though, strictly speaking, the term applies mainly to interwoven floral and plant motifs. I prefer the comprehensive definitions of "arabesque" given in some English dictionaries. *The Random House Dictionary* includes "linear motif," and *The American Heritage Dictionary* "geometric figures," as part of the definition.

Oleg Grabar describes this "form of nonrepresentational decoration" as "uniquely Islamic."[25] The genius is demonstrated in the richness and variety, and especially the significance, with which the arabesque has been invested. It is also clearly evident in the simplicity from which that richness has been derived. Here is just one example of that simplicity.

The artist draws a circle and then around and adjacent to it six more circles. The centers of all the circles are connected with straight lines and the result is a box in the midst of the circles. From there, the artist can draw other squares, triangles, diamonds, and then squares within squares, triangles within triangles, and diamonds within diamonds. Then the artist abstracts a motif that is attached to another, similar, motif, then to another, until an intricate, exquisite design emerges, which, with colors added, is what can be seen on the walls of the Dome of the Rock, Alhambra, and mosques and other buildings all over the Muslim world.

This is one of several methods in the creation of Islamic geometric designs. Another method is based simply on dividing a rectangle into squares and then adding colors to these squares to beautify them. A third method is the placing of numbers within these squares and then lines are drawn from one number to the same number in another square. Still another is based on the arrangement of pentagons. One of the most intricate is derived from the way triangles are linked within a given area.

Although the beginnings of geometric designs are basic, it is clear that the process itself becomes increasingly intricate. This is where the role of creativity is vital, in the interplay of perception and imagination. A vast amount of creativity is required in the selection and isolation of individual sections of the squares, triangles, and diamonds, and in their arrangement. The imagination is also at work in the choice of colors. It is true to say that colors make an enormous difference, for this is clearly evident when a comparison is made of the same design painted in different colors. An example is the interlace patterns on the walls of Alhambra and the same pattern, but rendered in different colors, on the walls of the mosques and other buildings in Morocco.

There is deep spiritual significance to the underlying concept of the geometric designs, as highlighted in a story told by Rumi. A group of Greeks and a group of Chinese confront each other, each proclaiming its superiority in art. The Sultan decides on a contest and the groups are assigned two rooms facing each other, with a door in between. The Chinese keep demanding more and more pigments of all colors, while the Greeks set to work cleaning and polishing the wall. At the end of their efforts, the doorway between the two is removed and the Sultan visits the Chinese first and marvels at the pictures they had painted. However, when he visits the Greeks, he sees the reflections of the Chinese colors on the wall that the Greeks had polished. He is astonished because the reflected colors are enhanced "through an endless variety of shades and hues." "The purity of the mirror," Rumi says, "is beyond doubt the heart which receives innumerable images...impressions from the firmaments and the starry sphere." He adds, "They that burnish [their hearts] have escaped from [mere] scent and color: they behold Beauty at every moment."[26]

The story illustrates and the statements make it clear that Rumi is focusing on the Sufi's mystical experience, which is possible only after the heart is cleared of all the dross of the world. However, he is also talking of inspiration. And is Rumi not himself the best example? It was inspiration, at times bordering on the ecstatic, which enabled him to create his literary masterpieces.

What is being emphasized here is the spirituality of Islamic art. It reflects the universe and the earth and nature, for in addition to the depiction of flowers, trees, and leaves, designs are often taken directly from natural features. Although the artwork might be geometric or abstract, nevertheless, one can recognize in it the faces of, for example, the tulip and the sunflower.

Decoration from the world of plants is often intertwined with calligraphy to enhance the script. Burckhardt believes this to be an "analogy" between two predominant symbols of Islam: "between the 'book of the world' and the 'world tree.'" Burckhardt adds, "The universe is both a revealed book and a tree whose leaves and branches unfold from a single trunk."[27]

Much Islamic geometric art resembles stars. However, the "stars" are not opaqued, but instead, are rendered in outline form so that one can see "through," beyond them, and around them. In Alhambra, for instance, as in many another beautiful Muslim building, the gaze shifts from the patterns on the wall to a fountain close by, to pools of water, lush green vegetation, and, in places, the area beyond – the city of Granada and the mountains surrounding it.

A particularly relevant feature of these designs is that they appear to have neither beginning nor end. It is, in Curatola's description, "the idea of the infinite, as the result of simple, perfectly rational operations." As Papadopoulo expresses it, "one gets…the feeling that this web of the universe continues indefinitely." Papadopoulo also points out that this art is not static, since it is "a kind of cosmos in which the abstract is endowed with that paradoxical attribute – movement."[28]

There is also a special harmony in this artwork, which Burckhardt describes as "a perfect transcription of the laws of rhythm into visual terms." The harmony enhances the serene atmosphere in a mosque. In the artwork, features are either taken directly or abstracted from the natural world. They are then assembled to form a harmonious whole, so that at its best it renders an ordered universe, or at least, a tranquil aspect of it. In that environment, the Muslim can pray or contemplate or meditate with ease.

At times, the observer of Islamic art is not fully aware of the extent to which the work of art reflects the universe and there is, therefore, a need for a much more knowledgeable person to explain it.

Judson, in his book, *The Search for Solutions*, provides a typical and highly significant example. He states that nineteenth-century crystallographers spent decades to produce "thirty-two different types of symmetry that can be seen in crystals." Then a crystallographer visited Alhambra and discovered all these types depicted on the walls. "Taking a theme," Judson writes, "and working out variations, the [Muslim] artists had exhausted the geometry of symmetry."[29]

The intricacies of the arabesque achieved further prominence when they were chiseled or incised into metal, stone, and walls as well as carved out of stone and marble. The outstanding examples are arabesque screens in mosques and other buildings. Most of it is highly delicate work, similar to filigree. How delicate, the British learned with disastrous consequences. There were two stone screens in the mosque of Sidi Said in Ahmedabad, India, depicting a tree with curling stems filled with leaves and flowers. A special feature of this work is that although it looks symmetrical, it is not. The British attempted to remove one to take back to England for display in a museum. It crumbled and the hole had to be filled in. It remains in that state – one half-circle filled with cement and the other filled with a delicate, intricate design exemplifying the beauty of nature.

A special characteristic of Islamic geometrical design is that it invariably has a center. This is uniquely Islamic because Islam is the only religion that has an identifiable geographic spiritual Center, namely, the Ka'bah in Makkah. The rest of the Muslim world is a circle around the Ka'bah, with every Muslim worshiper facing in its direction. Circles of worshipers surround the Ka'bah and the circle widens and widens, until it extends to the farthest reaches of the world. There is no need for the imagination to create this picture. It is possible to climb up one of the hills surrounding Makkah and look down or, for those who cannot or do not want to travel to Makkah, they can look at a photograph taken from a high vantage point of Muslims during the pilgrimage.

One major art form did become part of the center during the Abbasid era, when the custom was introduced of draping the Ka'bah with a black cloth richly embroidered with Arabic calligraphy in gold.

The lettering covers a centered band all around the Kaʿbah and below that band and all four sides are additional panels flanked by medallions. There are also squares of calligraphy at each corner. Much more elaborate is the part covering the doorway into the Kaʿbah, where silver thread is used in addition to the gold. The *Kiswah* (covering) is changed every year and, until recently, was brought from Egypt. It is now made in Makkah. A richly calligraphed panel of the doorway cloth is displayed at the United Nations headquarters in New York.

The presence of a center in Islamic geometrical design is clearly evident in a detailed work by Claude Humbert, an artist and professor of art from Geneva. He traveled to Spain, Syria, Egypt, Tunisia. and especially Morocco (which has a fondness for geometric art – see the massive two-volume *Traditional Islamic Craft in Moroccan Architecture* by André Paccard, which fully illustrates this). Humbert scrutinized buildings and other artwork and isolated 1,001 motifs, which he compiled in his book, *Islamic Ornamental Design*. Readers can examine his illustrations of the geometrical designs and see the center for themselves.[30]

Mosques

The geographical center is what is most significant in the life of the Muslims. It is the mosque, which encompasses all of Islam's other major arts, especially calligraphy and the arabesque. "In Islam everything is important," Curatola writes, "but there is a specific emphasis on the mosque, the house of God."[31] Beautification of the mosque led to similar efforts in the creation of other buildings with amazing results, such as the Dome of the Rock, Alhambra, and the Taj Mahal. Architecture is the art of Islam and deserves recognition accordingly.

As mentioned in Chapter 3, the Prophet's mosque in Madinah was the prototype of all Islamic buildings of worship, the only variation being dictated by direction. The *miḥrāb* (prayer niche) had to face the Kaʿbah in Makkah. This most strictly observed requirement of the mosque was hardly known in the West. Because the Muslims in Europe prayed facing toward the East, this was the direction established in Western minds. It led to misunderstanding during the Crusader occupation of the Holy Land, for when they saw Muslims facing southward, the Crusaders insisted on a change of direction to strictly east, at times enforcing their orders by manhandling the worshipers.

The part of the mosque where the Prophet led the prayers and delivered his sermons was protected. It was built of palm trunks and branches covered with earth, and was formed as a simple square with walls made of mud brick. Other mosques were built in Madinah during the Prophet's lifetime, soon followed by others wherever the Muslims ventured, and although they were more permanent structures, they followed the same basic pattern as the original.

Burckhardt draws attention to the subsequent aesthetic development in the building of mosques. From the very beginning, he says, a completely convincing unity of form "... [maintained] itself over the centuries." Although there might be variations – for example, in West Africa, China, and Indonesia – yet the structure can always be identified as a mosque. What is most notable about this, Burckhardt states, is that such a development and consistency are seemingly without scriptural foundation, while undeniably possessing "a profoundly Islamic character."

The reason is clear. There was very little Arab art that could be labeled as such before Islam. The Muslims initiated their arts by borrowing, mainly from Byzantium, though also from Persia and India. However, what did they borrow and to what extent? Burckhardt emphasizes one aspect overlooked in those discussions of Islamic art that focus primarily on "borrowing": "the arts [of these other countries] remained alien to their vital needs." What the Muslims borrowed were not the arts but the techniques, the craftsmanship.[32]

This is evident during the earliest years of the development of Islamic architecture. Art historians often focus on the first major mosque built by the Umayyads in Damascus and describe its prominent features, especially the mosaic panels, as derived from the Byzantine world. What they ignore is that the Muslims had by then already demonstrated originality in the first major Islamic building, the Dome of the Rock in Jerusalem, completed over a decade before the Mosque of Damascus. Here, too, Byzantine artisans were employed.

Nevertheless, most of the features of the building are distinctly Islamic and hence it is among the finest of Muslim architecture.

Why was the first of the exceptional buildings not a mosque? And why was it built in Jerusalem? The first "mosque" – the Ka'bah in Makkah – was already in existence and was the center of the Muslim world. Nothing was done to embellish it because there was no need to do so. It was and has always been maintained in all its simplicity, with the only decoration confined to the covering. The second mosque – the Prophet's mosque in Madinah – was already being transformed. While the earliest structure, the part where the Prophet is buried, was completely sealed, the rest of the building has been extended over the centuries. The different styles of those who worked on the mosque is reflected in the variation throughout the building in the four minarets, the arches, the calligraphy, and the tiles.

Jerusalem is, of course, after Makkah and Madinah, the third most sacred place in Islam. It has the added distinction of being called simply *al-Quds*, the Holy or the Sacred. It is also for Islam the City of the Prophets to whom the Qur'an refers in various places, including Abraham, Moses, David, Solomon, and Jesus. Their presence is still strong in the city, especially in the area known as the Noble Sanctuary. The Prophet's presence is also associated with this area, for this was where his Night Journey took place. That is why Islam's first mosque outside Arabia was built here, close to where the Dome of the Rock was later erected. This mosque was known as the Masjid al-Aqsa (the Farthest Mosque), the name given to it by the Qur'an. That early structure has since been replaced by the current, bigger mosque.

The Dome of the Rock was so named because the Muslims wanted to cover this particular rock with a dome. The significance of the rock has lasted through the millennia, for it is recognized as the place where Abraham intended to sacrifice his son in response to God's command. If there is one act common to all the prophets, it is that they made sacrifices. That a rock commemorates Abraham's sacrifice is also highly significant, in that their *faith* (emphasis on the singular) has been as firm as a rock and has withstood every assault against it.

The Dome of the Rock is a monument to all the prophets from Abraham to Muhammad, and the Dome is, from the Muslim viewpoint, also extremely important. It was to become one of the two most prominent features of almost all the mosques throughout Islamic history. In the seventh decade after the establishment of the Islamic community, Abd al-Malik, the Ummayad Caliph, requested that a dome be raised over the Rock. A model was built, which still exists across from the Dome of the Rock. The model was named Dome of the Chain after prophet David's "chain of judgment, which could be grasped by the innocent but would evade the touch of the guilty."[33] When the Dome of the Rock was nearing completion, 10,000 gold dinars remained from the amount allocated for the work. The Caliph offered the money to the two overseers of the work, but they refused it. Instead, they added to it family jewels and surplus dinars of their own. All this gold was melted down to gild the entire dome.

The Dome was the creation of the Muslims in another respect, namely, that there was no other similar dome designed before Islam. Although the artisans who worked on the building might have come from Byzantium, the designers and, as the above story about the gold indicates, the overseers were Muslim. For example, one can compare the dome of the Dome of the Rock with those already in existence from before Islamic times. The dome on the Pantheon in Rome, built between 120 and 124 AC, looks like a pyramid of flat discs placed on top of one another. It is as low as the other, more prominent dome on the Hagia Sophia, built in Constantinople between 532 and 536 AC. This dome resembles a quarter of an enormous sphere. It is an attractive dome, and the entire building was a model for Sinan, the architect of Ottoman Turkey, who built many of the outstanding mosques of Istanbul. Sinan did not simply copy, but, according to Glasse, he "[made] of the model a more perfectly geometric form."[34]

The dome of the Dome of the Rock is more rounded and appears to float just above the rest of the building. It must have been a model or an inspiration for all future architects of the Muslim world. The dome became part of virtually every major mosque as well as other Muslim buildings. In some cases it was almost completely spherical. Together with the minaret, the dome is the most widespread characteristic of Muslim cities or communities, for example, Baghdad, Cairo, Isfahan, Istanbul, Lahore, and Delhi.

Almost all domes are exceptional and many of them have their own distinctive features. Because they are made of white marble, the Mughal domes (of the Badshahi mosque in Lahore, for example, and the Taj Mahal) have the appearance of floating pearls, especially in the dusk. Judson chooses the dome of the Masjid-i-Jami in Isfahan as "one of the most beautiful of early Muslim buildings." He also describes the Madrasah-yi-Madar-i-Shah as "lofty, slender, elegant" and "all but transformed into a spire that leaps up into immateriality."

Judson also emphasizes the genius of the Muslim architects who created the dome, a recognition that needs to be more widely known: "...centuries before the necessary mathematics were developed, [the Muslim architect] managed to create a dome of almost perfect proportions. The feat was not equaled in Europe for almost a thousand years."[35] The dome is not predominant, however, in traditional Islamic architecture in al-Andalus and North and West Africa. In addition, many of the mosques of West Africa do not have minarets, just elevated areas from which the call to prayer is made.

The minaret is the other most prominent feature of the exterior of the mosque. The question arises here of whether it was modeled on a church tower. Its origin already existed in the early mosques in Madinah, that is, a place from which to proclaim to the community that it was time for prayers. Those mosques in Madinah had elevated platforms on which a person stood to make the call. Two subsequent events must have led to the realization that height was essential for the call to be an audible reminder that it was time for the obligatory prayers. The first event took place immediately after the Prophet rid the Ka'bah in Makkah of its idols. Bilal, the African Companion to the Prophet, ascended the sacred building and from there voiced the first call to prayer made from the Ka'bah. The second event, which was the expansion of the Muslim community, began soon afterward and continued over the centuries. The minaret was thus created so that the call would reach the ever-widening circle of the faithful.

The earliest true minaret is recognized as the one atop the Mosque of Damascus, built during the first century AH. Its design was possibly derived from a church in the West, perhaps Old St Peter's in Rome, built by Constantine around 326 AC, which had a tower in one corner. Another prominent church tower, that of San Vitale in Ravenna, built by Justinian between 526 and 547 AC, appears to have been added later and looks more like a minaret. The other model for a minaret – the Babylonian *ziggurat* – was short-lived. From it was created the spiral minarets of the mosques of Samarra. The only other place where it was used was in the Ibn Tulun Mosque in Cairo. Art historians agree that this spiral minaret is not in keeping with the splendid architecture of the rest of the building.

Eventually, each region had its individual type of minaret, somewhat easy to identify. In the Maghreb (North Africa west of Egypt) and al-Andalus, the minaret is square, either from the base to the top, or with a low dome as its highest point. The tops of Turkey's minarets resemble sharpened pencils. Those of Egypt, and especially Cairo, have the appearance of an oval bead in a rosary. Iran's minaret is rounded at the top, and that of the Indian subcontinent has a miniature dome.

Whereas some mosques consist mainly of closed areas and others with courtyards open to the sky, all the mosque interiors share certain features. Of these, the two most important are a recessed area in the front, the *miḥrāb*, facing the Kaʿbah in Makkah, where the Imam positions himself when he is leading the prayers; and the *mimbar*, an open pulpit consisting mainly of steps, from where sermons are given.

Also common in most mosques are the other major Islamic arts that are incorporated into their structures: calligraphy, geometric patterns, woodwork, ceramics, glassware, and carpets. Of these, calligraphy is the most significant. In many cases, it is restricted to a single name or a series of names. The single name is, of course, Allah (God). Often, the next is Muhammad, the Messenger of God. In Shiʿite mosques, Ali and his sons Hassan and Hussain dominate. In Sunni mosques, the names of the first three Caliphs – Abu Bakr, Umar, and Uthman – accompany that of the fourth Caliph Ali. The other dominant calligraphic inscription is the *Shahādah* (the declaration of faith): "There is no [other] deity but God and Muhammad is His Messenger." In some mosques and other buildings, entire passages from the Qur'an are inscribed, in places as borders around arches. The calligraphy bordering the entrance to the Taj Mahal has been carefully designed in that the characters are gradually enlarged as they reach the top, so that to a person stationed in front of the building, seeing it whole, all the characters appear to be of the same size.

The next dominant art form in the mosque and other buildings is the arabesque, which ranges from the simple to the highly complex. It could even be said that every kind of arabesque ever created by a Muslim could be found on Muslim buildings, not only on walls and ceilings, but also on domes and minarets. These decorations also reflect the vast communication network of artists and artisans all across the vast Muslim world. A design created, for example, for a building in Muslim Spain was also found, within a few years, on a mosque in Cairo, then in Baghdad, and then in China.

Glass occupied two places in the mosques – as windows and as lamps. Many windows consist of latticework through which the air circulates. A few windows were made of stained glass, invariably following an arabesque design. The mosque lamps, as already mentioned above, are among the finest works of Islamic art.

The floors of nearly every mosque are covered with carpets, usually of the best quality. Here, too, there is a reflection of the far reaches of the Muslim world. Often, especially in the bigger mosques, there are carpets of all kinds, brought to the mosque as contributions from different regions. Mechanization has changed this, however, for there are now lengths of prayer carpets of uniform design. Nevertheless, they serve their function in protecting the faithful from the hardness of a stony surface. And the carpets certainly muffle footsteps, so that every Muslim in a mosque is treading softly.

14

OTTOMAN CONTRIBUTION TO ISLAMIC CIVILIZATION

Art and Architecture

OTHMAN ALI [1]

THE TURKIC PEOPLE, especially the Ottomans, left their imprint on the formation and maturation of Islamic civilization in its later period. This chapter examines the role of the Ottoman Empire and its contribution to Islamic civilization, especially in art and architecture. It aims to shed light on the Ottoman mosque architecture and Ottoman interaction with the Byzantine and European Renaissance in art and architecture. Since most Ottoman achievements and contributions took place between the fourteenth and eighteenth centuries, this chapter will not cover the nineteenth century, when the Ottomans were at the receiving end of the impact of Western civilization.

Pre-Ottoman Turkic Art and Architecture: Seljuks and Emirates (1098–1308 AC)

The grand tradition of Ottoman architecture, established in the sixteenth century, derived from two main sources. One was the rather complex development of new architectural forms that occurred all over Iran, Mesopotamia, Egypt, and Syria. The other was the Anatolian-Byzantine tradition that was formulated under the Seljuks of Rum, especially at Manisa, Iznik, and Bursa, during the fourteenth and early fifteenth centuries. Since the development of art and architecture in non-Anatolian regions has already been described in Chapter 13, this chapter will focus on the Anatolian background to Ottoman art and architecture.

The cultural history of Islam, with its wealth and magnificence, spread like a vast ocean over the countries that constituted the majority of the Old World. The architecture of the Muslim countries developed in the same manner. Its wide variety reflects the difference in natural conditions such as climate, materials yielded by the terrain, historical events, traditions, and innovations. At the same time, its common features allow it to be identified as Islamic architecture.[2]

The Turkish contribution to Islamic architecture starts with the establishment of the Turcoman Emirates. The Karahanids were the first in central Asia to construct a mosque with a central dome and spatial layout, which became a central feature of Islamic architecture. The Muslim Turkish Emirates brought to Islamic architecture many features and innovations that have their roots in the Turkish culture of Central Asia.[3]

The Turkish Muslim dynasties had created a completely new type of minaret, peculiar to the Muslim world. The Central Asian minarets of brick, extremely rich ornamentation, and elegant design were very different from the early Islamic rectangular minarets, related to Mediterranean Christian form. Later in the Seljuk and Ottoman eras, the cylindrical long, thin type of minaret underwent numerous developments and its design spread to the farthest corners of Europe.

In addition to the central court, four *īwānāt*[4] became the standard layout in the Muslim world for Seljuk tombs and caravanseries,[5] and this style was imposed on mosque architecture. The combination of the dome and monumental cubic space was an innovation in the Muslim world. Its most splendid examples are the Seljuk *mesjidi* and *jumas* in the Iranian cities of Isfahan, Zafare, and Ardistan.

Another addition is the tomb that takes the popular form of tomb towers. The transition from block to dome in the Seljuk style, whether in tombs or mosques, gave rise to the creation of new, aesthetic values specific to Islamic architecture. After the conquest of Anatolia, the Seljuks united the newly developed Islamic forms with Anatolian elements of antique or Byzantine origin. This can be seen in the Konia Aladdin Mosque and the Ulu Mosque in Mardin.[6] In addition to the usual mosques, mausoleums, and *madāris*, some buildings called *tekkes* were constructed to accommodate dervishes (members of Sufi fraternities) and other holy men who lived communally. The *tekke* (or *zeviye*) was often joined to a mosque or mausoleum. The entire complex was called a *külliye*. All these buildings continued to develop the domed, central-plan structure constructed by the Seljuks in Anatolia.

In their homeland in Central Asia, the Turks lived in dome-like tents appropriate to their natural surroundings. These tents later influenced Turkish architecture and ornamental arts. When the Seljuks arrived in Iran, they encountered an architecture based on old traditions. Integrating this with elements from their own traditions, the Seljuks produced new types of structures, most notably the *madrasah* or Islamic theological school. The first *madāris*, known as *niẓāmīyyah*, were constructed in the eleventh century by the famous minister Nizam al-Mulk, during the time of the two most influential Seljuk Sultans, Alp Arslan and Malik Shah I. The most important examples are the three government *madāris* in Nishapur, Tus, and Baghdad.

Another aspect of architecture to which the Seljuks contributed is that of the tomb monument. It can be divided into two types: vaults and large dome-like mausoleums. Seljuk buildings generally incorporate brick, while the inner and outer walls are decorated in a material made by mixing marble, powder, lime, and plaster. In typical buildings of the Anatolian Seljuk era, the major construction material was wood, laid horizontally, except alongside windows and doors, where columns were considered more decorative.[7]

Perhaps the *madāris* were originally the houses of the teachers. It was not long before the idea was produced on a monumental scale appropriate to the Seljuk empire, whose needs the new installation was intended to serve. The great vizier Nizam al-Mulk, who was the real leader of the Islamic empire during Malik Shah's reign, realized the unique potential of the *madāris* for training cadres of administration, without which the state could not combat the heresies that menaced its existence. From its inception, indeed, from the first word, Islam (revelation) had the character of a literary and learned civilization. The acquisition of knowledge and its transmission were paramount, and therefore, the *madāris* were the instruments of education in every town and city.

The three-*īwān madrasah* was of a simple design and numerous *madāris* of this type were constructed throughout the Seljuk era. A typical example was the Nizamiya of Baghdad, which was established in 1067 AC. It was based on Shafi'ite jurisprudence and Asharite theology. It had six thousand students, hundreds of professors, both full- and part-time, and an elaborate system of scholarships, grants, and academic disciplines to an advanced level. However, this establishment was eclipsed by the Mustansiriyyah Madrasah, founded in Baghdad in 1234. Of the four-*īwān madrasah*, there were only thirty examples in Baghdad. In addition to the *madāris*, there was the *khanqah* or the Sufi mosque. The Ayyubites built many of these mosques in Egypt. Each had an enormous circular main ceremonial hall for the performance of the dervish dances, spectator galleries on the first floor, and separate galleries for the musicians.[8]

The earliest Anatolian mosques followed the Arab prototypes, and gradually, some of them were influenced by Iranian designs, especially in their free use of *īwānāt* for portals and sanctuary entrances. By the thirteenth century, the single dome was becoming the dominant feature of mosque architecture. During the Seljuk era, a consistent emphasis on the dome as the main architectural feature created the necessary visual unity to achieve the integration of the building with its surroundings.[9]

The Ottoman State

The Ottomans originally came from a Turkic tribe called the Oghuz, which settled in Anatolia in western Turkey during the reign of the Seljuks (1098–1308 AC). This tribe initially organized itself as warriors (*ghāzī*) against the Byzantine Empire, which was largely hostile to

Islam. The Ottomans soon ruled a small military state in western Anatolia by 1300, about the time when the Seljuk state was disintegrating. This small state was in conflict with several other small Muslim states, all fighting one another for territory. By 1400, the Ottomans had managed to extend their influence over much of Anatolia and even into Byzantine territory in Eastern Europe, Macedonia, and Bulgaria. In 1402, the Ottomans moved their capital to Edirne in Europe, where they threatened the last great bastion of the Byzantine Empire, its capital Constantinople. However, the city seemed to defy the great expansion of Islam. No matter how much territory fell to the Muslims, Constantinople resisted every siege and every invasion.[10]

The Ottoman Empire was a world power until the end of the seventeenth century. At its zenith during the sixteen and seventeenth centuries, it spanned three continents, controlling much of southeastern Europe, the Middle East, and North Africa. It stretched from the Strait of Gibraltar (and in 1553, the Atlantic coast of Morocco beyond Gibraltar) in the west to the Caspian Sea and the Gulf in the east. In the north, it was bounded by Austria, Slovakia, and parts of Ukraine, and in the south by Sudan, Eritrea, Somalia, and Yemen. The Ottoman Empire contained 29 provinces, in addition to the tributary principalities of Moldavia, Transylvania, and Wallachia.

The Empire was at the center of interaction between the East and the West for six centuries. In many respects it was a Muslim successor to the earlier Mediterranean empires of Rome and Byzantium. Therefore, the Ottomans regarded themselves as the heirs to both Roman and Muslim traditions, and hence rulers of a "Universal Empire" with the unification of cultures. One can argue that the Ottoman state was, in a manner similar to that of the Abbasid Caliphate in Baghdad, a cosmopolitan empire, a civil state, and very inclusive in its main tendencies. The framework of the state enabled every individual, regardless of race, class, sex, color, and religion, to develop his/her potential and serve the state. This framework was based on numerous ingenious institutions established by the government.

The *millet* system divided the empire into communities based upon religious affiliation. Each *millet* was granted a large measure of autonomy, in which it was ruled by its own religious leader, and was allowed to retain its own laws and customs. The religious leader, in turn, was responsible to the sultan or his representatives for details such as the payment of taxes. There were also organizations that united these diverse groups of people. Particularly important were the guilds of artisans, which often cut across the divisions of religion and location.[11] Therefore, Western scholars, and some modern Turkish scholars, have erroneously labeled the Ottoman Empire as Turkish. This was not so. "If they wished to…unify their empire, the Ottomans had their best chance then. Instead, they welcomed into their empire…" the Jews, and others from different ethnic and religious minorities to be full citizens of their state.[12]

The Ottomans inherited a rich mixture of political traditions from vastly disparate ethnic groups such as the Turks, Persians, Mongols, Mesopotamians, and, of course, Islam. The Ottoman state, like the Turkish, Mongol, and Mesopotamian states, rested on the principle of absolute authority vested in the monarch. The nature of Ottoman autocracy, however, is greatly misunderstood and misinterpreted in the West, particularly in textbooks on world history.

The central function of the ruler or sultan in Ottoman political theory was to guarantee justice (ʿ*adālah* in Arabic) in the land. All authority hinged on the ruler's personal commitment to justice. This idea has both Turco-Persian and Islamic aspects. In Islamic political theory, the model of a just ruler was Solomon in the Hebrew histories (Suleiman is the Arabic version of Solomon). The justice represented by the Solomon-like ruler is distributive, being a system based on fairness and equity, which comes closer to the Western notion of justice. In addition, ʿ*adālah* has Turco-Persian origins in this tradition, for it is the protection of the helpless from the rapacity of corrupt and predatory government. In this sense, justice entails protecting the least powerful members of society, such as the peasantry, from unfair taxation, corrupt magistracy, and inequitable courts.[13]

The primary task of the sultan was to personally protect his people from the excesses of government, such as predatory taxation and the corruption of local officials. For the Ottomans, the ruler could guarantee this level of justice only if he had absolute power. If he was not an absolute ruler, then he would be dependent on others and so subject to corruption. Absolute authority then was at the service of building a just government and laws rather than elevating the ruler above the law, which is how Europeans have interpreted the sultanate.

In addition to their military abilities, the Ottomans had a special talent for organization. Toward the end of the Ottoman Empire, this talent fossilized into a moribund bureaucracy. At the beginning, however, when its institutions were responsive to the needs of the people and the state, the Ottoman Empire was a model of administrative efficiency. This, together with a series of brilliant sultans, culminating in the undoubtable Suleiman the Magnificent, established the foundations of an empire that at its height was comparable to that of the Romans.

Ottoman Economic System as World Model

The Ottoman government deliberately pursued a policy for the development of the successive Ottoman capitals of Bursa, Edirne (Adrianople), and Istanbul into major commercial and industrial centers, for it considered that merchants and artisans were indispensable in creating a new metropolis. To this end, Mehmet II and his successor Bayezid also encouraged and welcomed the immigration of the Jews from many parts of Europe, where they were suffering persecution at the hands of the Christians. These Jewish immigrants settled in Istanbul and other port cities like Salonica.

The tolerance displayed by the Ottomans was welcome to the immigrants. The largest Jewish population in the Empire was in Istanbul, its administrative, financial, and economic center. However, the Jews constituted a much smaller proportion of the total here than in Salonica, where they were in the majority. The Jewish migration from Spain included 36,000 settlers in Istanbul alone. Immigration from Western Europe and from the newly conquered territories of Serbia, Greece, and Iraq brought this number to 56,490. The Ottoman Jewish community was not only the largest, but also the most prosperous in the world during the sixteenth and the early seventeenth centuries.

In addition, Mehmet II wanted his new capital in Constantinople to be the world's biggest economic center. Therefore, he invited the members of the Greek community, who had fled after the conquest, to return and be granted full freedom. Sultan Mehmet told the new Greek Orthodox patriarch of Istanbul, "Be [a] patriarch with a good fortune, and be assured of our friendship, keeping all the privileges that the patriarchs before you enjoyed." The Sultan was eager to see the Greek population not only content but prosperous too.[14] The Ottomans were pioneers in their emphasis on the significance of free world trade. For instance, Sinan Pasha in the second half of the fifteenth century was quoted as advising the Ottoman Sultan: "Look with favor on merchants in the land, always care for them, and let no one harass them, for through their trading the land becomes prosperous." Ottoman capitulation to France had contributed greatly to the growth of European capitalism.[15]

The Ottoman Empire stood between the West and the East, blocking the land route eastward and forcing Spanish and Portuguese navigators to set sail in search of a new route to the Orient. The Empire controlled the spice route once used by Marco Polo. When Christopher Columbus journeyed to America in 1492, the Ottoman Empire was at its zenith, an economic power that extended over three continents. Modern Ottoman studies demonstrate that the change in relations between the Ottomans and Central Europe was caused by the opening of the new sea routes. It is possible to see the decline in significance of the land routes to the East (as Western Europe opened the ocean routes that bypassed the Middle East and Mediterranean) as parallel to the decline of the Ottoman Empire itself.[16]

Ottoman Art and Architecture

Ottoman art and architecture reflected an interesting blending of numerous civilizations: Asian, Persian, Arab, Muslim, and Byzantine. The blend generated vitality and creativity that were uniquely Ottoman. Their language was Turkish, although enriched with sophisticated Persian and Arabic poetic narrative tradition and vocabularies. It also created a privileged class that had no basis in ethnicity, race, or religion. Its members included Arabs, Greeks, Italians, Jews, Slavs, Turks, and others.[17]

The Ottoman religious tolerance and sensibility were similarly reflected in architecture, mosque building, and colleges. Their unique ties to Islam were ever present. Ottoman design, featured on mosque buildings, such as single large domes, tall minarets, and colonnaded courtyards, was derived from Aya Sophia (Hagia Sophia), the greatest of Byzantium's churches. Although Ottoman mosques mimicked the great Eastern Christian traditions, nevertheless, like the Dome of the Rock in Jerusalem, it also portrayed the victory of Islam over Christianity.[18]

In the arts, there is a paucity of extant objects from the early Ottoman period, yet it is apparent from the surviving buildings that Byzantine, Mamluk, and Persian traditions were integrated to form a distinctly Ottoman artistic vocabulary. Significant changes emerged with the establishment of the new capital in former Byzantine Constantinople.

During the Ottoman era, calligraphy as an Islamic art became one of the most important art forms. There was new excellence to achieve with *tugras*, the embellished signatures of the sultans, equivalent to the great seals of European monarchs. The art of calligraphy became so important that it began to pervade every material and surface in Muslim life. Helmets, swords, magical talismanic garments, crockery, and all walls and windows were open to inscription. *Tugras* and the decorative arts had also come under Byzantium influence.[19] The Ottomans and their sultans were particularly interested in the art of calligraphy. The sixteenth-century writer, Mustafa Ali, devoted most of his book *Menakibi Hunerveran* (Tales of Artists) to the calligraphers. His officials in the court were most lavish patrons of the arts.[20] M. Ugur Derman describes the Ottoman contribution in this field: "... it was the good fortune of the Ottoman Turks to be capable of this very interesting art with the painstaking and meticulous labor of Islamic script."[21]

In painting, there emerged a clear-cut Ottoman style from the Herat and other schools, while the designs of ceramics and textiles were the result of influences from China to Byzantine territory. Fabrics, for example, permitted the use of ever bolder and more self-confident displays, producing sun-spanned symbolic robes for ceremonial occasions. These were quite different from the Sassanid and Byzantine eagles, along with the gold-embroidered blue and red of the royal court uniforms. The two great masters, Abdullah and Hafiz Osman, established for this art form an elaborate tradition of purity, simplicity, and harmony, as echoed in the Qur'an.[22] Although large metal objects of the early Islamic period were inspired mostly by Sassanid art, they also revealed the influence of Central Asian. Many of the motifs decorating the metal art of that time originated in Turkish lands.

The palace employed hundreds of artisans known as *ahli hirf* (community of the talented), including partisans, painters, goldsmiths, and bookbinders. The far-reaching role of the designers can be seen in the designs of the large medallion Ushak carpets. The development in Ottoman luxury textiles, many of which were exported to Europe, would have been inconceivable without the active role of the court.

The reign (1520–1566 AC) of Sulayman the Lawgiver at the heart of the sixteenth century was without doubt a golden age for Ottoman literary works and Islamic culture. His greatness was not confined to talent for legislation but also included his appreciation for language. This was an age of great wealth and power, and also a time when one of the most highly developed literary languages in the world was imbued with a sense of spiritual and intellectual mastery. The age of Sulayman was the zenith of Ottoman art and culture.

During the late fifteenth and sixteenth centuries, there were developments in every artistic field, especially architecture, calligraphy, manuscript painting, textiles, and ceramics. Apart from Istanbul, various cities in the provinces were also recognized as major artistic and commercial centers: Iznik for ceramics, Bursa for silks and textiles, Cairo for carpets, and Baghdad for the book arts. Ottoman visual culture left its influence on the different regions of the Empire. Despite local variations, the legacy of sixteenth-century Ottoman artistic tradition can still be seen in monuments from the Balkans to the Caucasus, from Algeria to Baghdad, and from Crimea to Yemen, incorporating characteristic elements such as hemispherical domes, slender pencil-shaped minarets, and enclosed courts with domed porticoes.[23]

The great literary figures of this period include Hayali, Mesut, Latefi, Baki, and Kesfi. These were great poets of mysticism, love, and differences in ethnic backgrounds. Their achievement was similar to that of Sa'di and Hafiz, the two great literary figures in Persian literature. The poets were favored by both the Sultan and the Grand Vizier Ibrahim Pasha, and they achieved wealth and status at court. Thus, the golden age of Sulayman manifests a cultural maturity created from the magic of art, language, building, decoration, and representation of lore and legend.

Byzantine Influence on Ottoman Mosque Architecture

The Ottoman Empire, in a manner similar to the Islamic state that preceded it, paid special attention to mosque building because the mosque continued to play an important part in the Ottoman state and society. Mitchell elegantly points out the significance of the mosque in Muslim societies of the classical period:

> At the center of Islam, both geographically and spiritually, stands the Ka'bah. The *miḥrāb* of every mosque is aligned with it, and to it every Muslim turns to pray, thus the whole of Islam can be seen as a wheel with the spokes radiating from Ka'bah. But as well as this horizontal axis there is a vertical one, that of the spirit. The Muslim world is so read like a gigantic wheel with Makkah as the hub, with lines drawn from all the mosques in the world forming the spikes. These lines converge on a city and within a city on a point. The city is Makkah and the point is the Ka'bah at its center.[24]

The Ottomans achieved the highest level of architecture in their territory. They mastered the technique of building vast inner spaces confined by seemingly weightless yet massive domes, and achieved perfect harmony between inner and outer spaces, as well as light and shadow. Until that time, Islamic religious architecture had consisted of simple buildings with extensive decoration. The Ottomans transformed buildings with a dynamic architectural vocabulary of vaults, domes, semi-domes, and columns. The mosque evolved from a cramped and dark chamber with arabesque-covered walls into a sanctuary of aesthetic and technical balance, refined elegance, and a hint of heavenly transcendence. The Ottomans developed the monumental centralized mosque, covered by a dome and buttressed by semi-domes.

The Sultan Ahmet Mosque in Istanbul was begun in 1609 and finished in 1617. Four minarets flank the sanctuary and two more in the courtyard to the right, though logistically only one was needed. In the foreground are the *madāris* and the mausoleum of the pious young Sultan who labored beside the builders every Friday. Among the most outstanding achievements of this period were the mosques and religious complexes built by Sinan (1492–1588 AC), one of the most celebrated Muslim architects. In the period following Sulayman's death, architectural and artistic activity resumed under patrons from the imperial family and the ruling élite. Hundreds of public buildings were designed and constructed throughout the Ottoman Empire, contributing to the dissemination of Ottoman culture. Commissions continued outside the imperial capital, with many pious foundations established across the realm.[25]

The fall of the city of Constantinople in 1453 marked the beginning of a profound Byzantine influence on Ottoman art and architecture. The influence was credited to Sultan Mehmet II and Sulayman the Magnificent's self-image, world vision, and the pre-existence of numerous religious and secular buildings, Hagia Sophia Church in particular, which the Ottomans had inherited from the Byzantine Empire. There is controversy among scholars on the extent of this impact. Whereas Turkish scholars tend to underestimate the Byzantine archaeological impact on Ottoman architecture, Western scholars tend to exaggerate it.

The conquest by Mehmet II (r. 1451–1481 AC) had given him possession of one of the great cities of the world, and he saw himself not just as the heir of the Caliphs and sultans who had preceded him, but also as the successor to the Byzantine emperors and the heir of Caesar and Alexander. Mehmet II employed Greek painters, collected Greek icons, hired scholars of Greek and Latin to read to him from the classics, and took measures to preserve the city's sanctuary. He also encouraged some Italian artists to work in Istanbul. However, the influence of Western artists on Ottoman art should not be overestimated. In the long term, developments pioneered by the palace workshops and indigenous industries were certainly more significant.

Indeed, Islamic art can be seen as much an heir to the culture of the late classical period as the art of Christendom in the West and that of Byzantium itself. In architecture, the cultural inheritance from Byzantium was of great importance. The *miḥrāb*, or prayer niche, had a forerunner in the use of niches in Byzantine secular architecture. The *minbar*, or Muslim pulpit, probably derived from the Byzantine *ambo*, or lectern, while the *maqṣurah*, a special enclosure in the mosque for the ruler and his entourage, is likely to have been modeled on Byzantine atheism, or the "Royal Box," and the use of the dome as a honorific marker of a holy place was an imitation of the later Byzantine marking of holy places.[26]

To return to the debate between Turkish and Western scholars on the extent of the influence of the great Byzantine monument, Hagia Sophia Church, on Ottoman mosques. Western scholars held the view that most mosques built after the conquest either copied Hagia Sophia Church or borrowed from its architectural ingredients.

After the conquest, Hagia Sophia Church was transformed into an imperial mosque and became a source of inspiration for Ottoman architects. Fatih Mehmet II ("the Conqueror," r. 1444–46, 1451–81) envisaged the city as the center of his growing world empire and began an ambitious rebuilding program. He commissioned two palaces (the Old and the New, later Topkapi palaces) as well as a mosque complex known as the Mehmetiye, later Fatih complex, which combined religious, educational, social, and commercial functions. In his commissions, Mehmet drew from Turkic, Perso-Islamic, and Byzantine artistic repertoires. He was also interested in developments in Western Europe. Ottoman, Iranian, and European artists and scholars flocked to Mehmet's court, making him one of the greatest Renaissance patrons of his time.

Subsequent to the conquest of Constantinople, the architects of mosques commissioned by sultans in Istanbul would engage in dialog with those of Hagia Sophia to focus on shared gemmology and imperial iconography. The building that initiated the dialog was the mosque Mehmet II had commissioned as a part of a broader campaign to revive the former splendor of Constantinople. Kritovoulos, a Greek authority, wrote that the Sultan's new important mosque was meant to rival the city's most famous temples: "The Sultan himself selected the best site in the middle of the city and commanded them to erect a mosque in height, beauty, and size that would compete with the largest and finest temple already existing there." This grandiose complex, which would eventually contain the Sultan's posthumously built domed mausoleum, replaced the celebrated Church of the Holy Apostles, with its adjoining mausoleum housing the body of the city's founder of Constantinople. Sultan Mehmet's complex integrated selected elements from Romano-Byzantine and Italian Renaissance building traditions with an Ottoman architectural vocabulary to fabricate a new imperial idiom. The style had been considered a modern synthesis.[27]

Mehmet's complex was unprecedented in its numerous facilities: eight *madāris* with preparatory schools, an elementary school, library, hospital, hospice, guest house, caravansary, and a bathhouse. The eight *madāris* integrated the ʿulamāʾ into the administrative hierarchy of the centralized state and subordinated them to the Sultan's absolute power. This move may have been inspired partly by the memory of the Byzantine patriarchal college, which was once attached to the Church of the Holy Apostles, sited in the middle of a huge plaza laid out to hold large crowds of pilgrims. With colleges and preparatory schools dedicated to the study of the trivium and quadrivium, this was the foremost education institution of Byzantium.[28]

Mehmet the Conqueror had the Fatih Mosque designed by Sinan and constructed on the ruins of the Church of the Holy Apostles, which had been built by Emperor Constantine. The structure reflects the transition from Byzantine to Ottoman art.[29] The second Ottoman type of mosque used several domes of different sizes. On various scales, the domes had a spacious layout in cruciform, stepped or inverted T-Type. This feature emphasizes increased concentration on the central dome, which is enveloped by vaults on the main axes and diagonals, the whole preceded by a three-domed portico. This combination cannot fail to recall the standard quincunx plan, complete with narthex, of mid-Byzantium churches.[30]

The steady Byzantine influence affected the evolution of Ottoman architecture, even before the capture of Constantinople, an event that brought Ottoman architecture into a new era. Yet it would be grossly mistaken to regard the Ottoman mosques as mere derivatives of Hagia. Before a single dome was flanked by numerous smaller ones, after the fall of Constantinople, architects began to incorporate two full semi-domes along the *miḥrāb*. Once the decision was taken to make the largest dome the central feature of a much larger square, the way was open for the adoption of Byzantine features. At this time, the transformation and enrichment of the interior space was a foregone conclusion. The capture of Constantinople provided both a terminus and an impetus to radical rethinking of mosque design.[31] The Ottomans inherited the magnificent churches of Constantinople, which engendered a similar blending seen in the Romano-Byzantine classical heritage of the Eastern Roman Mediterranean. The golden age of Byzantium architecture inspired the Ottomans to redefine their concept of the imperial arch in the early Ottoman era.[32] Ekrem Akurgal, a Turkish scholar, attributes the Byzantine impact on Ottoman architecture to the openness and dynamism of the early Ottoman sultans to other cultures and pragmatic consideration. He writes: "Pragmatic reconstruction, alterations, and utilization of existing Byzantium buildings were common practice. Orhan's body, for example, was buried in a chapel in the citadel of Bursa. He ordered the conversion of many Christian convents into madrasas and Zaviya."[33]

The great tradition of stonemasonry in the territories was part of the Ottoman conquest. The Turkic nomads were able to absorb their large numbers into the existing settled population of the region and to use their skills as builders. Therefore, elements of Armenian, Georgian, and Byzantine influence appear to some degree.[34] Many Western scholars attribute this influence to Sinan, the most celebrated architect of the Muslim world. Some attribute it to his supposed Christian background, although others argue that he was a very dynamic artist who knew how to synthesize all the existing architectural traditions that he encountered in the Muslim East and in Byzantine architectural art.[35] Stratton writes that the celebrated Sulaymaniya complex clearly indicates the profound impact of Hagia Sophia Church on Sinan:

> But surely neither for incompetence nor for lack of imagination did Sinan or Sultan Sulayman choose to build the Sulamaniya Mosque on the floor plan of the Church of the Divine Wisdom. Both Sulaymaniya and Hagia Sophia rose from the circle inscribed in the square, extended on all four sides but roofed by a single great dome shouldered by two semi-domes in the main axis. The two side aisles, which rise only to the height of the four piers, are covered with cupolas and vaults. In both the church and the mosque, the high arches on either side are filled by fenestrated screen walls.[36]

Kuran argues that Sinan was not mimicking Hagia Sophia Church but drawing upon it in a very creative way. The building of the Bayezid II Mosque in Istanbul was the first important example of the influence of Hagia Sophia Church, which Mehmet II used for the Friday Mosque. Other mosques built by Ottoman architects who were similarly influenced were presented with the serious problem of compartmentalization, lack of precision, and little harmony between the exterior and the interior. It was Sinan with his architectural genius who solved these problems. Stratton adds:

In the time the dome of the mosque was flanked by two semi-domes to create a rectilinear central area for prayer but still with four small domes on each flank, equal in size to each other. The proportions were not precisely Byzantine since the mosque was built with the traditional Ottoman demand for exactitude that the great church never had, neither when it was built not remotely after a millennium of vicissitudes. The semi-domes failed to unify the compartmentalization spaces.[37]

Sinan had to carry out two tasks. The first was to rationalize the classical Ottoman building by unifying the various parts and creating harmony between the interior and exterior spaces. This created the magisterial calm, without which Ottoman architecture would have no soul. Secondly, he had to extend the limits of his intellect beyond the didactic bylaws of the parts and, in so doing, he became a man of his time and the Renaissance.[38]

Turkish scholars see Sinan's point of reference as an Ottoman, not a Byzantine, artistic ideal. The great Ottoman classical architects, especially Sinan and his disciples, were trying to transform Ottoman ideals and intellectual aspirations into the art of architecture. These ideals were reflected in mosque building. For instance, the centrality in Ottoman mosques was the function of unifying the inner space under a huge single dome. The great dome conveyed a dual message: on the religious plane, it symbolized the Oneness of God; at the temporal level, it portrayed an image of the absolute centralism in Ottoman state.[39]

Behcet Unsal, another Turkish scholar of Ottoman art, maintains that the impact of Hagia Sophia on Ottoman architecture has been overstated. He states that the Sultan Ahmet complex, built during the classical period, demonstrated that the Ottoman architects were merely building upon pre-existing Turkish and Islamic architectural traditions borrowed from Byzantine art. The arrangement comprised of one dome and two half–domes common to Hagia Sophia Church and Sultan Ahmet Mosque as a natural result of the historical Turkish architectural evolution. The Byzantine arch closely resembles the Graeco-Roman tradition and was greatly influenced by early Christian arches of Western Asia and Asia Minor. Ottoman Turkish architecture is allied to the early Far Eastern and Central Asian traditions, and is under the influence of not only Western Asian and Anatolian, but also Mesopotamian and Sassanid art. The two are distinct in culture and origin.[40]

Unsal maintains that Western scholars have overrated the impact of Hagia Sophia Church on Turkish architecture. To demonstrate his point, he makes the following comparison between Sultan Ahmet Mosque in Istanbul and Hagia Sophia:

Sultan Ahmet Mosque	Hagia Sophia Church
Plastic and stereometric form	Solid and unadorned mass
Conspicuous and hemispherical dome	Low and inconspicuous
Exterior takes its form from interior	Circular dome
Constructional elements disguised	Exterior rendered ponderous by buttress
Tiles of contrasting colors	Gilt mosaics
Geometric column-capitals and arcades	Round arches supported on columns with open workpitals
Perfect centralization in plan and spacing	
Central dome eccentric to general plan	Pointed arches
Surface unity and uniformity of Basilica plan	
Form uninterrupted by subdivisions	
Side naves cut off from central nave	

Ottomans and the Renaissance in Europe

Although there has been little questioning of the profound impact of pre-Ottoman Islamic civilization on the European Renaissance, very few scholars have examined the impact of the Ottoman Empire itself. The Ottomans both influenced and were influenced by the Renaissance in Europe. Ottoman cartographers and writers used the same sources as European Renaissance cartographers, that is, the works of classical antiquity, in particular, Ptolemy's *Geography*.[41]

For a brief time in the sixteenth century, Ottoman Turkey was close to taking a decisive step in the same direction as the European Renaissance, which was then in its early stages. Fatih Mehmet, the conqueror of Constantinople, had on various occasions demonstrated his unconventional spirit and scientific curiosity and surrounded himself with scholars, some of whom were of Greek origin. In 1465, the Sultan ordered them to make an Arabic translation of Ptolemy's *Geography*. In 1675, he ordered a Turkish translation of Belau's *Atlas*. In the fifteenth century, there had appeared Ulu Ali Kuscu, a graduate of Samarqand and a scholar who had a far superior knowledge of astronomy than his Renaissance counterparts.[42]

The transfer of the Ottoman capital to Constantinople engendered a new imperial vision of reviving the ancient glory of the Roman Empire. The Utopian project of reuniting Constantinople with Rome triggered a special receptiveness among the Ottomans to artistic development in Renaissance Italy. Until the project was abandoned, the sultans actively sponsored Italian artists and architects to promote a visual culture befitting the Ottoman multicultural world empire. However, when this dream proved to be unrealistic, foreign architects were no longer invited.[43]

Parallels between the Italian Renaissance churches and the Ottoman mosques have largely been obscured by the contemporary written discourses of these building traditions, each stressing an origin of a different historical past. The Italian humanists' preoccupation with a pure classical pedigree and the Ottoman emphasis on the Islamic dynastic heritage gave rise to exclusivist discourses on the arch that contained little reference to shared early modern sensibilities and cross-cultural exchanges. The discourse on humanism particularly accentuated this cultural divide. The monuments, however, suggest a more connected universe of architectural culture in the eastern Mediterranean world during the fifteenth and sixteenth centuries.[44]

The simultaneous emergence of centrally planned domed sanctuaries in Italy and the Ottoman Empire can be attributed partly to the concurrent revival of a mutual Romano-Byzantine architectural heritage. The knowledge each culture had of the other should not be underestimated as a factor contributing to the appearance of similar plans. Nevertheless, the Ottoman receptiveness to Italian architectural innovations is more readily recognized because of documented invitations to architects from Italy. Imagining the possibility of a fluid, two-way traffic in architectural concepts, however, is hindered by the lack of written evidence and by the great divide between the schools of Islamic and Western architecture.[45] The cross-cultural exchange of architectural ideas between Ottoman and Renaissance Italy was achieved through various channels: the artists who were appointed to European embassies in Constantinople; Ottoman diplomats; scholars employed in Europe; the Ottoman Sultan's vision of the establishment of world power and linking Rome to Constantinople; and Italian artists interested in seeking employment in prestigious and wealthy Constantinople. One example is the Danish artist Melchior, who was appointed to the Austrian Hapsburg embassy.

In addition to the artists who traveled to the embassies in Istanbul, some learned diplomats played a role in the transmission of architectural knowledge. One example was the Venetian Bailo Marcantonio Barbaro, who was particularly talented in sculpture and some aspects of architecture. His brother, Daniele Barbaro, had written on architecture and had been in correspondence with the Ottoman architect Sokollo. In many of his letters, Marcantonio praised the Sinan-designed mosques as *superbissime*. Sinan had also left his mark on the Western Palladio's Church of Redentore, which was designed by Marcantonio.

Many Western writers suggest that the two thin companili of that church could have been inspired by the Sinan minarets. Close mercantile, cultural, and diplomatic ties between the Ottomans and Venice had certainly attracted the Venetian diplomats' attention to Ottoman architecture, and it is likely that Sinan had access to the architectural treatises of the period.[46]

Throughout Ottoman rule, the sultans invited European experts on various disciplines to join their service. A special Chamber of European engineers was created in the sixteenth century. Leonard Da Vinci, for instance, applied to contribute to the Sultan his expertise in construction. Until the sixteenth century, Ottoman art was still the best in Europe.[47] The bilateral symmetrical, axial layout of the Fatih Mehmet II complex, built on a vast platform raised on vaulted substructures, seems to have been inspired by the Italian Renaissance concept of ideal planning. Its composition has been compared to the plan of the Ospedale Maggiore in Milan, which is one of the creations of Antonio Averlo. This Florentine architect had expressed an interest in visiting Constantinople during the reign of Mehmet II, whose architects must have had access to Italian architectural treatises and drawings. The immense complex and experimentation with the centrally planned styles trumpeted Mehmet's modernism by embracing the authority of ancient Rome.

Mehmet II's interest in the Italian Renaissance was continued by his successor Bayezid II. He sought the help of Michelangelo and Leonardo Da Vinci for the construction of the bridge spanning the Golden Horn. Leonardo Da Vinci submitted a sketch, and Michelangelo also gave serious consideration to visiting Istanbul.[48] Although the project never materialized, it indicated the attitude of Ottoman sultans toward the Renaissance.

The European influences were not confined to Italy. The Ottomans were open to artistic borrowing from other European countries as well, especially from France, with whom the Ottomans had generally peaceful ties throughout the seventeenth and eighteenth centuries. During the reign of Ahmed III (1703–1730) and under the impetus of his Grand Vizier Ibrahim Paşa, a period of peace ensued. Owing to its relations with France, Ottoman architecture began to be influenced by the Baroque and Rococo styles, which were popular in Europe. The Baroque style is noted as first being developed by the Seljuk Turks. From here it re-emerged in Italy, and later grew in popularity among the Turks during the Ottoman era.

Various visitors and envoys were sent to European cities, especially to Paris, to experience contemporary European life and customs. The decorative elements of the European Baroque and Rococo influenced even the religious Ottoman architecture. On the other hand, Mellin, a French architect, was invited by a sister of Sultan Selim III to Istanbul, where he designed the layout of the Bosphorus shores and the wooden pleasure mansions (*yalis*) along the coast. During a thirty-year period, known as the Tulip Period, all Ottoman eyes turned to the West, and instead of monumental and classical works, villas and pavilions were built around Istanbul. However, it was about this time that the Ishak Pasha Palace in Eastern Anatolia was under construction (1685–1784).[49]

Although Ottomans were on the verge of developing their own Renaissance further, its progress stopped and both Ottomans and state lapsed into a period of regression in all fields of knowledge. Art and architecture were in stagnation and this was a reflection of the general decadence and weakness of the state.

Nevertheless, there were a few individual reformists such as Katip Çelebi, Ibrahim Müteferriqa, and Piri Reis, who tried to push the wheels of progress, but in vain. When these efforts failed, military defeats awakened the Ottomans to the need for reform, but it was too late. One of the foremost reasons for the failure of internal reforms was the crisis of epistemology (paradigm dimension), which they had inherited from their predecessors' Islamic states. Ottoman statesmen of the later period rarely exhibited the dynamism and rationalist approach of the earlier period. Instead, they regressed in the name of orthodoxy. The later sultans were interested in learning the practical arts and sciences, but not in metaphysical speculation.

Scholars returning from the well-established *madāris* in Egypt, Iran, and Western Asia brought home an old controversy among the followers of Imam Ghazali and Ibn Rushd regarding the relationship of rational thinking to faith. Specifically, could the scientific realities of life contradict the truth of faith (pillars of belief)? Ottoman scholars, after some deliberations, decided in favor of Ghazali's *tahāfut* (incompatibility) argument against the counterviews held by Ibn Rushd, who left a far-reaching influence on the Renaissance in the West. The Sultan had apparently confirmed this position, which then became and remained the law of the land. It marked the end of all scientific inquiry and speculation that failed to conform or seemed totally contrary to the established Sunni orthodox faith.

The Ottoman state prosecuted many young and talented people on the grounds of would-be heresy or apostasy. However, the psychological factor should be borne in mind. Before the nineteenth century, the Ottomans felt far superior to the West. Lewis points out that this attitude blinded them to the harsh realities of their decline and the West's progress to the Renaissance and the Enlightenment. This writer finds compelling reasons to highlight the efforts of the above-mentioned Ottoman reformers. Katip Çelebi, who was a self-educated man of science, well ahead of his time, strove almost single-handedly for an Ottoman Renaissance and Enlightenment.[50] Among his dozens of books is *Kesh-fuz Zunun*, an annotated, encyclopedic dictionary of about 15,000 entries. He distinguished between rational politics and the Shariʿah (Islamic Law). Although he stood for a rational state, yet he was careful not to appear anti-Shariʿah. He emphasized the importance of the 3Rs (including mathematics), natural history, and the primacy of original sources in education. In a way reminiscent of Aristotle's "golden rule or ratio," he recommended moderation and reconciliation, rather than extremes and conflict. He was critical of the *madāris'* "instrumental sciences" (that is, the teaching of Arabic) and recommended going to the basic 3Rs instead. He probably visualized a modern "pyramid of learning," whose layers rested on one another.[51]

Ibrahim Müteferriqa was a Hungarian prisoner of war and a Unitarian turned Muslim. In 1727, he introduced and operated the first printing press in Turkey. Though the Jews (since 1492), Gregorian Armenians (since 1567), and Orthodox Greeks (since 1627) had their own printing presses, the Muslims were denied this privilege. Müteferriqa believed that obscurantism was the main reason for this delay. After its defeat at Vienna in 1689, Ottoman power was in decline. Ibrahim Müteferriqa seized on the favorable spirit known as *Lale Devri* (the "Tulip Era"). He was the first to print Turkish–Arabic dictionaries and natural and social science texts for the *madrasah* students. The total number of books printed amounted to 180 titles in the first hundred years, indicating that he was resourceful and ahead of his fellow statesmen.[52]

Besides these thinkers there are two prominent scientists. The cartographer Admiral Piri Reis in the early sixteenth century drew a set of the most accurate world maps. After losing a sea battle, however, he was executed.[53] The natural historian Ibrahim Hakki of Erzurum (1703–1780 AC), in his *Marifetname* (epistemology, 1756), anticipated Darwin's evolutionary theory. He cautiously noted, "Those who refute such knowledge may actually be committing a crime against their own faith." The fact that his book was first published in Mehmet Ali Pasha's Cairo in 1835 shows that he was not appreciated early on and his ideas were not the currency of the day.[54] Therefore, when these efforts were stifled in the name of orthodoxy and the protection of the faith, Ottomans had to surrender to Westernization, which was externally packaged and imposed in the name of Tanizimat. Consequently, this led to the inevitable decline and fall of the state.

To conclude, the study of Ottoman art and architecture demonstrates clearly that the Turkic people, especially the Seljuks and Ottomans, had a profound impact on the development of Islamic art. They excelled in their contribution to Islamic art and architecture in particular. This defies the conventionally held view that the Ottoman contribution was confined to the military aspect of Islamic civilization. Ottoman art and architecture had helped build an Islamic civilization based on the ideals of Islam, which was open to other cultures, universal in outlook, and very inclusive in nature. There is no doubt that Ottoman achievements left their imprint on the Renaissance and were, in turn, influenced by it to a significant degree.

Osman Gazi	(1299-1324/26)
Orhan Gazi	(1324/26-60)
Murat I	(1360-89)
Yildirim Bayazid I	(1389-1403)
Mehmet I	(1403-21)
Murat II	(1421-44 and 1446-51)
Fatih Mehmet II	(1444-46 and 1451-81)
Beyazid II	(1481-1512)
Yavuz Selim I	(1512-20)
Suleyman I	(1520-66)
Selim II	(1566-74)
Murad III	(1574-95)
Mehmet III	(1595-1603)
Ahmed I	(1603-17)
Mustafa I	(1617-18 and 1622-23)
Genc Osman II	(1618-22)
Murad IV	(1623-40)
Ibrahim	(1640-48)
Avci Mehmed IV	(1648-87)
Suleyman II	(1687-91)
Ahmed II	(1691-95)
Mustafa II	(1695-1703)
Ahmed III	(1703-30)
Mahmud I	(1730-54)
Osman III	(1754-57)
Mustafa III	(1757-74)
Abdulhamid I	(1774-89)
Selim III	(1789-1807)
Mustafa IV	(1807-08)
Mahmud II	(1808-39)
Abdulmecit	(1839-61)
Abdulaziz	(1861-76)
Murad V	(1876)
Abdulhamid II	(1876-1909)
Mehmed V	(1909-18)
Mehmed VI Vahdettin	(1918-22)

Spelling of names is in Ottoman Turkish whereas in the text modern Turkish is used. Dates given are Common Era.

15

ISLAMIC IMPACT ON
THE RENAISSANCE

HISTORY IS FULL of ironies. The European Christians, who most wanted to destroy Islam and the Muslim world, were the same people who benefited most from the achievements of Islamic civilization. A further irony is that of the Mongols, who devastated the Muslim world and whose help the Crusaders sought in their efforts to destroy Islam. The Mongols became Muslim instead and extended Islamic civilization for several centuries more. After devastating Baghdad, they established their own Muslim cities with their own Islamic institutions. They were also responsible for creating Mughal India, another Muslim state, which, together with Safavid Iran and Ottoman Turkey, kept Islamic civilization alive until the coming of European colonizers.

Medical Influence

The Muslim contribution in medicine has already been discussed in Chapter 10, and therefore, this chapter will give only a brief survey of the impact of Islamic medicine on the European Renaissance. Europe benefited from Islamic civilization in various areas, though notably in the sciences and medicine. Western medicine was, for centuries, the continuation of Islamic medicine. Muslim "medical literature," according to Campbell, "led to the rebirth of the medical system of Europe." An enormous number of books written by Muslims were translated from Arabic into European languages. "They were the works," Campbell states, "that exercised a dominating influence over the minds of the thinkers of the West from the twelfth to the fifteenth century." Of these works, more were translated on medicine than on any other subject, and the majority had been written by the most eminent medical scholars. Campbell adds that Ibn Rushd and al-Zahrawi "exercised a great influence over scholastic medical Europe in the persons of Roger Bacon (1214–1294), Guy de Chauliac (1300–1368), and many other Arabists." [1]

There is some recognition of Islam's achievements in the histories of medicine. The portraits of al-Razi and Ibn Sina, the greatest contributors of medical knowledge, are displayed in the great hall of the University of Paris School of Medicine. [2]

"The Arabians," Campbell writes, "raised the dignity of the medical profession from that of a menial calling to the rank of one of the learned professions." The Muslims were responsible, Campbell also states, for the preservation of "some of the works of Hippocrates and Galen." Unfortunately, Campbell adds, the translations that Hunain ibn Ishaq rendered into Arabic, the most accurate of the translations, especially those of Galen, never reached the West. Campbell gives no reasons why. [3]

According to Le Clerc, a French physician and authority on Arab medicine, the translation of other works from Arabic into Latin were poor. Campbell quotes Le Clerc describing these translations as "barbarous Latin versions," and adds that "he who judges Arabian medicine from [the Latin texts] will inevitably undervalue it and do it a great injustice." [4]

That is probably why Europe turned directly to Galen. The first Latin translation, presumably direct from the Greek, became available in 1476. For those who wanted the original Greek text, it was printed in Venice fifty years later. What is not understandable is that those who flocked to Galen totally ignored all the progress in medicine after him, notably the enormous strides of the Muslims. Boorstin labels it "The Tyranny of Galen," the title of a chapter in his book *The Discoverers*. Galen's books, Boorstin adds, "became sacred texts" and "Galenism" was "the physician's dominant dogma." [5]

Nevertheless, medical practice in Europe was based largely on Islamic medicine. Boorstin also states that while the Christians were traveling to the Crusades, "Christian physicians in Europe were daily curing bodily ills by the wisdom of modern Muslim and Jewish doctors."[6] There was, despite the verbal denial of deriving knowledge of medicine from the Muslim world, a continuation in the West of learning from the Muslims.

This fact is often overlooked. There is the example of Paracelsus (1493–1541), who, though he had the reputation of being a "charlatan," practiced as a physician in the sixteenth century. He is more famous as a "visionary" bent on reforming medicine. His proclamation of this aim was accompanied by the gesture of throwing the works of Galen and Ibn Sina's *Canon* into a bonfire. Were they his books or his father's? His father was a qualified physician and must have found Galen as well as Ibn Sina most helpful, both during his student years and in his practice.

Paracelsus succeeded in changing the course of European medicine, although that was to take years. Meanwhile, according to Campbell, until the seventeenth century the works of al-Razi, Ibn Sina, al-Zahrawi, Ibn Zuhr, and Ibn Rushd received more attention than those of Hippocrates and Galen. Ibn Sina's *Canon* was printed in Latin in more than thirty editions,[7] and there was also an edition available in the West in the original Arabic, printed in Rome.

Soon, however, there were more accurate translations available with the efforts of Archbishop Raymond I in Spain, who was the first to recognize the wealth of the Arabic works. With the conquest of Toledo, according to James Burke, the Christians "found a literary treasure beyond anything they could have dreamed of." To take advantage of the richness of the library, Archbishop Raymond formed a "society of translators."[8] Its members were among the most knowledgeable in Arabic and the accuracy of their translations was assured with the adoption of Arabic words where no Latin equivalent was available.

To the center in Toledo came scholars from other parts of Europe. Among the famous were Adelard of Bath, Robert of Chester, and Michael Scot, all from the British Isles. Scot also went to Sicily to work under Frederick II, who imposed on his employee the major task of translating the Aristotelian works on natural history with the commentaries of Ibn Rushd and Ibn Sina. In conquering Toledo, the Christians inherited from the Muslims, "a beacon of Graeco-Arab-Hebraic culture for the whole of the Latin West."[9]

Another very important place where the medical knowledge from the Muslim world entered the West was the School of Salerno. The city itself had been a health resort since ancient times, and its physicians had some acquaintance with Greek medicine. However, there is debate over when and how Islamic medicine reached Salerno. Sarton believes that "at the beginning Muslim influences were accidental."[10] There were Arabic teachers at Salerno and the Latin translations of Arabic texts helped considerably.

Later, according to Sarton, Muslim influences "were considerably increased by the activity of Constantine the African." Campbell, on the other hand, states that many Latin translations had reached Salerno long before Constantine the African. Nevertheless, Constantine the African certainly made a significant difference, for he was very well versed in Muslim culture.[11]

There should be no doubt that there was considerable Muslim influence at the School of Salerno. Sarton reveals its extent when he explains that surgery was "made available to Latin readers" owing to "the enormous amount of medical experience treasured in Arabic literature." There was the need, Sarton points out, for the assimilation of the medical knowledge available in Arabic, a task that "taxed the energy of Salernitan practitioners to the limit for more than a century." Then, there was the knowledge of surgery as practiced by Muslims, made available by the translations of Constantine the African. It was owing to all of these activities that Roger, "the earliest and greatest surgeon of Salerno," was able to write his own work of surgery, which was "truly the first monument of European surgery."[12]

The Crusades also enabled the School of Salerno to promote the efficacy of Islamic medicine, for the Crusaders established their base hospital in the city. Salerno and other contacts with Muslims thus "contributed to the spread" of Islamic medical knowledge in Europe.[13]

When Henry VI sacked Salerno in 1194, other universities took its place, notably the University of Naples, founded by Frederick II in 1224, and the universities of Palermo and Montpelier, the last being an Arabist center in the Middle Ages. In the same century, the University of Bologna, established in 1088, emerged as an outstanding institution for the study of medicine: it was "founded on the teachings of Avicenna [Ibn Sina]."[14] A century later, Islamic medicine was dominant at the University of Tübingen, where the curriculum included the works of Ibn Sina and al-Razi. Other universities were established in Paris, followed by Oxford and Cambridge. All of these institutions sought their learning from Arabic sources, being the only channel where the culture of Ancient Greece could be obtained.[15]

Islamic medicine reached Oxford via Paris. Students from Paris migrated to Oxford and, later, students from Oxford migrated to Cambridge. British scholars benefited from their studies at these universities and went on to write their own works. The books on medicine and surgery by John of Arden, a fourteenth-century physician of London, had as their sources Islamic medicine. The same is true of the works of John's contemporaries, Bernard de Gordon, Gilbertus Anglicus, and John of Gaddesden. Campbell describes their books as "Arabist."

Islamic medicine received literary endorsement, too, in the English-speaking world. Chaucer, in his description of the "Doctour of Physique" in *The Canterbury Tales*, lists the Muslim authorities from whom the good "doctour" took his knowledge: Ibn Sina, Ibn Rushd, and al-Razi. Shakespeare, too, alluded to Islamic medications, notably in *Othello*. Islamic pharmacology, according to Campbell, "survived the longest."

As late as the sixteenth century, Muslim works on pharmaceuticals were being translated into European languages other than Latin. The influence continues, for many of today's pharmacopoeias use methods of presenting medications in the manner established by Muslim physicians. Islamic medicine "culminating in Ibn Sina remained until the closing years of the Renaissance the most authoritative source of Western theory and practice."[16]

Philosophy and Translation

A number of authorities, including Roger Bacon, agree that it was also from the Islamic civilization that Europe acquired Greek philosophy. The commentaries of Muslim scholars were pivotal. The considerable interest in philosophy demonstrated by these scholars was due primarily to the Qur'anic counsel emphasizing that Muslims should use their intellect. The Muslims went even further in basing their thinking on a very close connection between philosophy and medicine.

Intellectual discourse began with the Companions of the Prophet, Aishah, his wife, and Ali, his son-in-law and the fourth Caliph of Islam. According to Sharif, they discussed "the practical ramifications of religious doctrines in the light of reason."[17] Incidentally, one of the founders of a school of Islamic law, Abu Hanifah, was also responsible for extending the quest for knowledge, so that the Muslims were "open" to learning from other cultures, especially that of the Greeks. According to Mahdi, al-Kindi "insisted that a purely human knowledge of all things is possible, through the use of various scientific devices, learning such things as mathematics and logic, and assimilating the contributions of earlier thinkers."[18]

Among those thinkers were the Greek philosophers, whose contributions were rejected by Byzantium. Emile Brounier, in his *Histoire de la philosophie*, says: "[Constantinople], the new capital of the [Roman] empire was scarcely favorable for philosophic studies...in the sixth and seventh centuries only a great silence reigned." However, it was not only Byzantium.[19] By the beginning of the ninth century, according to Sarton, "the West had gradually lost touch with the Greek springs of knowledge." Islamic civilization revived the West's interest in that knowledge and, as a result, the West also acquired some of the Muslim world's own contributions.[20]

Al-Farabi helped the West considerably in its renewed quest. Among Muslims, his enormous achievement earned him the title of, in Mahdi's words, "the greatest philosophical authority since Aristotle."[21] Muslims, as well as Jews and Christians, studied his works to extricate themselves from the difficulty of understanding the intricacies of philosophy.

He was, in fact, most knowledgeable about Aristotle, having read the Greek philosopher's texts repeatedly. Shustery reports him as having read Aristotle's *Physics* 400 times and *De Anima* 200 times.[22] He was also idealistic, especially with regard to politics.

Al-Farabi gives further details of the six different kinds of ʿaql (reason) in his *Epistle on the Intellect*. The following is an abstract of the summary by Netton in his book on al-Farabi. The first is of the "ordinary," everyday reasoning of all people. The second is that of the scholar. The third is the perception of *the certainty* "of some basic universal and necessary true principles." The fourth is "part of the soul…[derived] from experience," which is the "*developed* voice of conscience." The fifth is the most complex, which al-Farabi divides into four different types: Potential Intellect, Actual Intellect, Acquired Intellect, and Agent or Active Intellect. The sixth is Divine Reason, that which belongs to God.[23]

Al-Farabi's influence on Western thought was considerable. Less known is his Islamic contribution to Christianity. His works based on the Qur'an influenced both Albertus Magnus and St. Thomas Aquinas. Magnus certainly relied heavily on al-Farabi in his lectures, which made a deep impression on St. Thomas Aquinas, one of Magnus's students. Both used al-Farabi's works in reconciling Aristotle and Islamic philosophy with Christianity.

As a result, according to Hammond in his *The Philosophy of al-Farabi and Its Influence on Medieval Thought*, St. Thomas Aquinas's *Summa Theologia* and *Summa Contra Gentiles* contain material taken directly from al-Farabi, at times word for word. Hammond (as quoted in Myers) gives some examples, as follows:[24]

Al-Farabi	**St. Thomas Aquinas**
The uncaused being is infinite.	Being itself, being considered absolutely infinite.
God as the first cause is pure act.	God must be pure act.
The passive intellect…is in potentiality to things intelligible.	The human intellect is in potentiality with regard to things intelligible.

Another Muslim philosopher who impressed Thomas Aquinas was Ibn Rushd, who also influenced Roger Bacon and Albertus Magnus among other Christian and Jewish scholars. Ibn Rushd's works were translated into Latin and Hebrew. According to Urvoy, the Jews "preserved" his texts in "Arabic, Arabic written in Hebrew script, and Hebrew translation." Urvoy adds that "the influence of Ibn Rushd [among the Jews] equaled that of Maimonides."[25] Thomas Aquinas specifically quoted Ibn Rushd 503 times and, as a result, was accused of being an Averroist.[26] Palacios points out that "the positions of Ibn Rushd and Aquinas regarding the substantial accord between faith and reason were identical."[27] There was at the time a strong Christian opposition to Ibn Rushd as well as to Aristotle, Christian scholars describing both philosphers "as the same evil."[28] Despite the campaign led against them by popes and bishops, nevertheless, the Latin world recognized Ibn Rushd as an interpreter of Aristotle and also as an original thinker.

When Islamic philosophy is taken as a whole, Muslim philosophers did succeed to a great extent in "reconciling faith and reason, religion and science," according to Hitti, who adds that it was this synthesis that was "transmuted...to the Latin West." Hitti even goes so far as to state that "the influx into Western Europe of a body of new ideas [from the Muslim world], mainly philosophic, marks the beginning of the end of the 'Dark Ages' and the dawn of the scholastic period."[29]

What followed was that instead of translations being made from other languages into Arabic, the language of the Muslims at the time, it was the other way around – from the Muslim world to other cultures, especially the West. It must be emphasized here that the West, for centuries, acquired knowledge from the Muslim world, including "works" by Muslim scientists in various fields that dominated Western thought from the twelfth to the fifteenth century.[30]

There is no doubt that the West inherited an enormous amount of knowledge from the Muslims, for the evidence is overwhelming in the abundance of translations from the languages of the Muslim world, especially Arabic. "Until the Renaissance and the Reformation," Lewis points out, "...Arabic was probably the most widely translated language in the world,"[31] and most of these translations were into Latin.

Spain

It was mainly through Muslim Spain that a major proportion of Islamic knowledge entered the West. For centuries, Spain was certainly more like a country in the Muslim Middle East. Many non-Muslims adopted Muslim names, Muslim clothes, and Muslim customs, and in addition used Arabic in public and in private. Muslim as well as Jewish and Christian students traveled to study at the Islamic universities in Spain. One Christian student, Gerbert, who studied mathematics and the physical sciences in al-Andalus, later became Pope Sylvester II. There were records of a much more famous Christian student called Charlemagne, who was sent to Spain to be educated by the Muslims.[32]

An early king of Aragon, Peter I, could write only in the Arabic script, and many Christians also used the Arabic script when they wrote in Latin. They were also avid readers of Arabic literature, to the extent that Alvaro of Cordoba complained that Christians were spending too much time on Muslim books and neglecting the Gospels. Since these Christians insisted on reading Arabic books, John of Seville had the Bible translated into Arabic so that they would at least read about their religion.

It was also in Muslim Spain during the twelfth century AC, over five hundred years after the emergence of Islam, that the translation of Arabic works into Latin was begun. This beginning was largely due to the efforts of Domingo Gundisalvo, the archdeacon of Segovia, assisted by John of Seville. Gundisalvo's writings, including the classification of the sciences, all of which he declared to be his "original" ideas, were in fact derived from Muslim scholars. Other Westerners also "appropriated" Muslim writings and published them under their own names.

More translations followed those of Gundislavo. Those by Herman the Dalmatian were mostly scientific and included al-Majriti's

Arabic version of Ptolemy's *Planisphaerium*. Hugh of Santalla concentrated on scientific writings, as did Plato of Tivoli. More translations, almost all of them in astronomy, are attributed to John of Seville. At about the same time, Adelard of Bath, England, was also doing translations of his own.

Robert of Chester, an Englishman who settled in Spain and was the archbishop of Pamplona, went beyond the sciences to include the first Latin translation of the Qur'an. It had been commissioned by Peter the Venerable, who wanted to refute it. Another translation by Robert of Chester proved to be of great significance to the future of Europe, being the first of al-Khwarizmi's treatise on algebra. "Its importance can hardly be overestimated," according to Myers, for "it may be said to mark the beginning of European algebra."[33]

In his *Medieval Civilization 400–1500*, Le Goff describes the enormous wealth of knowledge that the Christians gained from Muslim Spain, ranging from Greek philosophy and science to Islam's own contributions in medicine and various other fields. Twelfth-century English clerics, Le Goff points out, "were eager for Arab culture." Certainly, all of Europe held Islamic culture in high esteem: according to Le Goff, Adelard of Bath stated that he attributed his own ideas to the Arabs so that they would be accepted.[34]

A favourite among the Christians in the West at this time was popular literature, much of which was derived from Baghdad. However, it was so popular that it interfered with serious work. Monks, bent on the task of translating Arabic works into Latin, were reprimanded for ignoring their translations and instead amusing themselves with these tales. Nevertheless, the tales were also influential, for they were the "models" for Spanish literature, particularly in "the wit of Cervantes' *Don Quixote*, whose author…jokingly claimed that the book had an Arabic original."[35]

The second half of the twelfth and the first half of the thirteenth century AC was the heyday of the translations, which were far too numerous to detail here. Most of them were of the sciences, medicine, and philosophy, although there were also other subjects, including theology. Gerard of Cremona is considered "the greatest" of the translators, with translations of well over seventy volumes credited to him, which has led Hitti to declare him "the most prolific of the Toledan translators."[36] Myers believes that he might have been "the head of a school of translation."[37] He translated books on logic, philosophy, mathematics, astronomy, medicine, and astrology. His career as a translator having begun with his devotion to science and love of learning, his aim was to translate *Almagest*, and so he traveled to Toledo to learn Arabic.

Another work of enormous importance translated by Gerard was Ibn Sina's *Qānūn*, the greatest medical work of Islamic civilization. Gabrieli says that Gerard worked on "the whole range of Hellenistic-Arab science." He lived in Toledo for most of his life, leaving it only after he achieved, according to Gabrieli, "an imperishable fame in the history of knowledge" for his translations of Muslim science.[38] "The impact of [Gerard's] work was enormous," Myers states, for it "opened to the Latin world the treasures of Greek and Arab philosophy, mathematics, astronomy, physics, medicine, and alchemy... [and] helped to pave the way for the founding of universities." It was the beginning, as has already been emphasized, of European science.[39]

For some decades, the translations consisted mostly of Arabic works into Latin, including books that had been translated from Syriac and Greek into Arabic and consisting of the wealth of knowledge from Classical Greece. As a result, the Muslims awakened – and in very few instances, reawakened – Christian interest in the classical works and inspired Christian scholars to translate directly from Greek into Latin.

There were also many translations of original Arab texts into Hebrew. In addition to transferring Islamic learning to the Jews, these translations enhanced their language with the adoption of Arabic words that did not exist in Hebrew. Lewis points out, "Much of the scientific and philosophy vocabulary of early modern Hebrew originated in this way."[40]

There could have been many more translations from the Arabic into Latin, had it not been for the fall of Granada, followed by a change in the Christian appreciation of Muslim knowledge. Cardinal Jimenez de Cisneros, who was responsible for starting a ruthless religious campaign against the Muslims, sought out Arabic books and burned them. However, Philip II succeeded in rescuing about two thousand volumes, which were deposited at the Escorial close to Madrid. His successor Philip III was able to acquire from Spanish pirates another three to four thousand books, which were also sent to the Escorial.

Nevertheless, Hitti states, "By the close of the thirteenth century [seventh century AH], Arabic science and philosophy had been transmitted to Europe, and Spain's work as an intermediary was done."[41] The universities of Spain made no further contributions after the conquest, that is, after the Muslims had been expelled.

The Muslim books and manuscripts that were neglected still exist, locked up in Western libraries belonging to church and state. There are still a large number in the libraries of the Muslim world that have yet to be uncovered. Al-Hassan and Hill estimate that these books and manuscripts total a quarter of a million, excluding unrecorded collections.[42] Meyerhof gives some details of these collections. In Istanbul alone, "there are more than eighty mosque libraries containing tens of thousands of manuscripts." He lists Cairo, Damascus, Mosul, and Baghdad as possessing sizable collections. He singles out the Escorial Library in Spain as the repository of "a large part of the wisdom of western Islam."[43]

Not all the translations were meant to engender learning. There was the Order of the Preachers, who established a school of Oriental Studies, the first such institution in Europe, whose sole purpose, according to Hitti, was to prepare "missionaries to Moslems and Jews."[44]

The contradictions in the Christians' attitude to Muslim learning is best demonstrated in the life of Ramon Lull. Because he studied Muslim sciences, he was designated, according to Fox, "a master of necromancy and alchemy." Fox adds that Lull learned Arabic "from an Arab slave"[45] and that he taught Arabic at a Franciscan institution in Majorca. Later, he used his knowledge of Arabic to preach Christianity to the Muslims of North Africa.

Christian Europe was also very reluctant to give recognition to Islamic learning, in many instances, simply refusing to acknowledge the Muslim origin of many translations. Max Meyerhof points to translations as coming "from the Greek rather than the Arabic. 'Hellenism' was opposed to 'Arabism,' though there was no fundamental difference between them."[46]

European Christians also plagiarized with impunity. Meyerhof states that he has read "an old German treatise on zoology of 1838" and discovered therein "all the legends relating to the poisonous nature of the gecko...[taken directly from the Arabic text of] adDimri's *Life of Animals*," without referring to adDimri at all.[47] Plessner points out that the discovery "of the lesser circulation of the blood," attributed to Michael Servetus, was by Ibn al-Nafis. The major plagiarist was the monk known as Constantine the African, who translated a number of Arabic works into Latin and claimed the authorship for himself.[48] Campbell believes he did this under "clerical pressure."[49] In Muslim Spain, a Muslim scholar, Ibn Abdun, tried to prevent the selling of books by Muslims to Christians "because they [the Christians] translate them and attribute them to their bishops."[50]

The West used other means to camouflage Muslim authorship or authority. As mentioned in Chapters 9 and 10, this was done by either Latinizing Muslim names or changing them entirely. For example, how can one recognize the original Arabic of the names of the following Muslim scholars? Al-Razi was Latinized into Averroes, al-Haytham into Alhazen, al-Sufi into Azophi, Ibn Yunus into Azarquiel.

Mention must be made of one major acknowledgment of the Muslim contribution to science concerning the features on the moon. At the time, all the features of the moon had been named after European royalty. However, a seventeenth-century Jesuit, Giambattista Riccioli, who was an Italian astronomer, discarded the royal names and replaced them with those of the major contributors to the sciences. Among the new names were those of thirteen Muslims, including the Caliph al-Ma'mun, who created a milieu for the exploration of the earth and the heavens and thus took a major step in engendering

Muslim science. The other twelve Muslims were, appropriately, astronomers. All thirteen names were confirmed by the International Astronomical Union in 1935.

Literature

Literature was another major influence of Islamic civilization on the West. "There would seem to be no doubt," says Gabrieli, "that throughout the Middle Ages and the Renaissance, down to the threshold of the modern era, *only* Arabic literature need to be taken into account when we are dealing with literature contacts with, and influence upon, the Christian world." He adds, "During the first thousand years of its existence, Islam was revealed and expressed to Europe almost exclusively through Arabic literature."[51]

Gabrieli cites as examples the testimony of Alvaro of Cordoba that Alvaro's "Christian contemporaries were assiduously cultivating Arabic literature," and then discusses in detail the considerable influence of Arabic poetry, pointing to Dante, Goethe, Wilhelm Hauff, and Victor Hugo as the major beneficiaries.[52]

Nevertheless, this is yet another area where the West has been very reluctant to recognize the contributions of Muslim learning, even while benefitting from these achievements. It has done so by insisting that the Muslims borrowed from others, or by ignoring the Muslims' accomplishments and concentrating on their wars instead. That the medieval Western scholars behaved in this way is understandable, since the attitude of most Christians toward Muslims in those days was overwhelmingly belligerent. They began by distorting the teachings of Islam and then went on to destroy Islamic civilization and learning, not only during the Crusades, but afterward, too. Having failed during the Crusades, they made every attempt to persuade the Mongols to ally themselves with the Christians, to totally destroy the Muslim world, and completely eliminate Islam.

However, of one thing there is no doubt whatsoever. No scholar, whatever his or her background and learning, will ever be able to alter or delete the achievements of Islamic civilization and its contribution to, and its place in, world history. All other civilizations, especially that of the West, which followed the Islamic example benefited from these achievements. As highlighted in various places in this book, the West borrowed overwhelmingly from Islam and the Muslim world and benefited immensely from those borrowings. Roberts emphasizes this several times in his *History of the World*. Christendom, he said, owes its "Christian cultural achievement...to Islam." A little later, he adds, "To no other civilization did Europe owe so much in the Middle Ages as to Islam."[53]

For these reasons, translations from the Arabic into European languages, as well as the enormous learning that the West acquired from the Muslims, whether as an addition to or a conveyer of Ancient Greek and Eastern sciences, were the important contributions to the Renaissance and the development of modern Western civilization.

NOTES

Notes to Preface

1 Gabriele Crespi, *The Arabs in Europe* (New York: Rizzoli, 1986), p.307.

2 G.S. Marshall Hodgson, *The Venture of Islam*, 3 vols. (Chicago, IL and London: The University of Chicago Press, 1974), vol.1, pp.95, 99.

Notes to Introduction

1 George Sarton, *Introduction to the History of Science*, 3 vols. Vol.1, *From Homer to Omar Khayyam* (Baltimore, MD: Williams & Wilkins for the Carnegie Institute of Washington, 1927; repr. 1962), p.746.

2 Karen Armstrong, *A History of God* (New York: Knopf, 1993), p.152.

Notes to Chapter 1

1 J.M. Roberts, *The Penguin History of the World* (Harmondsworth, Middx, UK: Penguin Books, 1980), p.378.

2 Ibid., p.62.

3 Bernard Lewis, *Islam and the West* (New York, and Oxford, UK: Oxford University Press, 1993), p.82.

Notes to Chapter 2

1 Franz Rosenthal, *Knowledge Triumphant* (Leiden, The Netherlands: E.J. Brill, 1970), p.70.

2 Zamakhshari and Razi, quoted by Muhammed Asad in *The Message of the Qur'an* (Gibraltar: Dar al-Andalus, 1980), p.933.

3 Ibid., p.9.

4 *Beyond the Written Word: Oral Aspects of Scripture in the History of Religion* (Cambridge, UK: Cambridge University Press, 1988), p.x. The remainder of the discussion of Dr. Graham's ideas is a summary of the section on the Qur'an.

5 Zamakhshari and Razi in Asad, *The Message of the Qur'an*, p.iii.

6 Roberts, *Penguin History of the World*, p.397.

7 Ibid., p.394.

Notes to Chapter 3

1 Seyyed Hossein Nasr, *The Encounter of Man and Nature* (London: Allen & Unwin, 1968), pp.94–98.

2 Ibid., pp.96–98.

3 Shabir Akhtar, *A Faith for All Seasons* (Chicago, IL: Ivan R. Dee, 1990), p.222.

4 Marshall G.S. Hodgson, *The Venture*, 3 vols. (Chicago, IL, & London, 1974), vol.1, p.104.

5 Charles Greville Tuetey (trans.), *Classical Arabic Poetry* (London: KPI Ltd, 1985), p.22.

6 Ira Lapidus, *A History of Islamic Societies* (Cambridge, UK: Cambridge University Press, 1988), p.55.

7 Hodgson, *The Venture*, vol.1, p.94.

8 Al-Ghazali, quoted by Ismail R. al-Faruqi in a lecture, 'al-Ghazali and the Modern World', given in South Africa. Cassette recording (n.d.).

9 E.H. Whinfield (trans. & abridged), *Masnavi i Ma'navi:The Spiritual Couplets of Maulāna Jalālu-'d-Dīn Muhammad Rūmī, 1207–1273* [Masnavi. English. Selections] (London: Routledge: 2002), p.34.

10 F.E. Peters, *Allah's Commonwealth* (New York: Simon and Schuster, 1973), p.129.

11 Hodgson, *The Venture*, vol.1, p.180.

12 Karen Armstrong, *Muhammad: A Western Attempt to Understand Islam* (London: Victor Gollancz, 1991), p.34.

13 Hodgson, *The Venture*, vol.1, p.182.

14 Ronald Eyre, *Ronald Eyre on the Long Search* (New York: William Collins, 1979), pp.149–150.

15 Al-Ghazali, quoted by al-Faruqi in 'al-Ghazali and the Modern World'.

16 Sawirus ibn al-Muqaffa, *History of the Patriarchs of the Coptic Church of Alexandria*, trans. Basil Evetts (Paris: Firmin-Didot, 1904), pt. I,

ch. 1, from Patrologia Orientalis, vol. I, pp.489-497, reprinted in Deno John Geanakoplos, *Byzantium: Church, Society, and Civilization Seen Through Contemporary Eyes* (Chicago: University of Chicago Press, 1984), pp.336-338; Philip Hitti, trans., *The Origins of the Islamic State* (New York: Columbia University Press, 1916), vol. I, pp.346-349, reprinted in Deno John Geanakoplos, *Byzantium: Church, Society, and Civilization Seen Through Contemporary Eyes* (Chicago: University of Chicago Press, 1984), pp.338-339.

17 Eric Schroeder, *Muhammad's People* (Portland, ME: Bond Wheelwright, 1955), p.157.

18 Zamakshari and Razi, quoted by Asad in *The Message of the Qur'an,* p.933.

19 Jim Hogshire, 'Animals and Islam', *The Animals' Agenda* (October 1991), pp.10–14.

20 R.V.C. Bodley, *The Quest* (London: R. Hale; and New York: Doubleday, 1947), p.34.

21 Sarton, *History of Science*, vol.1, p.520.

Notes to Chapter 4

1 Philip Khuri Hitti, *History of the Arabs: From the Earliest Times to the Present,* 9th edn. (London: Macmillan; & New York: St. Martin's Press, 1968), pp.144–55.

2 Hodgson, *The Venture*, vol.1, pp.200–201.

3 Paul Johnson, *Civilizations of the Holy Land* (New York: Atheneum, 1979), pp.169–170.

4 Ibid., p.170.

5 Schroeder, *Muhammad's People*, p.169.

6 Alexandre Papadopoulo, *Islam and Muslim Art*. Trans. Robert Erich Wolf (New York: Harry N. Abrams, 1979), p.32.

7 Philip K. Hitti, *Capital Cities of Islam* (Minneapolis, MN: University of Minnesota Press, 1973), p.69.

8 Hodgson, *The Venture*, vol.1, p.226.

9 Norman F. Cantor, *The Civilization of the Middle Ages: The Complete Revised and Expanded Edition of Medieval History: The Life and Death of a Civilization* (New York: HarperCollins, 1993), pp.133–134.

10 Johnson, *Civilizations*, p.170.

11 Abba Eban, *Heritage: Civilization and the Jews* (New York: Summit

Books, 1984), p.127.

12 Hitti, *History*, p.527.

13 Ibid., p.292.

14 Hitti, *History*, p.103.

15 Hitti, *Cities*, pp.510–512.

16 Geoffrey & Susan Jellicoe, *The Landscape of Man: Shaping the Environment from Prehistory to the Present Day* (Revd. edn. New York: Thames & Hudson, 1987), p.34; Hitti, *Cities*, p.103; Robert S. Lopez & Irving W. Raymond, 'Muslim Trade in the Mediterranean and the West', in Archibald R. Lewis (ed.), *The Islamic World and the West 622–1492 AD* (New York: Wiley, 1970), p.132-135.

17 Hitti, *History*, pp.619–620.

18 Titus Burckhardt, *Fez: City of Islam* (Cambridge, UK: Islamic Texts Society, 1992), pp.122-124.

19 Elizabeth B. Moynihan, *Paradise as a Garden: In Persia and Mughal India* (New York: George Braziller, 1979), pp.1–2.

20 Hitti, *History*, pp.220–221, 264–265.

21 Moynihan, *Paradise as a Garden*, pp.28–29.

22 Albert Hourani, *A History of the Arab Peoples* (Cambridge, MA: Belknap Press of Harvard University Press, 1991), pp.46–47.

23 Lewis, *Islam and the West*, p.12.

24 Richard Bulliet, *Conversion to Islam in the Medieval Period* (Cambridge, MA; and London: Harvard University Press, 1979), pp.33, 34, 37, 44, 82, 97, 109 & 124.

25 Philip Curtin, *Cross-Cultural Trade in World History* (Cambridge, UK: Cambridge University Press, 1984), p.107.

26 Dorothy Woodman, *The Republic of Indonesia* (London: Cresset, 1955), p.135.

27 Roberts, *Penguin History of the World*, p.327.

28 Hodgson, *The Venture*, vol.1, p.206.

29 Lewis, *Islam and the West*, p.182.

30 Curtin, *Cross-Cultural Trade*, p.107.

31 Robert Fox, *The Inner Sea: The Mediterranean and its People* (New York: Alfred A. Knopf, 1993), p.182.

32 Ismail R. al-Faruqi et al., *The Great Asian Religions* (New York: Macmillan, 1969), p.330.

33 Hitti, *History*, p.537.

34 Abba Eban, p.127.

35 Ibid., p.139-140.
36 Ibid., p.140.
37 Ibid., p.141.
38 Sarton, *Introduction to Science*, vol.1, p.520.
39 Cantor, *Civilization of the Middle Ages*, pp.367–368.
40 Vivian B. Mann et al. (eds.), *Convivencia: Jews, Muslims and Christians in Muslim Spain* (New York: George Braziller, in assoc. with the Jewish Museum, 1992), p.xi.

Notes to Chapter 5

1 Aly Mohamed Fahmy, *Muslim Sea-Power* (Cairo: National Publication and Printing House, 1961), p.27,81.
2 Isaac Asimov, *Asimov's Chronology of Science and Discovery* (New York: Harper & Row, 1989), p.82.
3 Colin A. Ronan, *Science: Its History and Development among the World's Cultures* (New York: Facts on File Publications, 1982), p.207.
4 Hitti, *History*, p.299.
5 Sarton, *Introduction to Science*, vol.1, pp.565–566.
6 Melvinger, A., 'Al-Madjus,' in *Encyclopedia of Islam*, 2nd edition, vol. V (Leiden 1986) pp.1118-1121; Melvinger, A., *Les premières incursions des Vikings en Occident d'après les sources arabes* (Uppsala 1955); Munis, H., 'Contribution à l'étude des invasions des Normands en Espagne,' *Bulletin de la Société Royale d'Etudes Historiques*, Egypte vol. II/1(1950).
7 Hitti, *Cities*, p.66.
8 Most of the information on Sicily has been derived from Hitti, *History*, pp.606–611; Sayyid Fayyez Mahmud, *A Short History of Islam* (Karachi, Pakistan: Oxford University Press, 1960), pp.208–209; and Crespi, *The Arabs*, p.298.
9 David Nicole, *The Armies of Islam: 7th–11th Centuries* (London: Osprey Publishing, 1982), p.27.
10 Roberts, *Penguin History of the World*, p.389.
11 Mahmud, *A Short History of Islam*, p.208.
12 Hitti, *History*, pp.606–607.
13 Ibid., p.609.
14 Ibid., p.608.
15 Ibid., p.610.
16 Mahmud, *A Short History of Islam*, p.209.
17 Crespi, *The Arabs in Europe*, p.298.

18 Mahmud, *A Short History of Islam*, p.209.

19 Hitti, *History*, p.611.

20 James & Thorpe, pp.523–525.

21 Ibid., pp.527–528.

22 Akbar S. Ahmed, *Discovering Islam: Making Sense of Muslim History and Society* (London & New York: Routledge, 1988), p.99.

23 Jamil Ahmad, *Hundred Great Muslims* (Karachi, Pakistan: Ferozsons, 1971), p.225.

24 Cyril Glasse, *The Concise Encyclopedia of Islam* (San Francisco, CA: Harper & Row, 1989), p.262.

25 Details for this and subsequent paragraphs are taken from Hamilton Gibb (ed. and trans.), *The Travels of Ibn Battuta*, 2 vols. (Cambridge, UK: Cambridge University Press for the Hakluyt Society, 1958, 1959 & 1971).

26 Ibid., p.149.

27 Curtin, *Cross-Cultural Trade*, p.107.

Notes to Chapter 6

1 Theodore Zeldin, *An Intimate History of Humanity* (London: Sinclair-Stevenson, 1994), p.156.

2 Andrew S. Ehrenkreutz, 'The Silent Force behind the Rise of Islamic Civilization', in C.E. Bosworth et al. (eds.), *The Islamic World* (Princeton, NJ: The Darwin Press, 1989), p.25.

3 Fox, *The Inner Sea*, p.311.

4 Ehrenkreutz, 'The Silent Force', p.25.

5 Hourani, *A History of the Arab Peoples*, p.115.

6 For information on the Arab trade routes, see, Irene M. Franck & David M. Brownstone, *To the Ends of the Earth: The Great Travel and Trade Routes of Human History* (New York: Facts on File, 1984), pp.169–186.

7 Curtin, *Cross Cultural Trade*, p.21.

8 Fox, *The Inner Sea*, p.164.

9 Lewis, *Islam and the West*, p.11.

10 Mahmud, *A Short History of Islam*, pp.433–434.

11 Curtin, *Cross Cultural Trade*, p.40.

12 Ibid., pp.51–52.

13 Description taken from an African art show at the Royal Ontario Museum in Toronto during the author's visit there in June 1990.

14 Fox, *The Inner Sea*, pp.332, 364.

15 Curtin, *Cross Cultural Trade*, p.27.

16 Mahmud, *A Short History of Islam*, p.131.

17 Roberts, *History of the World*, p.436.

18 Ibid., pp.439–440.

19 *The New York Times*, March 16, 1993.

20 Mahmud, *A Short History of Islam*, p.103.

21 Curtin, *Cross Cultural Trade*, p.105.

22 Roberts, *History of the World*, p.436.

23 Mahmud, *A Short History of Islam*, p.131.

24 Hodgson, *The Venture*, vol.1, p.233.

25 Dorothy Woodman, *The Republic of Indonesia* (London: Cresset, 1955), p.135.

26 Curtin, *Cross Cultural Trade*, pp.129–130.

27 Ibid., p.104

28 Ibid., pp.111–113.

29 Hourani, *History of the Arab Peoples*, p.110.

30 Asimov, *Science*, p.70.

31 J. and H. Kramers (eds.), *Shorter Encyclopedia of Islam* (Ithaca, NY: Cornell University Press, 1953), pp.103–105.

32 Kenneth Cragg & Marston Spreight, *Islam from Within* (Belmont, CA: Wadsworth Publishing, 1980), p.71.

33 Sir Thomas Arnold and Alfred Guillaume (eds.), *The Legacy of Islam* (Oxford, UK: Oxford University Press, 1931), p.102; Ahmad Y, al-Hassan and Donald R. Hill, *Islamic Technology: An Illustrated History* (Cambridge, UK: Cambridge University Press, 1986), p.102; Kramers, *Shorter Encyclopedia of Islam*, p.107-109.

34 James and Thorpe, *Ancient Inventions*, p.372.

35 Curtin, *Cross Cultural Trade*, pp.15, 21.

36 Mahmud, *A Short History of Islam*, p.291.

37 Lapidus, *A History of Islamic Societies*, p.249.

38 William MacNeill, *The Rise of the West* (Chicago, IL: University of Chicago Press, 1963), vol.1, p.583.

39 Fox, *The Inner Sea*, p.153.

40 Hourani, *A History of the Arab Peoples*, p.43.

41 Sarton, *Introduction to Science*, vol.1, p.620.

42 Crespi, *The Arabs in Europe*, p.94.

43 Hitti, *History*, p.307.

44 Donald Campbell, *Arabian Medicine and Its Influence on the Middle Ages*, vols.1 & 2 (London: Kegan Paul, Trench, Trubner, 1926), p.186.

45 Mahmud, *A Short History of Islam*, pp.217, 227, 235, 251.

46 Charles Corn, *Distant Islands* (New York: Viking, 1991), pp.157–158.

47 Mahmud, *A Short History of Islam*, p.131.

48 Roberts, *History of the World*, p.392.

49 Mahmud, *A Short History of Islam*, p.131.

50 Crespi, *The Arabs in Europe*, p.76.

51 Hitti, *History*, p.613.

Notes to Chapter 7

1   Andrew M. Watson, *Agricultural Innovation in the Early Islamic World* (Cambridge, UK: Cambridge University Press, 1983), p.2.

2   John McPhee, 'Oranges', in Donald Hall, ed., *The Contemporary Essay* (New York: St. Martins, 1984), p.300.

3   Janet L. Abu-Lughod, *Before European Hegemony: The World System AD 1250–1350* (New York, & Oxford, UK: Oxford University Press, 1989), p.233.

4   Watson, *Agricultural Innovation*, pp.62, 70–71.

5   Abu-Lughod, *Before European Hegemony*, p.43.

6   Watson, p.22.

7   Ibid., pp.10–11.

8   Ibid., pp.17–18.

9   Abu-Lughod, *Before European Hegemony*, p.233.

10 Fox, *The Inner Sea*, p.505.

11 Hitti, *History*, p.528.

12 Abu-Lughod, *Before European Hegemony*, p.43.

13 Watson, pp.83, 92.

14 Ibid., pp.90–92.

15 Al-Hassan and Hill, *Islamic Technology*, p.13.

16 James and Thorpe, *Ancient Inventions*, p.139.

17 Ibid., pp.126, 524.

18 Al-Hassan and Hill, *Islamic Technology*, p.45.

19 James and Thorpe, *Ancient Inventions*, pp.394–395.

20 Al-Hassan and Hill, *Islamic Technology*, pp.54–55.

21 Ibid., pp.13–14, 45, 60.

22 James and Thorpe, *Ancient Inventions*, p.405.

23 Al-Hassan and Hill, *Islamic Technology*, p.151.

24 Roy Genders, *Perfume through the Ages* (New York: G.P. Putnam, 1972), p.101.

25 Hitti, *History*, p.350.

26 Hourani, *A History of the Arab Peoples*, p.43.

27 Hitti, *Cities*, p.307.

28 Ibid.

Notes to Chapter 8

1 Hitti, *History*, p.255.

2 Hitti, *Cities*, pp.308–309.

3 Hugh Kennedy, 'When Intrigue Really Was Byzantine', *New York Times Book Review* (January 7, 1996), p.10.

4 Asimov, *Science*, p.82.

5 Campbell, *Arabian Medicine and Its Influence*, p.185.

6 Roberts, *History of the World*, p.436.

7 Hodgson, *The Venture*, vol.1, p.55.

8 William Hardy McNeill, *The Rise of the West: A History of the Human Community* (Chicago, IL: Chicago University Press, 1963), p.267.

9 Roberts, *History of the World*, pp.182, 208.

10 Cantor, *The Civilization*, p.358.

11 Hitti, *History*, pp.292–293.

12 Hodgson, *The Venture*, pp.298–299; Hitti, *Cities*, p.103; Campbell, *Arabian Medicine*, pp.48–49.

13 Hitti, *History*, p.313.

14 Sarton, *Introduction to Science*, vol.1, p.558.

15 James and Thorpe, *Ancient Inventions*, pp.326–328.

16 Al-Hassan and Hill, *Islamic Technology*, p.9.

17 Naila Minai, *Women in Islam: Tradition and Transition in the Middle East* (New York: Seaview Books, 1981), p.34.

18 Schroeder, *Muhammad's People*, p.157.

19 Najib Ullah, *Islamic Literature* (New York: Washington Square Press, 1963), pp.52–53; Minai, *Women in Islam*, pp.30–34.

20 Annemarie Schimmel, *As Through a Veil: Mystical Poetry in Islam* (New York: Columbia University Press, 1982), p.38; Hitti, *History*, p.439.

21 A.M.A. Shustery, *Outlines of Islamic Culture* (Lahore, Pakistan: Sh. Muhammd Ashraf, 1976), p.325.

22 For information on al-Nadim, see Sarton, *Introduction to Science*, vol.1, p.662; and al-Nadim and Ibn Abi Yaqub, *The Fihrist of al-Nadim*, ed.

and trans. George Bayard, 2 vols. (New York and London: Columbia University Press, 1970), pp.398, 338, 615–626, 349, 361.

23   Hitti, *History*, p.611; Ronan, *Science: Its History*, p.260.

24   Roberts, *A History of the World*, p.196.

25   Campbell, *Arabian Medicine and Its Influence*, vol.1, pp.58–59.

26   Ali ibn Ahmad, known as Asaʿdi of Tus, was a poet and nephew of Firdausi, one of the eminent poets of Iran.

27   Carlton S. Coon, *Saturday Review* (October 24, 1953), p.61.

28   Arnold and Guillaume, *The Legacy of Islam*, pp.257–263.

29   Hitti, *History*, pp.431–432.

30   Al-Faruqi, Lois Lamya', *The Cultural Atlas of Islam* (New York: MacMillan, 1986), pp.299–301.

31   Muhammad Asad, *The Message of the Qur'an* (Gibraltar: Dar al-Andalus, 1980), p.206.

32   Hodgson, *The Venture*, vol.2, pp.480–481.

33   M. Saeed Sheikh, *Islamic Philosophy* (London: Octagon Press, 1982), p.144.

34   Sarton, *Introduction to Science*, vol.3, p.294.

35   Arnold Toynbee, *A Study of History* (London: Oxford University Press, 1961), vol.10, pp.64–86, vol.9, pp.175–182.

36   Hodgson, *The Venture*, vol.2, p.478.

37   Anwar G. Chejne, *Muslim Spain: Its History and Culture* (Minneapolis, MN: University of Minnesota Press, 1974), p.275.

38   Shaukat Ali, *Intellectual Foundations of Muslim Civilization* (Lahore, Pakistan: Publishers United, 1977), p.114.

39   Hodgson, *The Venture*, vol.2, p.481; Muhsin Mahdi, 'Islamic Philosophy', *The New Encyclopaedia Britannica, Macropedia*, vol.22, pp.24–31.

40   Chejne, *Muslim Spain*, p.275.

41   Hodgson, *The Venture*, vol.2, pp.479, 482.

42   Roberts, *A History of the World*, pp.538-39.

43   Hitti, *History*, p.307.

44   Al-Faruqi, *Atlas*, p.308.

Notes to Chapter 9

1   Asad, *The Message of the Qur'an*, p.34.

2   Ibid., p.308.

3   Whinfield, *Masnavi i Ma'navi*, pp.19–20.

4   Roberts, *History of the World*, p.204.

5   Ibid., pp.205, 223.

6   Ronan, *Science: Its History*, p.203.

7   Hodgson, *The Venture*, vol.1, pp.314–315; Asimov, *Science*, p.109.

8   Ronan, *Science: Its History*, p.203.

9   Seyyed Hossein Nasr, *Science and Civilization in Islam* (New York: New American Library, 1968), p.148.

10 Timothy Ferris, *Coming of Age in the Milky Way* (New York: William Morrow, 1988), p.43.

11 Hitti, *History*, p.376.

12 Bernard Carra de Vaux, "Les sphères célestes selon Nasīr Eddin-Attusī." In Paul Tannery, *Recherches sur l'histoire de l'astronomie ancienne*, Appendix VI, pp.337–361, 396 Paris, 1893.

13 Hitti, *History*, p.572.

14 J. Casulleras and J. Samso (eds.), *From Baghdad to Barcelona: Studies in the Islamic Exact Sciences in Honour of Prof. Juan Vernet*, 2 vols. (Barcelona: Barcelona University, 1996), vol. 1, p.479.

15 Ferris, *Coming of Age*, p.43.

16 Ronan, *Science: Its History*, pp.212, 217–218.

17 Hitti, *History*, p.572.

18 Ibid., pp.254, 572–573.

19 Whinfield, *Masnavi i Ma'navi*, p.22.

20 Watson, *Agricultural Innovation*, p.65.

21 William J. Kaufmann III, *Universe* (New York: W.H. Freeman, 1991), p.140-143.

22 Ronan, *Science: Its History*, pp.236–237.

23 J. Casulleras and J. Samso, pp.475–476.

24 Sarton, *Introduction to Science*, vol.1, p.520.

25 Cyril Glasse, *The Concise Encyclopedia of Islam* (San Francisco, CA: Harper & Row, 1989), p.203.

26 *Encyclopedia Britannica*, vol.1, p.208.

27 Ronan, *Science: Its History*, p.237.

28 Ibid., p.239.

29 Asimov, *Science*, p.69.

30 Ronan, *Science: Its History*, p.239.

31 Asimov, *Science*, p.87.

32 Max Meyerhof, *Le monde islamique* (Paris: F. Rieder, 1926), p.327.

33 Sarton, *Introduction to Science*, vol.1, p.586.

34 Hitti, *History*, p.366.

35 Ronan, *Science: Its History*, p.238.
36 Ibid.
37 Sarton, *Introduction to Science*, vol.1, p.563.
38 Ferris, *Coming of Age*, p.388.
39 Sarton, *Introduction to Science*, vol.1, p.563.
40 Ibid., pp.666, 1022.
41 Carra de Vaux, p.388.
42 Ahmad, *Discovering Islam*, pp.346–238.
43 Sarton, *Introduction to Science*, vol.1, p.666.
44 Ronan, *Science: Its History*, p.225.
45 Carra de Vaux, p.388.
46 Sarton, *Introduction to Science*, vol.1, pp.666, 1022.
47 James and Thorpe, p.63.
48 Meyerhof, *Le monde islamique*, p.393.
49 Glasse, *Encyclopedia of Islam*, p.224.
50 Ronan, *Science: Its History*, p.227.
51 James and Thorpe, p.123.
52 Sarton, *Introduction to Science*, vol.1, p.740.
53 Hitti, *History*, p.570.
54 Sarton, *Introduction to Science*, vol.1, p.559.
55 Ibid., pp.559–560.
56 Ronan, *Science: Its History*, p.227; See also http://news.bbc.co.uk/1/hi/ sci/tech/7810846.stm (accessed 5 January 2008).
57 Meyerhof, *Le monde islamique*, p.229.
58 Ahmad, *Discovering Islam*, p.230.
59 Hitti, *History*, p.629.
60 Meyerhof, *Le monde islamique*, p.335.
61 Carra de Vaux, p.396.
62 Jamil Ahmad, *Hundred Great Muslims*, p.262.
63 Carra de Vaux, p.396.
64 Shustery, *Outlines of Islamic Culture*, p.138.
65 For more detailed information on Muslim geographers, see Sarton, *Introduction to Science*, vol.1, pp.546–547, 571, 586–587, 621–622, 631, 637, 675, 707–708.
66 Sarton, *Introduction to Science*, vol.2, pp.410–412.
67 Chejne, *Muslim Spain*, pp.284–286.
68 Sarton, *Introduction to Science*, vol.2, p.410.

69   Ronan, *Science: Its History*, p.233.

70   Sarton, *Introduction to Science*, vol.2, pp.410–412.

71   Chejne, p.287.

72   Sarton, *Introduction to Science*, vol.2, p.513.

73   Moynihan, p.29.

Notes to Chapter 10

1   *Concise Oxford Book of Quotations* (London: World Books & Oxford University Press, 1971), p.204, qu. 15. Quotation taken from William Shakespeare, *Much Ado About Nothing*, v, i, 35.

2   Sarton, *Introduction to Science*, vol.1, p.731.

3   Campbell, *Arabian Medicine and Its Influence*, vol.1, p. xiv.

4   Edward G. Browne, *Arabian Medicine* (Lahore, Pakistan: Hijra International Publishers, 1990), p.36.

5   Ibid., p.48.

6   Campbell, *Arabian Medicine and Its Influence*, vol.1, p.51.

7   Eugene A. Myers, *Arabic Thought and the Western World* (New York: Frederick Ungar Publishing, 1964), pp.13–14.

8   Reynold A. Nicholson, *Mathnawi of Jalauddin Rumi* (Lahore, Pakistan: Sang-e-Meel Publ., 2005), p.22.

9   Browne, *Arabian Medicine*, pp.51, 66.

10   Ibid., pp.47, 50.

11   Hitti, *History*, p.366.

12   Meyerhof, *Le monde islamique*, p.324.

13   Browne, *Arabian Medicine*, p.59.

14   Meyerhof, *Le monde islamique*, p.329.

15   Hitti, *History*, p.367.

16   Fielding H. Garrison, *An Introduction to the History of Medicine* (Philadelphia, PA & London: W.B. Saunders, 1929), p.129.

17   Sarton, *Introduction to Science*, vol.1, p.700.

18   Ahmad, *Discovering Islam*, p.221.

19   Meyerhof, *Le monde islamique*, p.329.

20   Sarton, *Introduction to Science*, vol.1, p.711.

21   Garrison, *Introduction to the History of Medicine*, p.130.

22   Campbell, *Arabian Medicine and Its Influence*, vol.1, p.78.

23   Cases taken from Browne, *Arabian Medicine*, pp.83–89.

24   Nicholson, *Mathnawi*, p.23.

25 Hitti, *History*, p.578.
26 Ibid., p.577.
27 Campbell, *Arabian Medicine*, vol.1, p.86.
28 Ibid., p.88.
29 Hitti, *History*, p.585.
30 Garrison, *An Introduction to the History of Medicine*, p.133.
31 Hitti, *History*, p.585.
32 Sarton, *Introduction to Science*, vol.1, p.534.
33 Garrison, *An Introduction to the History of Medicine*, p.133.
34 Campbell, *Arabian Medicine and Its Influence*, vol.1, p.55.
35 Browne, *Arabian Medicine*, pp.15–16.
36 James and Thorpe, p.7.
37 Sarton, *Introduction to Science*, vol.1, p.678.
38 Ibid., p.728.
39 Ibid., p.771.
40 Ibid., p.728.
41 Ibid., p.729.
42 J. Casulleras and J. Samso, p.479.
43 Meyerhof, *Le monde islamique*, pp.335, 349.
44 Garrison, *An Introduction to the History of Medicine*, p.136.
45 Ibid.; Campbell, *Arabian Medicine and Its Influence*, vol.1, p.56.

Notes to Chapter 11

1 Reynold A. Nicholson, *A Literary History of the Arabs* (Cambridge, UK: Cambridge University Press, 1966), pp.15–16.
 2 Ibid., p.323.
 3 Tuetey, *Classical Arabic Poetry*, p.3.
 4 Nicholson, *A Literary History of the Arabs*, p.71.
 5 Tuetey, *Classical Arabic Poetry*, p.21.
 6 Michael A. Sells (trans.), *Desert Tracings: Six Classic Arabic Odes* (Middletown, CT: Wesleyan University Press, 1989), p.4.
 7 Lewis, *Islam and the West*, pp.120–121.
 8 Tuetey, *Classical Arabic Poetry*, p.8.
 9 Ibid., p.98.
10 Julia Ashtiany, T. Johnstone, J. Latham, R. Serjeant, and G. Rex Smith (eds.), *The Cambridge History of Arabic Literature: 'Abbasid Belles-Lettres* (Cambridge, UK: Cambridge University Press, 1990).
11 Salma Khadra Jayyusi (ed.), *The Legacy of Muslim Spain* (Leiden, The

Netherlands; New York; Cologne: E.J. Brill, 1992), p.391.

12 Ibid., pp.387–396.

13 Ibid., pp.396–399.

14 Tuetey, *Classical Arabic Poetry*, pp.30, 35.

15 Ibid., pp.31, 40.

16 Nicholson, *A Literary History of the Arabs*, pp.243,327.

17 Ibid., p.243.

18 Jayyusi, *The Legacy of Muslim Spain*, p.401.

19 Tuetey, *Classical Arabic Poetry*, pp.169, 172.

20 Nicholson, *A Literary History of the Arabs*, pp.245–246.

21 Jayyusi, *The Legacy of Muslim Spain*, pp.406–409.

22 Ibid., pp.427, 429, 432.

23 Nicholson, *A Literary History of the Arabs*, p.246.

24 Jayyusi, *The Legacy of Muslim Spain*, p.324.

25 Ashtiany, p.197.

26 Ashtiany, p.83.

27 Nicholson, *A Literary History of the Arabs*, p.257.

28 Ibid., p.285.

29 Schroeder, *Muhammad's People*, pp.270–271.

30 Lillian Herlands Hornstein, *The Reader's Companion to World Literature* (New York: New American Library, 1956), p.329.

31 H.T. Norris "Fables and Legends," *The Cambridge History of Arabic Literature: 'Abbasid Belles-Lettres*, Ashtiany, p.48.

32 Ibid., p.57.

33 Ibid., p.63.

34 Nicholson, *A Literary History of the Arabs*, p.238.

35 H.T. Norris "Fables and Legends," *The Cambridge History of Arabic Literature: 'Abbasid Belles-Lettres*, Ashtiany, pp.137–138.

36 Muhsin Mahdi, 'Islamic Philosphy', in *The New Encyclopaedia Britannica*, Macropedia, vol.22 (Chicago, IL: Encyclopaedia Britannica Inc., 1987), pp.24–31.

37 Ullah, *Islamic Literature*, p.78.

38 Charles Pellat, *The Life and Works of Jahiz: Translations of Selected Texts*, trans. D.M. Hawke (London: Routledge & Kegan Paul, 1969), pp.78–79.

39 Ibid., pp.87, 90–91.

40 Ullah, *Islamic Literature*, p.79.

41 Pellat, *The Life and Works of Jahiz*, pp.83, 89, 108.

42 Ibid., pp.81, 94–96, 109.

43 Jon McGinnis, *Classical Arabic Philosophy: An Anthology of Sources* (Indianapolis, IN: Hackett, 2007), p.34.

44 C. Pellat, "Al-Sahib Ibn 'Abbad," *The Cambridge History of Arabic Literature: 'Abbasid Belles-Lettres*, Ashtiany, p.103-105.

45 Ibid., pp.105-106.

46 Ashtiany, pp.113, 119.

47 Bergé, *Les Arabes*, p.118.

48 Ibid., p.123.

49 Nicholson, *A Literary History of the Arabs*, p.328.

50 A.F.L. Beeston "Al-Hamadhani, al-Hariri and the Maqamat Genre," *The Cambridge History of Arabic Literature: 'Abbasid Belles-Lettres*, Ashtiany, p.127.

51 Beeston, "Al-Hamadhani, al-Hariri and the Maqamat Genre," pp.131–32.

52 Nicholson, *A Literary History of the Arabs*, p.329.

53 Ibid., pp.429–430.

54 Ibid., p.336.

55 Ibid., p.290.

56 M.M. Badawi, "Abbasid Poetry and Its Antecedents," *The Cambridge History of Arabic Literature: 'Abbasid Belles-Lettres*, Ashtiany, pp.149–150.

57 Nicholson, *A Literary History of the Arabs*, pp.295, 298.

58 Schoeler, G. "Banshar b. Burd, Abu 'l-'Atahiyah and Abu Nuwas," *The Cambridge History of Arabic Literature: 'Abbasid Belles-Lettres*, Ashtiany, p.296.

59 Ibid., p.270.

60 Nicholson, *A Literary History of the Arabs*, pp.298–303.

61 Schroeder, *Muhammad's People*, p.290.

62 Nicholson, *A Literary History of the Arabs*, pp.129–130.

63 Ibid., p.79.

64 Tuetey, *Classical Arabic Poetry*, p.73.

65 M.M. Badawi, *A Short History of Modern Arabic Literature*, (Oxford University Press, USA, May 27, 1993), p.156.

66 Ibid., pp.159–161.

67 Tuetey, *Classical Arabic Poetry*, p.240.

68 Ullah, *Islamic Literature*, p.59.

69 Nicholson, *A Literary History of the Arabs*, pp.311–312.

70 Tuetey, *Classical Arabic Poetry*, pp.80, 84.

71 Ashtiany, p.333.

72 Nicholson, *A Literary History of the Arabs*, p.317; Phillip Khurri Hitti,

    Islam: A Way of Life (Mineapolis, MN: University of Minnesota Press, 1970), p147.

73   Tuetey, *Classical Arabic Poetry*, p.86.

74   A'ishah Abd al-Rahman, *Rissalat-el Guphran* (Cairo: N/D, 1950), p.335.

75   Ibid., p.328.

76   Tuetey, *Classical Arabic Poetry*, p.87.

77   Ibid., p.90.

78   Nicholson, *A Literary History of the Arabs*, p.323.

79   Tuetey, *Classical Arabic Poetry*, p.18.

80   Ibid., p.184.

81   Ullah, *Islamic Literature*, p.40.

82   Tuetey, *Classical Arabic Poetry*, p.65.

83   Ibid., p.216.

84   Ullah, *Islamic Literature*, pp.52–53.

85   Hitti, *History*, pp.538–540.

86   Chejne, *Muslim Spain*, p.529.

87   Hitti, *History*, pp.535, 560.

88   *Muslim Spain* pp.558–559.

Notes to Chapter 12

1   Manoochehr Aryanpur, *A History of Persian Literature* (Tehran: Kayhan Press, 1973), pp.4, 23, 51.

2   Ibid., p.51.

3   Reuben Levy, *An Introduction to Persian Literature* (New York & London: Columbia University Press, 1969), p.15.

4   Aryanpur, *A History of Persian Literature*, pp.70, 72, 73.

5   Levy, p.36.

6   Aryanpur, *A History of Persian Literature*, pp.70, 72, 73.

7   A.J. Arberry, *Classical Persian Literature* (New York: Macmillan, 1958), p.34.

8   Aryanpur, *A History of Persian Literature*, p.77

9   Ibid.

10   Ibid., p.120.

11   Ibid., p.91.

12   James Kritzeck, *Anthology of Islamic Literature* (New York: Holt, Rinehart & Winston, 1964), pp.180–183.

13   Levy, p.39.

14   Arberry, *Classical Persian Literature*, p.84.

15   Aryanpur, *A History of Persian Literature*, p.131.

16   Ibid., pp.136–137.

17   Levy, p.38.

18   Ibid.

19   Idries Shah, *The Sufis* (Garden City, NY: Doubleday, 1964), p.164.

20   Aryanpur, *A History of Persian Literature*, pp.127, 134–142, 161.

21   Ibid., p.161.

22   Arberry, *Classical Persian Literature*, pp.90, 129.

23   Aryanpur, *A History of Persian Literature*, pp.167–169.

24   Annemarie Schimmel, *As Through a Veil: Mystical Poetry in Islam* (New York: Columbia University Press, 1982), p.53.

25   Arberry, *Classical Persian Literature*, p.132.

26   Aryanpur, *A History of Persian Literature*, p.164.

27   Shah, *The Sufis*, p.106.

28   Aryanpur, *A History of Persian Literature*, p.171.

29   Levy, p.82.

30   Aryanpur, *A History of Persian Literature*, p.171.

31   Ibid., p.192; Schimmel, *As Through a Veil*, p.83; Shah, *The Sufis*, p.115.

32   Levy, p.105.

33   Hodgson, *The Venture*, vol.2, pp.245, 246.

34   Nicholson, *Mathnawi*, Book 2.

35   Hodgson, *The Venture*, vol.2, p.248.

36   Shah, *The Sufis*, pp.117–125.

37   Arberry, *Classical Persian Literature*, p.64.

38   Aryanpur, *A History of Persian Literature*, p.208.

39   Levy, p.117.

40   Saʿdi, *The Gulistan or Rose Garden of Saʿdi*. Trans. Edward Rehatsek (London: George Allen & Unwin, 1964), p.83.

41   Arberry, *Classical Persian Literature*, pp.189–190.

42   Ibid., p.195.

43   Levy, p.61-62.

44   Arberry, *Classical Persian Literature*, pp.188–202.

45   Shah, *The Sufis*, p.98.

46   Levy, p.123.

47   W. G. Archer's "Preface" to Rehatsek's translation, trans. G. M. Wickens, *The Nasirean Ethics* (London: Allen and Unwin, 1964), p.216; and Aryanpur, *A History of Persian Literature*, p.219.

48 Ibid., p.221.
49 Aryanpur, *A History of Persian Literature*, p.226.
50 Levy, p.132.
51 Arberry, *Classical Persian Literature*, pp.346–349.
52 Aryanpur, *A History of Persian Literature*, p.243.
53 Arberry, *Classical Persian Literature*, p.426.
54 Ibid., p.431.
55 Ibid., p.430.
56 Arberry, *Classical Persian Literature*, p.441.
57 Ibid., pp.441–448.
58 Ibid., p.448.

Notes to Chapter 13
1   Hodgson, *The Venture*, p.98.
2   Issam El-Said and Ayse Parman, *Geometric Concepts in Islamic Art* (London: World of Islam Festival Publishing, 1976).
3   Giovanni Curatola, *The Simon and Schuster Book of Oriental Carpets*, trans. Simon Pleasance (New York: Simon and Schuster, 1981), p.93.
4   Ibid., p.106.
5   Ibid., pp.142–143.
6   Oleg Grabar, *The Formation of Islamic Art* (New Haven, CT & London: Yale University Press, 1973), p.192.
7   Curatola, *Book of Oriental Carpets*, pp.32–33.
8   Ibid., p.30.
9   Ibid., pp.42, 44, 45, 75.
10 Errol Manners, *Ceramics Source Book* (Secaucus, NJ: Chartwell Books, 1990), p.15.
11 Alan Caiger-Smith, *Lustre Pottery: Technique, Tradition and Innovation in Islam and the Western World* (New York: New Amsterdam Pottery, 1985); Alan Caiger-Smith, *Tin-Glaze Pottery in Europe and the Islamic World* (London: Faber & Faber, 1973), pp.22–23.
12 Manners, *Ceramics Source Book*, p.84.
13 Barbara Brend, *Islamic Art* (London: British Museum Press, 1991), pp.38, 40.
14 Grabar, *The Formation of Islamic Art*, p.25.
15 Brend, *Islamic Art*, p.38.
16 Alexandre Papadopoulo, *Islam and Muslim Art*, trans. from French by Robert Erich Wolf (New York: Harry N. Abrams, 1979), p.108.

17 Ibid., pp.111, 113.
18 Jean Jenkins and Poul Rovsing Olsen, *Music and Musical Instruments in the World of Islam* (London: World of Islam Festival Publishing, 1976).
19 James and Thorpe, p.166.
20 Ibid., p.601.
21 Curatola, *Book of Oriental Carpets*, pp.28–30.
22 Titus Burckhardt, *Art of Islam:Language and Meaning* (London: World of Islam Festival Publishing, 1976), pp.40–41.
23 Papadopoulo, *Islam and Muslim Art*, p.165.
24 James and Thorpe, pp.276–277.
25 Grabar, *The Formation of Islamic Art*, p.18.
26 Whinfield, *Masnavi i Ma'navi*, p.52.
27 Burckhardt, *Art of Islam*, pp.51, 60.
28 Papadopoulo, *Islam and Muslim Art*, p.179.
29 Horace Freeland Judson, *The Search for Solutions* (New York: Holt, Rinehart & Winston, 1980), p.40.
30 Claude Humbert, *Islamic Ornamental Design*, English trans. Alison Martin (New York: Hasting House Publishers, 1980); André Paccard, *Traditional Islamic Craft in Moroccan Architecture*, English trans. Mary Guggenheim (Saint-Jorioz, France: Atelier 74, 1980).
31 Curatola, *Book of Oriental Carpets*, p.28.
32 Burckhardt, *Art of Islam*, pp.8, 117–174.
33 Jerry M. Landay and the editors of the *Newsweek* Book Division, *Dome of the Rock* (New York: Newsweek, 1972), p.67.
34 Glasse, *The Concise Encyclopedia of Islam*, p.372.
35 Judson, *The Search for Solutions*, p.188.

Notes to Chapter 14

1 Dr. Othman Ali is currently a lecturer in Middle Eastern Studies at Ryerson University, Toronto, Canada.
2 M. Olus Arik, Sami Güner, Adair Mill, Maggie Quigley Pinar, and Graham Clarke, *The Turkish Contribution to Islamic Art* (Istanbul: Yapi ve Kredi Bankasi, 1976), p.19.
3 Ibid., p.22.
4 An *iwān* is a house typically built on a cruciform layout with four arched entrances.
5 Caravanseries were built along the lines of a fortress during the Seljuk

era, with turrets strengthening three massive outer walls. These buildings were located at about fifty-mile intervals, or the distance of a day's travel, on the main trade routes and were designed to offer merchants and travelers comfort, recreation, and protection. See, Aptullah Kuran, *The Mosque in Early Ottoman Architecture* (Chicago, IL: Chicago University Press, 1968), p.22.

6 Arik, *The Turkish Contribution to Islamic Art*, p.23.

7 Juan Campo, ed., *The Encyclopedia of Islam* (New York: Facts on File Publications, 2008), p.67.

8 Arik, *The Turkish Contribution to Islamic Art*, pp.38–39.

9 Robert Hillenbrand, *Islamic Architecture: From Its Function and Meaning* (New York: Columbia University Press, 1994), pp.26–28.

10 S. Shaw, *History of the Ottoman Empire and Modern Turkey*, 2 vols. Vol.1: *Empire of the Gazis: The Rise and Decline of the Ottoman Empire 1280–1808* (Cambridge, UK, and New York: Cambridge University Press, 1976–1977), pp.22–25.

11 Seyyed Hossein Nasr, *Science and Civilization in Islam* (New York: New American Library, 1968), Introduction.

12 Avigdor Levy, *Jews, Turks, Ottomans: A Shared History, Fifteenth Through the Twentieth Century* (Syracuse University Press, 2003).

13 Ibid.

14 Stanford J. Shaw and Ezel Kural Shaw, *History of the Ottoman Empire and Modern Turkey*. Vol. 2: *Reform, Revolution and Republic: The Rise of Modern Turkey* (Cambridge, UK, and New York: Cambridge University Press, 1976–1977).

15 Halil Inalcik, *Turkey and Europe in History* (Istanbul: Eren, 2006), p.124.

16 Anthony Black, 'The State of the House of Osman (devlet-i al-it Osman)', in Anthony Black, *The History of Islamic Political Thought: From the Prophet to the Present* (Edinburgh, Scotland, UK: Edinburgh University Press, 2001), p.199; Halil Inalcik and Donald Quarter, *An Economic and Social History of the Ottoman Empire: 1300 to 1914* (Cambridge, UK: Cambridge University Press, 1971), p.120.

17 Daniel Gorman, *The Ottoman Empire and Early Modern Europe* (Cambridge, UK: Cambridge University Press, 2002), p.67.

18 Lapidus, *A History of Islamic Societies*, p.263.

19 Halil Inalcik and Cemal Kafadar, eds., *Suleyman the Second and His Time* (Istanbul: Isis Press, 1993), pp.300–301.

20 Robert Irwin, *Islamic Art in Context: Art, Architecture, and the Literary*

World (New York: Harry N. Abrams, 1997), p.99.

21   M. Ugur Derman, *Contributions to Islamic Art* (Istanbul: 1976), p.59.

22   Ibid., pp.60–61.

23   Inalcik and Kafadar, *Suleyman the Second*, pp.334–336.

24   George Mitchell, *Architecture Of The Islamic World: Its History and Social Meaning* (Thames and Hudson, New edition, 1995) p.123."*Mihrab*: An acoustic device, resonator, shaped to bounce sound back and magnify it for seamen. At the point where the qiblah's axis meets the wall of the mosque, an indentation is produced, a directional niche called a *mihrab*."

25   Ibid., p.18. Koca Sinan is compared to Michelangelo (1475–1564) and the English architect Christopher Wren (1632–1723). Sinan was born in Central Anatolia in 1490. At the age of 22, he was brought to Istanbul and instructed at the Palace. From 1514 to 1516, he traveled with Selim I and inspected the Turkish and Persian domed buildings of Tabriz, and the works of arabesque art in Cairo. For 52 years he worked with his colleague in the construction of buildings and erected around 360 monuments.

26   Irwin, *Islamic Art in Context*, p.124.

27   Gulru Necipoglu, *The Age of Sinan* (London: Reaction Books, 2005), pp.84–85.

28   Ibid., pp.86–87.

29   Franz Babinger, *Mehmet der Eroberer und Seine Seit* [*Mehmet the Conqueror and His Time*]. Trans. Ralph Manheim, ed. with a preface by William C. Hickman, 2nd edn. (Princeton, NJ: Princeton University Press, 1992), pp.293–294.

30   Hillenbrand, *Islamic Architecture*, pp.27–28.

31   Babinger, *Mehmet der Eroberer und Seine Seit*, pp.120–121.

32   Necipoglu, *The Age of Sinan*, p.77.

33   Ekrem Akurgal, ed., *The Art and Architecture of Turkey* (New York: Rizzoli, 1980).

34   Inalcik, *Suleyman II and His Time*, pp.306–307.

35   Arthur Stratton, *Sinan: The Biography of One of the World's Greatest Architects and a Portrait of the Golden Age of Ottoman Empire* (London: Macmillan, 1972), p.120.

36   Ibid.

37   Ibid., p.134.

38   Inalcik, *Suleyman II and His Time*, p.310; Kuran, *The Mosque in Early*

Ottoman Architecture, p.23.

39 Inalcik, *Sulayman II and His Time*, p.320.

40 Behcet Unsal, *Turkish Islamic Architecture in Seljuk and Ottoman Times 1071–1923* (London: St Martin's Press, 1973), pp.92–93.

41 Inalcik, *Sulayman II and His Time*, p.348.

42 Ibid., p.350.

43 Necipoglu, *The Age of Sinan*, p.82.

44 Ibid., p.83.

45 Ibid.

46 Ibid., pp.98–100.

47 Inalcik, *Turkey and Europe in History*, p.58.

48 Necipoglu, *The Age of Sinan*, pp.86–89.

49 Ernest Kühnel, *Islamic Arts*. Trans. Katherine Watson (London: G. Bell, 1970), pp.133–134.

50 Bernard Lewis, *The Emergence of Modern Turkey* (London: Oxford University Press, 1961), pp.50–51.

51 E. Birnbaum, *The Questioning Mind: Kātib Chelebi 1609–57* (Toronto, Canada: TSAR, 1994), p.45.

52 Stefan Reichmuth, *Islamic Reformist Discourse in the Tulip Period (1718–30)* (Istanbul: International Congress on Learning and Education in the Ottoman World, 1999), pp.12–15; Ali Çaksu, ed., *Studies and Sources on the Ottoman History Series*, 6 (Istanbul: Research Center for Islamic History, Art, and Culture [IRCICA], 2001), pp.149–161.

53 S. Soucek, ed., *Piri Reis and Turkish Mapmaking after Columbus: The Khalili Portolan Atlas* (London: Nour Foundation and Azimuth; and Oxford, UK: Oxford University Press, 1996), pp.192–195.

54 Berna Kilinç, ed., *Ottoman Science Studies: A Review*; Robert S. Cohen, Jürgen Renn, Kostas Gavroglu, Gürol Irzik, and Güven Güzeldere, *Turkish Studies in the History and Philosophy of Science*, vol.244, pp.251–263.

Notes to Chapter 15

1 Campbell, *Arabian Medicine*, vol.1, pp.155–156, xii, 43.

2 Hitti, *History*, p.365.

3 Campbell, *Arabian Medicine*, vol.1, pp. xiv, 14, 62.

4 Ibid., p.118.

5 Daniel J. Boorstin, *The Discoverers* (New York: Random House, 1983), pp.344–347.

6   Ibid., p.347

7   Campbell, *Arabian Medicine*, vol.1, pp.167, 121.

8   James Burke, *The Day the Universe Changed* (Boston, MA: Little, Brown, 1985), p.36.

9   Francesco Gabrieli, 'The Transmission of Learning and Literary Influences to Western Europe', in P.M. Holt, ed., *The Cambridge History of Islam*, vol.2 (London: Cambridge University Press, 1976), p.853.

10 For further information on the subsequent paragraphs, see Sarton, *Introduction to Science*, vol.1, pp.725, 742, 73.

11 Campbell, *Arabian Medicine*, vol.1, p.121.

12 Sarton, *Introduction to Science*, vol.2, pp.72–73.

13 Browne, *Arabian Medicine*, p.26.

14 Campbell, vol.1, p.159.

15 Ibid., pp.203–206.

16 Gabrieli, 'Transmission of Learning', p.862.

17 Sharif, *Islamic Philosophy*, p.1.

18 Mahdi, 'Islamic Philosophy', *Encyclopaedia Britannica*, vol.22, p.24.

19 Papadopoulo, *Islam and Muslim Art*, p.33.

20 Sarton, *Introduction to Science*, vol.2, p.559.

21 Mahdi, 'Islamic Philosophy', *Encyclopaedia Britannica*, vol.22, pp.24–25.

22 Shustery, *Outlines of Islamic Culture*, p.325.

23 Richard Netton, *Al-Farabi and His School* (London: Routledge, 1992), pp.43–47.

24 Myers, *Arabic Thought*, p.30.

25 Dominique Urvoy, *Ibn Rushd (Averroes)* (London & New York: 1991), pp.124–125.

26 Ibid., p.127.

27 Ibid.

28 Myers, *Arabic Thought*, pp.48–49.

29 Hitti, *History*, pp.580–581.

30 Browne, *Arabian Medicine*, pp.118–119, 135.

31 Lewis, *Islam and the West*, p.61.

32 Crespi, *The Arabs in Europe*, p.62.

33 Myers, *Arabic Thought*, p.81.

34 Jacques Le Goff, *Medieval Civilization 400–1500*. Trans. from French by Julia Barrow (Oxford, UK: Basil Blackwell, 1988), p.147.

35 Hitti, *History*, p.559.

36   Ibid., p.588.
37   Myers, *Arabic Thought*, pp.92–93.
38   Gabrieli, 'Transmission of Learning', p.855.
39   Myers, *Arabic Thought*, p.96.
40   Lewis, *Islam and the West*, p.62.
41   Hitti, *History*, p.589.
42   Al-Hassan and Hill, *Islamic Technology*, pp.21–22.
43   Max Meyerhof "Science and Medicine" in Arnold and Guillaume, ed. *The Legacy of Islam*, p.311
44   Hitti, *History*, p.588.
45   Fox, *The Inner Sea*, pp.42–43.
46   Meyerhof, *Le monde islamique*, pp.346, 352–353.
47   Ibid.
48   Joseph Schacht and C.E. Bosworth, eds., *The Legacy of Islam*, 2nd edn. (Oxford, UK: Clarendon Press, 1974).
49   Campbell, *Arabian Medicine*, vol.1, p.124.
50   J. Casulleras and J. Samso, p.486.
51   Gabrieli, 'Transmission of Learning', p.868.
52   Ibid., pp.70–71.
53   Roberts, *History of the World*, p.365.

BIBLIOGRAPHY

Abu-Lughod, Janet L., *Before European Hegemony: The World System A.D. 1250–1350* (New York & Oxford, UK: Oxford University Press, 1989).

Ahmad Aijaz, ed., *Ghazals of Ghalib* (New York & London: Columbia University Press, 1971).

Ahmed, Akbar S., *Discovering Islam: Making Sense of Muslim History and Society* (London & New York: Routledge, 1988).

_____, *Postmodernism and Islam: Predicament and Promise* (London & New York: Routledge, 1992).

Ajram, K., *The Miracle of Islamic Science* (Cedar Rapids, IA: Knowledge House Publishers, 1992).

Akhtar, Shabbir, *A Faith for All Seasons* (Chicago, IL: Ivan R. Dee, 1990).

Akurgal, Ekrem, ed., *The Art and Architecture of Turkey* (New York: Rizzoli, 1980).

Albarn, Keith, et al., *The Language of Pattern: An Enquiry Inspired by Islamic Decoration* (New York: Harper & Row, 1974).

Ali, Shaukat, *Intellectual Foundations of Muslim Civilization* (Lahore, Pakistan: Publishers United Ltd, 1977).

Anderson, William, 'The Great Memory,' *Noetic Sciences Review* (Spring 1992).

Arberry, A.J., *Classical Persian Literature* (New York: Macmillan, 1958).

Arik, M. Olus, et al., *The Turkish Contribution to Islamic Art* (Istanbul: Yapi ve Kredi Bankasi, 1976).

Armento, B.J., et al., *Across the Centuries* (Boston: Houghton Mifflin, 1991).

Armstrong, Karen, *A History of God* (New York: Knopf, 1993).

_____, *Muhammad: A Western Attempt to Understand Islam* (London: Victor Gollancz, 1991).

Arnold, Sir Thomas, and Alfred Guillaume, eds., *The Legacy of Islam* (Oxford, UK: Oxford University Press, 1931).

Aryanpur, Manoochehr, with Abbas Aryanpur Kashani, *A History of Persian Literature* (Tehran: Kayhan Press, 1973).

Asad, Muhammad, *The Message of the Qur'an* (Gibraltar: Dar al-Andalus, 1980).

Ashtiany, Julia, T.M. Johnstone, J.D. Latham, R.B. Serjeant and G. Rex Smith, eds., *The Cambridge History of Arabic Literature: 'Abbasid Belles-Lettres* (Cambridge, UK: Cambridge University Press, 1990).

Asimov, Isaac, *Asimov's Chronology of Science and Discovery* (New York: Harper & Row, 1989).

Atasoy, Nurhan, Afif Bahnassi, and Michael Rogers, *The Art of Islam* (Paris: UNESCO/Flammarion, 1990).

Babinger, Franz, [*Mehmed der Eroberer und seine Zeit*] *Mehmed the Conqueror and His Time*. Trans. from the German by Ralph Manheim; ed. with preface by William C. Hickman, 2nd edn. (Princeton, NJ: Princeton University Press, 1992).

Bammate, Haidar, *Muslim Contribution to Civilization* (Brentwood, MD: American Trust Publications, n.d.c. 1970).

Barakat, Halim, *The Arab World: Society, Culture and State* (Berkeley, CA: University of California Press, 1993).

Barraclough, Geoffrey, ed., *The Times Atlas of World History* (Maplewoods, NJ: Hammond, 1979).

Bergé, Marc, *Les Arabes: histoire et civilisation des Arabes et du monde musulman. Des origines à la chute du royaume du Grenade, racontées par les témoins: IXe siècle av. J.-C. – XVe siècle,* préf. de Jacques Berque (Paris: Lidis, 1978).

Billings, Malcolm, *The Cross and the Crescent: A History of the Crusades* (London: BBC Books, 1987).

Birnbaum, E., The *Questioning Mind: Kātib Chelebi, 1609–57: A Chapter in Ottoman Intellectual History* (Toronto, Canada: TSAR, 1994).

Black, Antony, 'The State of the House of Osman (devlet-i al-it Osman)', in Antony Black, *The History of Islamic Political Thought: From the Prophet to the Present* (New York: Routledge, 2002).

Bodley, R.V.C., *The Quest* (London: R. Hale, and New York: Doubleday, 1947).

Boorstin, Daniel J., *The Discoverers* (New York: Random House, 1983).

Boyle, John Andrew, *The Mongol World Empire* (London: Variorum Reprints, 1977).

Brend, Barbara, *Islamic Art* (London: British Museum Press, 1991).

Briffault, Robert, *Rational Evolution: The Making of Humanity* (New York: Macmillan, 1930).

Broadhurst, R.J.C., trans. & ed., *The Travels of Ibn Jubayr* (London: Jonathan Cape, 1952).

Browne, Edward G., *Arabian Medicine: Being the Fitzpatrick Lectures Delivered at the College of Physicians in November 1919 and November 1920*, repr. (Lahore, Pakistan: Hijra International Publishers, 1990).

_____, *Literary History of Persia* (Cambridge, UK: Cambridge University Press, 1964).

Bulliet, Richard W., *Conversion to Islam in the Medieval Period* (Cambridge, MA, and London: Harvard University Press, 1979).

Burckhardt, Titus, *Art of Islam: Language and Meaning* (London: World of Islam Festival Publishing, 1976).

_____, *Fez: City of Islam* (Cambridge, UK: The Islamic Texts Society, 1992).

Burke, James, *The Day the Universe Changed* (Boston, MA: Little, Brown, 1985).

Caiger-Smith, Alan, *Lustre Pottery* (New York: New Amsterdam Books, 1985).

_____, *Tin-Glaze Pottery* (London: Faber & Faber, 1973).

Çaksu, Ali, ed., *Studies and Sources on the Ottoman History*. Series, 6. (Istanbul, Turkey: Research Center for Islamic History, Art and Culture (IRCICA), 2001).

Campbell, Donald, *Arabian Medicine and Its Influence on the Middle Ages*, vols. 1 & 2 (London: Kegan Paul, Trench, Trubner and Co., 1926).

Campo, Juan, ed., *The Encyclopedia of Islam* (New York: Facts on File, 2008).

Cantor, Norman, *The Civilization of the Middle Ages* (New York: HarperCollins, 1993).

Cantacuzino, Sherban, ed., *Architecture in Continuity: Building in the Islamic World Today* (New York: Aperture and Islamic Publications, 1985).

Casulleras J. and Samso J., (eds.), *From Baghdad to Barcelona: Studies in the Islamic Exact Sciences in Honour of Prof. Juan Vernet* (Barcelona: Barcelona University, 1996).

Chejne, Anwar G., *Muslim Spain: Its History and Culture* (Minneapolis, MN: University of Minnesota Press, 1974).

Cohen, Mark R., 'Islam and the Jews', *Jerusalem Quarterly* (38), 1986.

Copplestone, Trewin, ed., *World Architecture* (New York: McGraw-Hill, 1963).

Corn, Charles, *Distant Islands* (New York: Viking, 1991).

Cragg, Kenneth, and Marston Spreight, *Islam from Within* (Belmont, CA: Wadsworth Publishing, 1980).

Crespi Yor, Gabriele, *The Arabs in Europe* (New York: Rizzoli, 1986).

Critchlow, Keith, *Islamic Patterns* (New York: Schocken Books, 1976).

Curatola, Giovanni, *Book of Oriental Carpets* (New York: Simon & Schuster, 1982).

Curtin, Philip D., *Cross-Cultural Trade in World History* (Cambridge, UK: Cambridge University Press, 1984).

Daniel, Norman, *The Arabs and Medieval Europe*, 2nd edn. (London & New York: Longman, 1979).

_____, *Islam, Europe and Empire* (Edinburgh, UK: Edinburgh University Press, 1966).

Danner, Victor, *Islamic Tradition: An Introduction* (Amity, NY: Amity House, 1988).

Derman, M. Ugur, *Contributions to Islamic Art* (Istanbul, Turkey: 1976).

Duncan, Alistair, *The Noble Sanctuary* (London: Middle East Archive, 1981).

Eaton, Charles Le Gai, *Islam and the Destiny of Man* (Albany, NY: State University of New York Press, 1985).

Eban, Abba, *Heritage, Civilization and the Jews* (New York: Summit Books, 1984).

Edwards, Paul, ed. in chief, *The Encyclopedia of Philosophy* (New York: Macmillan, 1967).

Ehrenkreutz, Andrew S., 'The Silent Force Behind the Rise of Islamic Civilization,' in C.E. Bosworth et al., eds., *The Islamic World* (Princeton, NJ: The Darwin Press, 1989).

El-Abbadi, Mostafa, *The Life and Fate of the Ancient Library of Alexandria* (Paris: UNESCO/UNPD, 1990).

El-Said, Issam and Ayse Parman, *Geometric Concepts in Islamic Art* (London: World of Islam Festival Publishing, 1976).

Embree, Ainslee, *Alberuni's India*. Abr. edn. repr. (New York: W.W. Norton, 1971).

_____, 'Foreign Interpreters of India: The Case of al-Biruni,' in Peter J. Chelkowski, ed., *The Scholar and the Saint* (New York: New York University Press, 1975).

Esposito, John L., *The Islamic Threat: Myth or Reality?* (New York & Oxford, UK: Oxford University Press, 1992).

Eyre, Ronald, *Ronald Eyre on the Long Search* (New York: William Collins, 1979).

Fahmy, Aly Mohamed, *Muslim Sea-Power in the Eastern Mediterranean* (Cairo: National Publication & Printing House, 1966).

al-Faruqi, Ismail Raji, et al., *The Great Asian Religions* (New York: Macmillan, 1969).

_____, ed., *Islamic Thought and Culture* (Washington, DC: International Institute of Islamic Thought, 1402/1982).

al-Faruqi, Lois Lamya', *The Cultural Atlas of Islam* (New York: MacMillan, 1986).

Ferris, Timothy, *Coming of Age in the Milky Way* (New York: William Morrow, 1988).

Fletcher, Sir Bannister, *A History of Architecture*, 17th edn. (New York: Charles Scribner's Sons, 1961).

Fletcher, Richard, *The Quest for El Cid* (London: Hutchinson, 1989).

Fox, Robert, *The Inner Sea: The Mediterranean and Its People* (New York: Alfred A. Knopf, 1993).

Franck, Irene M., and David M. Brownstone, *To the Ends of the Earth: The Great Travel and Trade Routes of Human History* (New York: Facts on File, 1984).

Freeman-Grenville, G.S.P., *The Muslim and Christian Calendars* (London: Rex Collings, 1977).

Frye, Richard N., *The Golden Age of Persia* (New York: Harper & Row, 1975).

Gabrieli, Francesco, 'The Transmission of Learning and Literary Influences to Western Europe,' in P.M. Holt, *The Cambridge History of Islam*, 2 vols. (London: Cambridge University Press, 1970).

Garrison, Fielding H., *An Introduction to the History of Medicine*. 4th edn. (Philadelphia, PA & London: W.B. Saunders, 1929).

Gearing, Lloyd, *Faith's New Age* (London: Collins, 1980).

Genders, Roy, *Perfume Through the Ages* (New York: G.P. Putnam, 1972).

Gibb, H.A.R., trans. and ed., *The Travels of Ibn Battuta*, 3 vols. (Cambridge, UK: Cambridge University Press for the Hakluyt Society, 1958, 1959, 1971).

Glasse, Cyril, *The Concise Encyclopedia of Islam* (San Francisco, CA: Harper & Row, 1989).

Goldstein, Thomas, *Dawn of Modern Science* (Boston. MA: Houghton Mifflin, 1980).

Goodman, Lenn E., *Avicenna* (London & New York: Routledge, 1992).

Gorman, Daniel, *The Ottoman Empire and Early Modern Europe* (Cambridge, UK: Cambridge University Press, 2002).

Grabar, Oleg, *The Formation of Islamic Art* (New Haven, CT & London: Yale University Press, 1973).

Graham, William, *Beyond the Written Word* (Cambridge, UK: Cambridge University Press, 1987).

Haddawy, Husain, trans., *The Arabian Nights* (New York: Norton, 1990).

Hart, Michael H., *The One Hundred: A Ranking of History's Most Influential Persons* (New York: Citadel Press, 1987).

Al-Hassan, et al., *Islamic Technology: An Illustrated History* (Cambridge, UK: Cambridge University Press, 1986).

Hillenbrand, Robert, *Islamic Architecture: From Its Function and Meaning* (New York: Columbia University Press, 1994).

Hitti, Philip K., *History of the Arabs: From the Earliest Times to the Present*. 9th edn. (London: Macmillan, & New York: St. Martin's Press, 1968).

_____, *Capital Cities of Islam* (Minneapolis, MN: University of Minnesota Press, 1973).

Hodgson, Marshall G.S., *The Venture of Islam*, 3 vols. (Chicago, IL, & London: University of Chicago Press, 1974).

Hornstein, Lillian Herlands, *The Reader's Companion to World Literature* (New York: The New American Library, 1956).

Horrie, Chris and Peter Chippindale, *What is Islam?* revd. edn. (London: Virgin Books, 1991).

Hourani, Albert, *A History of the Arab Peoples* (Cambridge, MA: The Belknap Press of Harvard University Press, 1991).

Humbert, Claude, *Islamic Ornamental Design* (New York: Hastings House, 1980).

Hussein, Muhammad A., *Origins of the Book* (Greenwich, CT: New York Graphic Society, 1972).

Ibn al-Arabi, Hadrat Muhyiddin, *What the Seeker Needs*, ed. Shaikh Tosun Bayrak al-Jeharri al-Halveti and Rabia Terri Harris (Putney, VT: Threshold Books, 1992).

Ikram, S.M., *Muslim Civilization in India* (New York & London: Columbia University Press, 1964).

Inalcik, Halil and Donald Quarter, *An Economic and Social History of the Ottoman Empire, 1300 to 1914* (Cambridge, UK: Cambridge University Press, 1971).

Inalcik, Halil, *Turkey and Europe in History* (Istanbul, Turkey: Eren, 2006).

_____, and Cemal Kafadar, eds., *Sulayman the Second and His Time* (Istanbul, Turkey: Isis Press, 1993).

Iqbal, Muhammad, *Javid-Nama*. Intro. & Notes by A.J. Arberry (London: Allen & Unwin, 1966).

Irwin, Robert, *Islamic Art in Context: Art, Architecture, and the Literary World* (New York: Harry N. Abrams, 1997).

Jayyusi, Salma Khadra, ed., *The Legacy of Muslim Spain* (Leiden, The Netherlands; New York; & Cologne: E.J. Brill, 1992).

Jellicoe, Geoffrey and Susan, *The Landscape of Man* (New York: Thames & Hudson, 1987).

Jenkins, Jean, and Poul Rovsing Olsen, *Music and Musical Instruments in the World of Islam* (London: Music Research, 1976).

Johnson, Paul, *Civilizations of the Holy Land* (New York: Atheneum, 1979).

Judson, Horace Freeland, *The Search for Solutions* (New York: Holt, Rinehart & Winston, 1980).

Kabbani, Rana, *Europe's Myths of the Orient* (Bloomington, IN: Indiana University Press, 1986).

Kassis, Hanna E., *A Concordance of the Qur'an* (Berkeley, CA: University of California Press, 1983).

Kaufmann, III, William J., *Universe* (New York: W.H. Freeman, 1991).

Keen, Maurice, 'Robin Who?' *The New York Review of Books* (May 9, 1985).

Kennedy, Paul, *Preparing for the Twenty-First Century* (New York: Random House, 1993).

Khatibi, Abdelkebir, and Mohammed Sijelmassi, *The Splendour of Islamic Calligraphy* (London: Thames & Hudson, 1976).

Khawam, Rene R., trans., *The Subtle Ruse: The Book of Arabic Wisdom and Guile* (London & The Hague: East–West Publications, 1976).

King, David A., *Islamic Astronomical Instruments* (London: Variorum Reprints, 1987).

Kramers, J. and H., eds., *Shorter Encyclopedia of Islam* (Ithaca, NY: Cornell University Press, 1953).

Kritzeck, James, ed., *Anthology of Islamic Literature* (New York: Holt, Rinehart & Winston, 1964).

Kühnel, Ernst, *Islamic Arts*. Trans. from the German by Katherine Watson (London: G. Bell, 1970).

Kuran, Aptullah, *The Mosque in the Early Ottoman Architecture* (Chicago, IL: Chicago University Press, 1968).

Landay, Jerry M. and the editors of the *Newsweek* Book Division, *Dome of the Rock* (New York: Newsweek, 1972).

Lane-Pool, Stanley, *The Moors in Spain* (Lahore, Pakistan: Publishers United, 1953).

Lapidus, Ira M., *A History of Islamic Societies* (Cambridge, UK: Cambridge University Press, 1988).

Le Goff, Jacques, *Medieval Civilization 400–1500*. Trans. Julia Barrow (Oxford, UK: Basil Blackwell, 1988).

Levy, Reuben, *An Introduction to Persian Literature* (New York & London: Columbia University Press, 1969).

Lewis, Bernard, *The Emergence of Modern Turkey* (London: Oxford University Press, 1961).

_____, *Islam and the West* (New York & Oxford, UK: Oxford University Press, 1993).

Lewis, I.M., ed., *Islam in Tropical Africa* (Oxford, UK: Oxford University Press, for the International African Institute, 1966).

Lichtenstadter, Ilse, *Introduction to Classical Arabic Literature* (New York: Schocken Books, 1976).

Lloyd, Seton, et al., *World Architecture* (New York: McGraw-Hill, 1963).

Lombard, Maurice, *The Golden Age of Islam* (Amsterdam, & Oxford, UK: North-Holland Publishing, 1975).

Lopez, Robert S., and Irving W. Raymond, 'Muslim Trade in the Mediterranean and the West', in Archibald Lewis, ed., *The Islamic World and the West 622–1492, A.D.* (New York: John Wiley, 1970).

Mabro, Judy, *Veiled Half-Truths: Western Travellers' Perceptions of Middle Eastern Women* (London & New York: I.B. Tauris, 1991).

Mahdi, Muhsin, 'Remarks on the 1001 Nights', *Interpretation*, 2 (2-3) (Winter 1973).

_____, 'Islamic Philosophy', *The New Encyclopaedia Britannica, Macropedia*, vol. 22 (Chicago, IL: Encyclopaedia Britannica, Inc., 1987).

Mahmud, Sayyid Fayyaz Mahmud, *A Short History of Islam* (Karachi, Pakistan: Oxford University Press, 1960).

Malik, Hafeez, ed., *Iqbal: Poet-Philosopher of Pakistan* (New York & London: Columbia University Press, 1971).

Mann, Vivian B., et al., eds., *Convivencia: Jews, Muslims and Christians in Medieval Spain* (New York: George Braziller, in assoc. with The Jewish Museum, 1992).

Manners, Errol, *Ceramics Source Book* (Secaucus, NJ: Chartwell Books, 1990).

Mantran, Robert, ed., *Les Grandes Dates de l'Islam* (Paris: Larousse, 1990).

Masud-ul-Hasan, *History of Islam* (Lahore, Pakistan: Islamic Publications, vol. 1, 1987; vol. 2, 1988).

_____, *Life of Iqbal*, Book 2 (Lahore, Pakistan: Ferozsons, 1978).

Matthews, D.J., et al., *Urdu Literature* (London: Third World Foundation, 1985).

McNeill, William, *The Rise of the West* (Chicago, IL: University of Chicago Press, 1963).

McPhee, John, 'Oranges,' in Donald Hall, ed., *The Contemporary Essay* (New York: St. Martin's Press, 1984).

Mernissi, Fatima, *The Forgotten Queens of Islam* (Minneapolis, MN: University of Minnesota Press, 1993).

Meyerhof, Max, *Le monde islamique* (Paris: F. Rieder, 1926).

Middleton, Christopher and Leticia Garza-Falcon, trans., *Andalusian Poems* (Boston, MA: David R. Godine, 1993).

Minai, Naila, *Women in Islam: Tradition and Transition in the Middle East* (New York: Seaview Books, 1981).

Mirza, Muhammad R. and Muhammad Iqbal Siddiqi, eds., *Muslim Contribution to Science* (Lahore, Pakistan: Kazi Publications, 1986).

Mitchell, George, *Architecture of the Islamic World: Its History and Social Meaning* (Thames and Hudson, New edition 1995).

Morgan, David, *The Mongols* (Oxford, UK: Basil Blackwell, 1986).

Mostyn, Trevor, exec. ed., *The Cambridge Encyclopedia of the Middle East and North Africa* (Cambridge, UK: Cambridge University Press, 1988).

Moynihan, Elizabeth B., *Paradise as a Garden: In Persia and Mughal India* (New York: George Braziller, 1979).

Myers, Eugene A., *Arabic Thought and the Western World* (New York: Frederick Ungar Publishing, 1964).

al-Nadim, ibn Abi Yaʿqub, *The Fihrist of al-Nadim*, ed. and trans. George Bayard, 2 vols. (New York & London: Columbia University Press, 1970).

Nagel, Thomas, *What Does It All Mean?* (New York, & Oxford, UK: Oxford University Press, 1987).

Nasr, Seyyed Hossein, *The Encounter of Man and Nature: The Spiritual Crisis of Modern Man* (London: Allen & Unwin, 1968).

_____, *Science and Civilization in Islam* (New York: New American Library, 1968).

_____, *Science and Civilization in Islam*, 2nd edn (Cambridge, UK: The Islamic Texts Society, 1987).

Necipoglu, Gulru, *The Age of Sinan* (London: Reaction Books, 2005).

Netton, Ian Richard, *Al-Farabi and His School* (London & New York: Routledge, 1992).

Nicholson, Reynold A., *A Literary History of the Arabs* (Cambridge, UK: Cambridge University Press, 1966).

_____, *Mathnawi of Jalauddin Rumi* (Lahore, Pakistan: Sang-e-Meel Publ., 2005).

_____, *Translations of Eastern Poetry and Prose* (London: Curzon Press; NJ: Humanities Press, 1987).

Nicole, David, *The Armies of Islam: 7th–11th Centuries* (London: Osprey Publishing, 1982).

Nuland, Sherland B., *The Doctors: The Biography of Medicine* (New York: Alfred A. Knopf, 1988).

Numani, Shibli, *Al-Farooq: Life of Umar the Great* (Lahore, Pakistan: Sh. Muhammad Ashraf, 1939).

Paccard, Andre, *Traditional Islamic Craft in Moroccan Architecture*. Trans. Mary Guggenheim, 2 vols. (Saint-Jorioz, France: Editions Atelier 74, 1980).

Papadopoulo, Alexandre, *Islam and Muslim Art*. Trans. Robert Eric Wolf. (New York: Harry N. Abrams, 1979).

Peters, F.E., *Allah's Commonwealth* (New York: Simon & Schuster, 1973).

_____, *Jerusalem* (Princeton, NJ: Princeton University Press, 1985).

_____, 'Science, History, and Religion: Some Reflections on the India of Rayhan al-Biruni,' *The Scholar and the Saint* (New York: New York University Press, 1975).

Qadir, C.A., *Philosophy and Science in the Islamic World* (London & New York: Routledge, 1988).

Rahman, Fazlur, 'Islamic Philosophy,' in Paul Edwards, ed. in chief, *The Encyclopedia of Philosophy*, vol. 4 (New York: Macmillan, 1967).

Reichmuth, Stefan, *Islamic Reformist Discourse in the Tulip Period (1718–30)* (Istanbul, Turkey: International Congress on Learning and Education in the Ottoman World, 1999).

Rice, David Talbot, *Islamic Art*, rev. edn. (London & New York: Thames & Hudson, 1975).

Roberts, J.M., *The Pelican History of the World* (Harmondsworth, Middx, UK: Penguin Books, 1980).

Robinson, Francis, *Atlas of the Islamic World Since 1500* (New York: Facts on File, 1982).

_____, *The Cambridge Encyclopedia of India, Pakistan, Bangladesh, Bhutan and the Maldives* (Cambridge, UK: Cambridge University Press, 1989).

Ronan, Colin A., *Science: Its History and Development Among the World's Cultures* (New York: Facts on File, 1982).

Rosenthal, Franz, *Knowledge Triumphant* (Leiden, The Netherlands: E.J. Brill, 1970).

Russell, Ralph and Khurshidul Islam, *Three Mughal Poets* (Cambridge, MA: Harvard University Press, 1968).

Sachau, Edward C., *Alberuni's India*, repr. (New Delhi: Mushiram Manoharilal Publishers, 1992).

Saʿdi, *The Gulistan or Rose Garden of Saʿdi*. Trans. Edward Rehatsek. (London: Allen & Unwin, 1964).

Sadiq, Muhammad, *A History of Urdu Literature* (Delhi: Oxford University Press, 1984).

Safadi, Y.H., *Islamic Calligraphy* (Boulder, CO: Shambhala, 1979).

Said, Edward, *Culture and Imperialism* (New York: Knopft, 1993).

_____, *Orientalism* (New York: Pantheon Books, 1978).

Sarton, George, *Introduction to the History of Science*, vol.1: *From Homer to Omar Khayyam* (Washington, DC: Carnegie Institution of Washington, 1927).

_____, *From Rabbi Ben Ezra to Roger Bacon*, vol. 2, Parts 1 and 2, (1931).

Savory, Roger, *Iran under the Safavids* (Cambridge, UK: Cambridge University Press, 1980).

Schacht, Joseph, and C.E. Bosworth, eds., *The Legacy of Islam*, 2nd edn. (Oxford, UK: Clarendon Press, 1974).

Schimmel, Annemarie, *As Through a Veil: Mystical Poetry in Islam* (New York: Columbia University Press, 1982).

Schroeder, Eric, *Muhammad's People* (Portland, ME: Bond Wheelright, 1955).

Sells, Michael A., trans., *Desert Tracings: Six Classic Arabian Odes* (Middletown, CT: Wesleyan University Press, 1989).

Settle, Mary Lee, 'A Sacred Spa Where Sultans Led an Empire,' *The New York Times*. Travel Section (July 8, 1990).

Shah, Idries, *The Sufis* (New York: Doubleday, 1964).

Sharif, M.M., *Islamic Philosophy* (London: Octagon Press, 1982).

Shaw, Stanford J., *History of the Ottoman Empire and Modern Turkey*, 2 vols. Vol.1: *Empire of the Gazis: The Rise and Decline of the Ottoman Empire 1280–1808* (London: Cambridge University Press, 1976).

_____, *History of the Ottoman Empire and the Turkish Republic*, vol. 2. (London and New York: Macmillan Press, 1977).

Sheikh, M. Saeed, *Islamic Philosophy* (London: The Octagon Press, 1982).

Shustery, A. M. A., *Outlines of Islamic Culture* (Lahore, Pakistan: Sh. Muhammad Ashraf, 1976).

Soucek, S., ed., *Piri Reis and Turkish Mapmaking After Columbus*: *The Khalili Portolan Atlas* (London: Nour Foundation and Azimuth, and Oxford, UK: Oxford University Press, 1996).

Southern, R.W., *Western Views of Islam in the Middle Ages* (Cambridge, MA: Harvard University Press, 1962).

Stratton, Arthur, *Sinan: The Biography of One of the World's Greatest Architects and a Portrait of the Golden Age of the Ottoman Empire* (London: Macmillan, 1972).

Temple, Robert, *The Genius of China* (New York: Simon & Schuster, 1986).

Trachtenberg, Marvin and Isabelle Hyman, *Architecture: From Prehistory to Post-Modernism/The Western Tradition* (Englewood Cliffs, NJ: Prentice-Hall; and New York: Harry N. Abrams, 1986).

Tuetey, Charles Greville, trans., *Classical Arabic Poetry* (London: KPI, 1985).

Ullah, Najib, *Islamic Literature* (New York: Washington Square Press, 1963).

Unsal, Behcet, *Turkish Islamic Architecture in Seljuk and Ottoman Times 1071–1923* (London: St. Martin's Press, 1973).

Unsworth, Barry, *Sacred Hunger* (New York: Random House, 1992).

Urvoy, Dominique, and Olivia Stewart, trans., *Ibn Rushd (Averroes)* (London & New York: Routledge, 1991).

Vahid, Syed Abdul, *Iqbal: His Art and Thought* (London: John Murray, 1959).

Voegelin, Eric, *The Ecumenic Age*, vol. 4: *Order and History* (Baton Rouge, LA: Louisiana State University Press, 1974).

Von Grunebaum, Gustave E., *Medieval Islam: A Study in Cultural Orientalism*. 2nd edn. (Chicago, IL: The University of Chicago Press, 1954).

Waddy, Charis, *Women in Muslim History* (London & New York: Longman, 1980).

Wade, David, *Pattern in Islamic Art* (Woodstock, NY: The Overlook Press, 1976).

Waldhorn, Arthur, et al., eds., *Good Reading*. 22nd edn. (New York: New American Library, 1985).

Walther, Wiebke, *Women in Islam* (Montclair, NJ: Abner Scram; & London: George Prior, 1981).

Watson, Andrew M., *Agricultural Innovation in the Early Islamic World* (Cambridge, UK: Cambridge University Press, 1983).

Welch, Anthony, *Calligraphy in the Arts of the Muslim World* (New York: The Asia Society, 1979).

Welch, Stuart Cary, *Persian Painting* (New York: George Braziller, 1976).

Wilford, John Noble, *The Mapmakers* (New York: Alfred A. Knopf, 1981).

Woodman, Dorothy, *The Republic of Indonesia* (London: Cresset, 1955).

INDEX